JUSTICE AND PEACE
EDUCATION

MODELS FOR COLLEGE
AND UNIVERSITY FACULTY

Edited by

David M. Johnson

Associate Director of the
Association of Catholic Colleges and Universities,
National Catholic Educational Association

ORBIS BOOKS
Maryknoll, New York 10545

The Catholic Foreign Mission Society of America (Maryknoll) recruits and trains people for overseas missionary service. Through Orbis Books Maryknoll aims to foster the international dialogue that is essential to mission. The books published, however, reflect the opinions of their authors and are not meant to represent the official position of the society.

© 1986 by Orbis Books, Maryknoll, NY 10545
Manufactured in the United States of America

Manuscript editor: Lisa McGaw

Permission to reprint given by:
New Directions Publishing Company for lines from William Carlos Williams's "Asphodel, That Greeny Flower," from *Pictures from Brueghel and Other Poems* © 1962

Houghton Mifflin Company for lines from Anne Sexton's *The Awful Rowing Toward God* © 1975

Library of Congress Cataloging in Publication Data

Main entry under title:

Justice and peace education.

Includes bibliographies.
1. Sociology, Christian (Catholic)—Study and teaching (Higher)—Addresses, essays, lectures.
2. Christianity and justice—Study and teaching (Higher)—Addresses, essays, lectures. 3. Peace—Religious aspects—Catholic Church—Study and teaching (Higher)—Addresses, essays, lectures. 4. Catholic Church—Doctrines—Study and teaching (Higher)—Addresses, essays, lectures. I. Johnson, David M. (David Michael), 1949-
BX1753.J87 1985   261.8'07'11   85-25808
ISBN 0-88344-247-7 (pbk.)

Contents

Preface

This book has a history, as all books do. The initial forces behind it date to 1964, and its immediate genesis to 1977. It is a history worth relating at least briefly here, as it encapsulates many of the changes occurring in both the church and Catholic higher education.

Vatican Council II serves as the 1964 benchmark in this story, as it has for so much of the recent history of Roman Catholicism. It was a point from which the church began to move in a new direction, its path irretrievably altered. For Vatican II was above all else a call for change, most particularly in the way the church and its followers related to the world around them. The council called upon the faithful to be "artisans of a new humanity" and to recognize that "all temporal activity continues the earthly task of the Savior." Specifically, Catholics were called to "work to overcome sin, disease, famine, pollution . . . and to change the structures of affairs flawed by . . . sin."[1]

The 1971 Synod of Bishops continued this call for social justice, stating that "Action on behalf of justice and participation in the transformation of the world fully appear to us as a constitutive dimension of the preaching of the Gospel."[2] At the same time, the synod called for a transformation in Catholic education to meet this end. Education, the synod agreed, must bring "renewal of heart," prepare "a critical sense," and challenge "the society in which we live and . . . its values."[3]

This call for educational transformation was made even more explicit in 1976 when, in the final assembly of the United States Catholic Bishops' Bicentennial "Call to Action" conference in Detroit, the delegates called upon Catholic educators to produce an education for justice, "which touches a Christian in all aspects of life while placing every sector of society under judgment of the Gospel." The National Catholic Educational Association (NCEA) was specifically seen by the delegates as the agency to continue efforts "to develop new models of justice education at all levels."[4]

One of the organizers of the 1976 Call to Action, Alice Gallin, O.S.U., returned to Washington, D.C., immediately afterward as the associate executive director of NCEA's College and University Department (now the Association of Catholic Colleges and Universities—ACCU). Among the duties of her new office was the development of justice and peace education at the 235 Catholic colleges and universities in the United States.

The colleges themselves were in a state of flux at that point, influenced not only by Vatican II and its progeny, but also by the civil rights, student, and peace movements of the late 1960s and by their increasing reliance upon state and federal sources of financial assistance. Many of the visible trappings of "traditional" Catholic higher education—required minors in theology and philosophy, mandatory attendance at Mass, boards of trustees dominated by men and women religious—had been left behind, lost to the "academic revolution" described so well by Christopher Jencks and David Reisman.[5] Where once it had been easy to describe what was "Catholic" about Catholic higher education, now it was increasingly difficult. Many of the faithful, both within academe and without, wondered what was left to distinguish Catholic colleges from any other independent institutions of higher education.

To Alice Gallin, Msgr. John Murphy (then the executive director of ACCU), and many of their colleagues on the campuses, at least a partial answer was clear: Catholic colleges and universities could and should be distinguished by a commitment to, and an education for, justice and peace. So, with the advice and support of the ACCU Advisory Council on Justice and Peace Education, they identified seven campuses to develop model programs in justice education.

The model programs operated for three years (1977–80), and a report of their successes and failures is available elsewhere.[6] For the purposes of this narrative, it will suffice to say that one of the clear outcomes of that pilot process was a realization that the task of educating for justice could not be adequately accomplished simply through the introduction of new majors or minors in "Peace Studies" and "Social Justice." Such programs would, after all, be of interest to only a limited number of students (particularly in a time of increasing careerism among youth), and would require the allocation of resources that many colleges and universities did not possess.

Along with that conclusion came an apparent solution: rather than setting up separate programs for a few, it would be measurably better to center efforts on incorporating justice concerns into the already existing courses of study in the various disciplines. More students—indeed, every student—could be presented with justice issues for discussion, and the discussions would occur in the context of their major fields of study, where they should have the greatest effect on the formation of life (and career) values. As a side benefit to the college, such a method would require little in the way of new resource allocations.

What this method does require is a commitment on the part of faculty who teach these courses to alter or to expand their syllabi and reading lists in order to consider how justice issues touch upon the particular subject matter of their disciplines. It is often not an easy commitment to make. Many faculty members have yet to be convinced that this type of values education has a place within the academic model. Others may question their own ability to present materials from outside the strict confines of their discipline in a fair and complete manner. Still others, who may think it should be done and are confident of their own ability to do it, find that the rewards are few. Promotion and tenure committees look more closely elsewhere.

This book is an attempt to deal with those concerns. Our method is again through the presentation of models; in this case, of faculty colleagues who have infused their teaching with justice concerns and who have found that this additional focus enhances both the academic rigor and human relevance of their courses.

It was not difficult to find such faculty in each of the disciplines considered in this volume. Indeed, it was exhilarating to discover that there were more such people on our campuses than we had imagined, the result of several years of steady growth in justice education at Catholic colleges and universities. Over 100 of these institutions now offer some regularly scheduled courses or programs in justice education. Over 135 institutions devoted special attention to study and reflection on the United States Catholic Bishops' pastoral letter on war and peace in 1984 and a similar number examined the draft of the bishops' letter on the American economy in 1985.

This heightened interest in justice education should not be surprising. The humanities are enjoying a resurgence of sorts as well. Both developments point to a renewed search for meaning through education, and perhaps, as David Walsh suggests, are evidence of a basic intellectual and moral dissatisfaction with scholarship that fails to address the purpose of human existence.[7] It is the thesis of this volume that that search for meaning can and should occur in *all* academic disciplines, and should not be confined to a few.

The volume begins with an introduction by Joseph Fahey, whose Peace Studies Institute at Manhattan College is known to all in this field as an exemplar of the academic study of justice and peace issues. Thirteen essays addressing major disciplines in the humanities, social sciences, and professional education follow. The book concludes with two essays on commonly offered interdisciplinary courses in the field, and an afterword by Donald McNeill, C.S.C., of the University of Notre Dame's Center for Social Concerns.

The instructions to these essayists were simple. They were asked to address their essays to colleagues in their discipline who teach undergraduate courses. They were asked to address the incorporation of justice themes into that discipline as a whole and then to present a model course within that discipline. They were encouraged to select as that model the basic introductory course in their discipline. They were asked to include some discussion of interdisciplinary efforts that could be pursued with faculty in related areas, and to suggest appropriate experiential learning activities, designed to bring concepts discussed in the classroom more directly into students' consciousness.

They have done these things well. The careful reader, however, will note significant differences in each contributor's approach. Not all agree, for example, on the essential elements of "justice," nor does a consensus emerge on the proper handling of peace concerns when they conflict with perceived justice imperatives. But this is as it should be. Our intention is simply to raise these issues in the minds of faculty and to suggest that they have a duty to consider these concerns and respond to them in accord with their consciences.

It is our hope that colleagues will see in these efforts new possibilities for better education and a better world.

Grateful acknowledgment is due: most especially to Alice Gallin, O.S.U., now the executive director of ACCU, whose faith, support, and friendship literally made this book possible. To Msgr. John Meyers, president of the NCEA, for the same reasons. To the ACCU Advisory Council on Justice and Peace Education, whose critique of the early proposal for the book was so important. To Rita Hofbauer, G.N.S.H.; Paul Steidl-Meier, S.J.; and Stephanie Russell—all of whom served as critical readers of the first drafts of these essays. To the late Philip Scharper, who encouraged this effort from the beginning, and to those who continue his ministry at Orbis Books. To Lisa McGaw, who took this collection of eighteen separate works and turned it into a coherent whole. To the contributors whose works fill these pages, teachers and scholars in the best tradition of higher education. And to Fr. Emmanuel, also known as Charles McCarthy, who made me see the potential for change through education.

DAVID M. JOHNSON

NOTES

1. Vatican Council II, *The Documents of Vatican II,* ed. Walter M. Abbott (New York: The America Press, 1966).

2. Synod of Bishops, Second General Assembly, "Justice in the World" (1971), no. 6, in *The Gospel of Peace and Justice,* ed. Joseph Gremillion (Maryknoll, N.Y.: Orbis Books, 1976),p. 514.

3. Ibid., no. 51, in Gremillion, *Gospel of Peace and Justice,* p. 524.

4. National Conference of Catholic Bishops, *To Do the Work of Justice* (Washington, D.C.: United States Catholic Conference, 1978), p. 5.

5. Christopher Jencks and David Reisman, *The Academic Revolution* (Garden City, N.Y.: Doubleday Anchor Books, 1969).

6. *Current Issues in Catholic Higher Education* 1, no. 2 (Winter 1981).

7. David J. Walsh, "Restoring the Lost Center of Education," *Thought* 58, no. 231 (December 1983): 363–74.

Introduction

The Nature and Challenge
of Justice and Peace Education

JOSEPH J. FAHEY
MANHATTAN COLLEGE

Although each generation should know its past, nevertheless each generation is ultimately responsible to generations yet unborn. A major problem of this—the nuclear—generation is that it demonstrates painfully little awareness of the long history of war and peace, and consequently is delinquent in its obligations to the future. This generation lives in the present, a present that is distinguished by paralyzing fear, "nuclear numbness," and a profound despair over its ability to do justice and to act for peace. This nuclear generation, separated from its past, is uncertain that it even has a future.

On May 3, 1983, the Roman Catholic bishops of the United States reminded this generation that it indeed has a past rooted in justice and peace. The bishops offered hope for the future based on God's design for the universe. In their pastoral letter on war and peace, "The Challenge of Peace: God's Promise and Our Response," the bishops provide an analysis of the past, a description of the present "new moment," and a visionary yet practical program for peace and justice for the future. Future generations will thank the bishops for their prophetic leadership and rigorous analysis of the problems and opportunities of this age.

This volume, although conceived before the pastoral letter on war and peace was published by the bishops, is nevertheless firmly rooted in the concern of the bishops that justice—not armaments races—can alone be the basis for the future peace that so many desire. In their pastoral letter the bishops offer many challenges to this generation and specifically call for the establishment of educational programs in justice and peace: "With Pope John Paul II, we call upon educational and research institutes to take a lead in conducting peace studies: 'Scientific studies on war, its nature, causes, means, objectives and risks have much to teach us on the conditions for peace.' "[1]

In this context the bishops endorse the establishment of a National Academy of Peace and Conflict Resolution and they "urge all citizens to support training in conflict resolution, non-violent resistance, and programs devoted to service to peace and education for peace." Concerning Catholic colleges and universities, the bishops state: "We urge universities, particularly Catholic universities, in our country to develop programs for rigorous interdisciplinary research, education and training directed toward peacemaking expertise." Finally, the bishops demonstrate the urgency of their concern:

> Every effort must be made to understand and evaluate the arms race, to encourage truly transnational perspectives on disarmament and to explore new forms of international cooperation and exchange. No greater challenge or higher priority can be imagined than the development and perfection of a theology of peace suited to a civilization poised on the brink of self-destruction. It is our prayerful hope that this document will prove to be a starting point and inspiration for that endeavor.

The challenge is before us. It is time to educate, to act, and to have hope for the future. This volume, based on the practical educational and research experience of professors in Catholic colleges and universities, is an immediate response to the challenge of the Catholic bishops and, it is hoped, will ultimately result in a new generation of American leaders who will do the work of justice so that the divine gift of peace may be granted the children of tomorrow.

THE NATURE OF JUSTICE AND PEACE EDUCATION

Before proceeding to examine the many excellent essays in this volume that deal with the perspectives of various academic disciplines on justice and peace education, the reader will be aided in this reading by understanding the "macro" nature of justice and peace education.

It should be noted that although the terminology used in justice and peace education is new—the categories "Faith and Justice," "Peace Studies," "Nonviolent Studies," and "Peace Science" have been developed since the start of the 1970s—the concept is old. Elements of education for justice and peace can be found in ancient "primitive" religions and philosophies, in the thought of Confucius and the Buddha, in the ethics of Aristotle and the drama of Aristophanes, in the Hebrew prophets and the teaching of Jesus, in the view of the universe held by Native Americans, in the practice of peacemaking by Francis of Assisi, Thomas Aquinas, Erasmus, Mahatma Gandhi, Martin Luther King, Jr., and Dorothy Day, and in the research and teaching of many scholars over the past several centuries. Literally millions of philosophers, theologians, political scientists, ethicists, economists, scientists, and especially "ordinary" people have contributed to an understanding of the concepts currently being investigated in justice and peace education. Like any science, justice and peace education is the heir of a long history of dedicated people who have prepared for its inception. In one sense we can say, with Gandhi, "I have nothing new to say to you about nonviolence. It is as old as the hills."

The "new" aspect is that an academic discipline, or field of study, is emerging that is clarifying its basic concepts, developing an appropriate research methodology, producing its own unique literature, institutionalizing itself through courses, departments, and degree programs, and, finally, leading to praxis that is innovative in nature. As stated above, the name of this new field varies among its disciples, but there seems to be a general consensus found among its practitioners in the Consortium on Peace Research, Education, and Development (COPRED), and in the Association of Catholic Colleges and Universities, that *justice and peace education constitutes a multidisciplinary academic and moral quest for solutions to the problems of war and injustice with the consequential development of institutions and movements that will contribute to a peace that is based on justice and reconciliation.* Thus justice and peace education is academic in nature, multidisciplinary in method, global in perspective, and oriented toward action that is intelligent, constructive, and creative. Above all, however, it should be stressed that the emerging field of justice and peace education is still very much experimental in nature; to rush to a definition that is exclusive in practice would be detrimental to the very nature of this experiment. In the words of the Hindu proverb, "Truth is One. The paths to it are many."

Having reached toward a definition of justice and peace education, we shall now attempt to answer the question "But what does one study in justice and peace education?"

An analysis of the theorists in the field, of the over 100 colleges and universities in the United States that teach justice and peace education in one or another form, and of the fifty or so research institutes that deal with the issues of justice and peace reveals five broad areas constituting the study of justice and peace: war, peace, and arms races; social, political, and economic justice; conflict regulation; the philosophy and practice of nonviolence; a just world order. We shall deal with each of these in turn.

War, Peace, and Arms Races

An examination of war, its causes, arms races including the present global arms race by East and West, North and South (arms races, contrary to popular opinion, are major causative factors of war), and the history of disarmament and arms control are obvious imperatives for justice and peace education. Clearly, these concerns need to be examined in a multidisciplinary manner, since the study of history, politics, economics, and culture individually cannot give adequate answers to these problems. The study of war is leading to a major fundamental insight: war does not make peace, just as arms races (in their conventional and nuclear manifestations) do not "deter" war; only an infusion of human justice can serve as a true basis for peace and as a deterrent to war. In the words of "The Challenge of Peace": "Reason and experience tell us that a continuing upward spiral even in conventional arms, coupled with an unbridled increase in armed forces, instead of securing true peace will almost certainly be provocative of war."[2]

Finally, it should be noted that although there is abundant literature to document the study of war, there is comparatively little to document the study of peace. But the history of peace activity is as long as that of war, and it is the task of justice and peace education to document more fully this disregarded history.

Social, Political, and Economic Justice

The insight that injustice is a major cause of violence and war is as old as the teaching of the Hebrew prophets and Jesus. If we would avoid war, we must first examine the causes of injustice and the denial of fundamental human rights. To ignore the "widows and orphans," the politically, economically, and sociologically oppressed, the poor, the hungry, and the refugees is to sow the seeds for future violence and war. To place our faith and hope in armaments races instead of justice will result in the very ruin that we seek to prevent. In the words of the prophet Hosea: "Because you have trusted in your chariots and in the multitude of your warriors, therefore the tumult of war shall arise among your people, and all your fortresses shall be destroyed" (10:13–14).

How often, when faced with a conflict, we hear the cry "Send in the marines!" Rather than sending the marines as an almost automatic response to a conflict situation, we should send in a peace corps—engineers, teachers, scientists, agricultural experts, doctors, nurses. Only when we understand that true national and international defense must be based on the work of justice shall we begin to realize the peace of God that is such an elusive reality in the twentieth century.

While justice and peace education has often popularly been associated with the humanities and the social sciences, we should not overlook the indispensable role of the physical sciences and engineering in working to end injustice and thus war itself. In a remarkable address to the world's scientists, Pope John Paul II urged scientists to pursue "the love of knowledge that builds peace":

Truth, freedom, justice and love: such, gentlemen, must be the cornerstones of the generous choice of a science that builds up peace. These four values, the cornerstones of science and of the life of civilized society, must be at the basis of that universal call of scientists, of the world of culture, of the citizens of the world, which the Pontifical Academy of Sciences, with my full and convinced approval, desires to address to the world for the reconciliation of peoples, for the success of the only war that must be fought: the war against hunger, disease and the death of millions of human beings whose quality and dignity of life could be helped and promoted with 7 percent of the amount spent each year for the incessant and threatening rearmament of the richest nations.[3]

As with the United States bishops' pastoral letter on war and peace, these words of Pope John Paul II should inspire Catholic colleges and universities to examine all of their academic programs in order to promote "truth, freedom, justice and love."

Conflict Regulation

A third constitutive element in justice and peace education is the theory and practice of conflict regulation (also known as "conflict resolution" and "dispute settlement"). The elimination of war through the work of justice must make use of the many techniques of conflict regulation, which include conciliation, mediation, arbitration, legal sanctions, and negotiation. To train students in the art and science of conflict regulation is an imperative if we are to equip them with the tools or—in Gandhian terminology—the "weapons" to settle disputes without violence. Too often the very people who ridicule the techniques of conflict regulation (especially world leaders) do so out of ignorance or because they believe that what works at home cannot work abroad.

The United States Catholic Bishops' support for a National Academy of Peace and Conflict Resolution was noted earlier in this essay.[4] Rigorous academic analysis of conflict and of the most effective methods for avoiding violence is essential in order to provide a means to regulate conflict among individuals, social groups, or nations that is commensurate with our end: the abolition of war. Whereas the abolition of conflict is *not* desirable (since conflict may be healthy for the human animal), Catholic universities, especially, should seek creative ways to regulate conflict to result in a minimum of violence and a maximum of justice. To provide training in such conflict-regulation techniques as mediation and arbitration should therefore be an essential function of a justice and peace educational program.[5]

The Philosophy and Practice of Nonviolence

Closely linked to the methods of conflict regulation is the practice of nonviolent resistance (defense) against injustice. Generally, nonviolence is regarded as a form of "force" that will secure justice against an unwilling opponent. The goal of nonviolence, however (unlike that of violence), is to provide a victory for *both* sides in a struggle. Nonviolence seeks a win/win rather than a win/lose resolution of a given conflict and clearly seeks reconciliation between opponents. (Rather than the word "enemy," the practitioner of nonviolence prefers to use the word "opponent.")

Nonviolence has been used as a successful defense against injustice not only in the India of Mohandas K. Gandhi and the United States of Martin Luther King, Jr., Dorothy Day, and Thomas Merton, but also against Nazis and Communists and in many third-world situations. The studies of Gene Sharp, Joan Bondurant, Severyn Bruyn and Paula Rayman, and Karl Schonborn, among others, provide abundant examples of how nonviolence has been successfully used in the cause of justice.[6]

One of the excellent contributions of "The Challenge of Peace" to a positive philosophy and strategy for peace is the section entitled "Efforts to Develop Non-Violent Means of Conflict Resolution" (sec. III. 5.) The bishops state that "Non-violence is not the way of the weak, the cowardly or the impatient" and they see in nonviolence a positive form of defense against "insurgency, counterinsurgency, 'destabilization' and the like." The bishops point out that the principles of nonviolence "are thoroughly compatible with—and to some extent derived from—Christian teachings and must be part of any Christian theology of peace." It is useful to quote the bishops' view of nonviolence at some length:

> Non-violent resistance, like war, can take many forms depending upon the demands of a given situation. There is, for instance, organized popular defense instituted by government as part of its contingency planning. Citizens would be trained in the techniques of peaceable non-compliance and non-cooperation as a means of hindering an invading force or non-democratic government from imposing its will. Effective non-violent resistance requires the united will of a people and may demand as much patience or sacrifice from those who practice it as is now demanded by war and preparation for war. It may not always succeed. Nevertheless, before the possibility is dismissed as impractical or unrealistic, we urge that it be measured against the almost certain effects of a major war.[7]

Can the practice of conflict regulation and nonviolence successfully defend against and deter nuclear war itself? The question certainly remains open for analysis and research. But how many readers of this volume can name even ten of the 198 methods of nonviolence as researched by Gene Sharp in *The Politics of Non-Violent Action?* Further, what does Paul mean by putting on the "whole armor of God" in resisting the "flaming darts" of the evil one (Eph. 6:11, 16, RSV)? It may be in the end that the practice of nonviolence will save the human race. If this is to be the case, Catholic colleges and universities have an essential and pivotal role to play in the research, education, and action of nonviolence.

A Just World Order

There are many who believe that even if we reduce armaments, engage in the work of justice, pursue conflict regulation and nonviolence, we still shall not secure global peace because of the present state of "anarchy" among nations. This conviction has compelled these theorists to posit that the only solution is the formation of a global community of nations based on law with its consequent rights, duties, and responsibilities.[8] Truly, our problems are global in nature and yet we do not have the necessary structures or institutions endowed with the necessary power to regulate right relations between communities and nation-states.

From the time of Hugo Grotius (1583–1645) to the present many have urged that "natural law" requires that we form a community of nations based on law. All the popes since Leo XIII have urged the creation of an international public authority as the only secure method to abolish war and promote basic human rights. The basis of "natural law" according to popes, theologians, and some political scientists is the unity of the human family. In the words of the bishops in "The Challenge of Peace": "The fundamental premise of world order in Catholic teaching is a theological truth: the unity of the human family—rooted in common creation, destined for the kingdom and united by moral bonds of rights and duties. This basic truth about the unity of the human family pervades the entire teaching on war and peace." With this as their basic premise, the bishops further state: "An important element missing from world order today is a properly constituted political authority with the capacity to shape our material interdependence in the direction of moral interdependence."[9] Also, despite its many hostile critics, the United Nations receives warm support from the bishops for what it can be, as it has from every pope since Pius XII.

The implications for research and education are obvious here. Is the bishops' assertion correct that there is such a reality as the "unity of the human family"? All too many theorists hold that there can be no fundamental basis for world community (not to mention even simple negotiations) because there is a *substantive* difference in the humanity found in some cultures from that of another. (Obviously, these theorists argue that their own culture or nation represents "true" humanity with its consequence that "God is on our side.") Researchers in biology, anthropology, psychology, and theology have much to contribute to this discussion. What is humanity? Are cultural, political, and economic differences so severe that they have resulted in an *essential* difference between, for example, the Russian people and those of the United States? Must the relations between states be based forever on the threat of mutual destruction rather than on trust, cooperation, and law? At times one has the impression that the human race prides itself on thinking the worst of itself—or at least of part of itself. The teaching of popes, bishops, and theologians on "natural law" as the basis of world community has a long and beleaguered history. It is certainly not the basis of the foreign policy of the first world. Will the graduates of Catholic colleges and universities help to reform what is in essence a racist foreign policy? The Catholic teaching on world order must be the starting point for the reformation of foreign policy and the formation of—let us say—the united states of the world.[10]

Thus we have answered the question (on an experimental and introductory basis) of "What does one study in justice and peace education?" No discipline can be excused from examining the questions raised above. It is the task of the *entire* university—faculty, students, administrators, campus ministers, and support staff—to cooperate together in the "holistic" education of students and of the world. The contents of this volume provide an excellent starting point.

JUSTICE AND PEACE EDUCATION PROGRAMS

Donald McNeill, C.S.C., in his afterword to this volume, presents some actual university programs that engage in justice and peace education. Here it will be helpful to discuss some models of university development in this area.

Incorporation of Justice and Peace Dimensions into Existing Courses

Most colleges and universities begin education for justice and peace by examining their present curriculum for courses that already deal in a substantive way with one or more of the five content areas of justice and peace education described above. After these courses are identified (some have estimated that in the average liberal-arts college 25 percent of presently existing courses already deal with the issues of justice and peace in some form), other courses are then examined for their potential to deal with these issues. A course on the sociology of minorities, for example, can deal with economic and political justice as well as nonviolence and conflict regulation, while a course on international relations can deal with world order and economic justice. The opportunities to add a justice and peace dimension to almost any field of study are amply demonstrated by the essays in this volume.

New Courses

In even the smaller college, requirements or electives can be instituted that deal directly with a major area of justice and peace education. At Manhattan College, for example, the courses "Religious Dimensions of Peace," "Economics of Peace," "Literature of the Great War," "War, Peace and the Arts," "Anatomy of Peace," and "Nonviolent Revolution" have all been added to the regular curriculum in response to the need for them on that campus. It is also ideal to offer some or all of these courses as team-taught interdisciplinary enterprises.

Degree Programs

In response to the need for justice and peace studies, many universities (Catholic and non-Catholic) are investigating degree-granting programs in the area of justice and peace education. These programs typically include the following elements: *(a)* interdisciplinary or multidisciplinary seminars for

PEACE STUDIES MAJOR, MANHATTAN COLLEGE
General Requirements for All Students

Each student must take thirty credits (one course equals three credits) divided as follows:

1. Nine required credits:
   a. Three credits from Peace Studies 201 or 202
   b. Three credits from Peace Studies 401 or 402
   c. Three credits from Peace Studies 451 or 452
2. Twenty-one elective credits chosen from among the courses listed below

REQUIRED COURSES

1. Peace Studies 61–201/202: Problems of Peace and Social Justice
2. Peace Studies 61–401/402: Senior Seminar in Peace Studies
3. Peace Studies 61–451/452: Peace Studies Field Project

ELECTIVES

1. Biology 215: Biology of Human Behavior
2. Economics 320: Economics of Peace
3. Economics 331: World Economic Geography
4. Economics 412: Economic Growth and Development
5. Fine Arts 335: War, Peace, and the Arts
6. Government 441: International Relations
7. Government 442: International Organization
8. Government 445: Latin American Politics
9. Government 446: Government and Politics of Africa
10. History 431: Anatomy of Peace
11. History 473: The Art of War to 1713
12. History 474: The Art of War since 1713
13. History 479: Cold War, Detente, and After
14. History 452: American Foreign Relations
15. Managerial Sciences 450: Behavioral Dynamics
16. Peace Studies 301: Seminar: Pilgrimage to Humanity
17. Peace Studies 302: Seminar on Current Topics
18. Peace Studies 421–422: Independent Studies
19. Philosophy 413: Philosophies of War and Peace
20. Philosophy 414: Philosophies of Nonviolence
21. Religious Studies 357: Religions of China and the Far East
22. Religious Studies 358: Religions of India
23. Religious Studies 433: Religious Dimensions of Peace
24. Religious Studies 434: Nonviolent Revolution
25. Religious Studies 438: Business Ethics
26. Sociology 301: Sociology of Social Problems
27. Sociology 302: Sociology of Minorities
28. World Literature 307: Literature and the Great War

majors or minors in the field; *(b)* traditional course work in those courses that were created especially for the program or that have been given an added dimension through the incorporation method; *(c)* independent research (similar to a junior or senior thesis) on a topic of student interest; *(d)* field work at local or international justice and peace organizations at home and abroad.

The following outline describes the "Peace Studies" major at Manhattan College and is offered as an example of one such program in the field. The major has been available at Manhattan College since 1971; as of this writing, over one hundred students have fulfilled its requirements.

Justice and Peace Research

One of the ways to help faculty members to develop expertise in this area is through the solicitation of campus or foundation grants to conduct what could be called a Faculty Development Seminar. Ten to fifteen faculty members and selected students in existing courses gather together three or four times a semester to hear a faculty person present a research paper on some topic of his or her interest, which relates to justice and peace education and which will enhance the teaching of an already existing course or a new one in this area. (This procedure can be used at undergraduate or graduate levels.)

In addition to faculty development, graduate students can be encouraged to choose a research topic for a paper or dissertation that will contribute significantly to the growing body of literature in justice and peace concerns. (Clearly, the nature of research that graduate students pursue at a Catholic university should have some distinctive mark because it is pursued at a Catholic university.) Although many topics for possible research are mentioned in this volume, professors are limited only by their vision, commitment, and curiosity in selecting research areas that will prepare people for professional work in justice and peace whether they pursue a traditional form of work or work in one of the emerging professions (e.g., dispute settlement) in justice and peace ministry.

Campus Activity and Outreach

Although it is the conviction of this author that the academic rigor and excellence of justice and peace education must distinguish any program in this area, it is nevertheless essential that justice and peace concerns pervade the *total* life of the campus and its surrounding community. Student-sponsored events on campus that deal with hunger, human rights, or third-world issues; student activity off campus in a justice and/or peace center; student/faculty trips to third-world situations at home and abroad—all are activities that should distinguish the academic and outreach programs of the college or university. Campus liturgies, especially, should focus on justice and peace concerns on the Catholic campus. In addition, the granting of awards or honorary degrees and the appointment of trustees, faculty, or administrators can signify the commitment of the institution to justice and peace.

In the pursuit of the activities above, one can expect to meet heated opposition at times from those who either are threatened by justice and peace education or sincerely disagree with the idea that the college or university should be involved in such work. Some will argue that justice and peace education is "unpatriotic"; others will posit that it is a collection of "Mickey Mouse" courses. It is my personal experience in seventeen years of this work, that once people—especially skeptical faculty members—are exposed to the research and options involved in justice and peace education, they often become staunch supporters and activists in the program. Therefore, it would be worthwhile to treat these opponents with respect, goodwill, and firmness in the realization that those who are opposed to the program may one day be among its friends. Make a special effort to invite the skeptics and opponents into the program, as they will often provide valuable insights that can prove especially challenging to the students.

CONCLUSION

How many of us daily face young students and hear them ask whether or not they have a future? How many children in Western nations and throughout the world are prevented from full human potential through inhumane governmental or economic problems? What shall we in the Catholic college and university community do for generations yet unborn? Does the university exist for itself or for God's world? Shall we pursue our own interesting but often irrelevant hobbies in the classroom, or shall we accept the challenge of the Catholic bishops to make education count for the poor, the oppressed, and the victims of violence and war?

The challenge before the Catholic university and all educational institutions today is whether we shall forge a new future based on the Christian and human imperative to serve the needs of people in every land and culture, or not. The words of the spiritual "We Shall Overcome" should not be restricted to chapel services but should find their way into the daily academic life of universities. Unless this generation of college and university teachers offers students hope along with the tools to make a better world, it will fail many generations to come. The calling of the professor is as much a spiritual ministry as an intellectual one. We simply cannot be morally neutral in a nuclear age, nor can we contribute to the apocalypse that is being prepared for today's students by some of the best minds in the world.

As one reads the essays in this volume it is well to keep in mind the words that Anne Frank inscribed in her diary on July 15, 1944:

I still believe that people are really good at heart. I simply can't build up my hopes on a foundation consisting of confusion, misery, and death. I see the world gradually being turned into a wilderness, I hear the ever approaching thunder, which will destroy us too, I can feel the sufferings of millions and yet, if I look up into the heavens, I think that it will all come right, that this cruelty too will end, and that peace and tranquillity will return again.[11]

Anne Frank sits daily in our classrooms. Let us not fail her.

NOTES

1. This quotation and those that follow from the pastoral letter on war and peace are found in "The Challenge of Peace: God's Promise and Our Response" (Washington, D.C.: United States Catholic Conference, 1983), sec. III.A.5.

2. Ibid., sec. III.A.3.

3. John Paul II, "Excerpts from Talk on Military Research," *New York Times,* Nov. 13, 1983, p. 36.

4. See *To Establish the United States Academy of Peace* (Washington, D.C., United States Government Printing Office, 1981).

5. For a fine book on this subject see Paul Wehr, *Conflict Regulation* (Boulder, Colo. Westview Press, 1979).

6. For an analysis of some of these (and other) struggles see Wehr (cited in n. 5); Gene Sharp, *The Politics of Non-Violent Action,* 3 vols. (Boston: Porter Sargent, 1973); Joan V. Bondurant, *Conquest of Violence: The Gandhian Philosophy of Conflict* (Berkeley, Calif.: University of California Press, 1971); Severyn T. Bruyn and Paula M. Rayman, eds., *Nonviolent Action and Social Change* (New York: Irvington Publishers, 1979); Marjorie Hope and James Young, *The Struggle for Humanity: Agents of Nonviolent Change in a Violent World* (Maryknoll, N.Y.: Orbis Books, 1977); Karl Schonborn, *Dealing with Violence: The Challenge Faced by Police and Other Peace-keepers* (Springfield, Ill.: Charles C. Thomas Publishers, 1975).

7. United States Catholic Bishops, "The Challenge of Peace," sec. III.A.5.

8. See Richard Falk, Samuel S. Kim, and Saul H. Mendelovitz, eds., *Toward a Just World Order,* vol. 1 (Boulder, Colo.: Westview Press, 1982); Robert C. Johansen, *The National Interest and the Human Interest* (Princeton, N.J.: Princeton University Press, 1980); Gerald and Patricia Mische, *Toward a Human World Order* (New York: Paulist Press, 1977). Also, the encyclicals *Pacem in Terris* and *Populorum Progressio* are particularly helpful in addressing the need for a global juridical community.

9. United States Catholic Bishops, "The Challenge of Peace," sec. III.B.1.

10. An excellent background book on this subject is E. B. F. Midgley, *The Natural Law Tradition and the Theory of International Relations* (New York: Harper & Row, 1975).

11. *Anne Frank: The Diary of a Young Girl,* trans. B. M. Mooyaart— Doubleday (New York: Pocket Books, 1969), p. 237.

PART I

THE HUMANITIES

1

Religious Studies

MONIKA K. HELLWIG
GEORGETOWN UNIVERSITY

No academic discipline offers a better or more fitting context for social justice and peace education than religious studies. Almost all imaginable courses in this field must include some observation of and reflection on lifestyle, values, social choices and decisions, relationships among groups, attitudes to wealth and power, and responses to suffering and violence, because all of these are dependent upon faith and beliefs. Moreover, there is much in the present trends in the religious studies field that encourages and aids explicit and scholarly attention to questions of peace and social justice: the interest of undergraduate students in these questions, a great deal of recent scholarship concerning past attitudes to these questions within the various traditions, the religious motivation behind the great liberation and peace movements of our time, and the availability of great numbers of suitable books in paperback.

There is, of course, also some reluctance on the part of conscientious college professors in the field of religious studies to change tried and successful courses that have not explicitly addressed questions of social justice and peace. There are the established patterns, which have become tradition. Much work and research has gone into the construction of the courses, and perhaps a good deal of earlier experimenting. However, perhaps the greatest reason for a certain reluctance on the part of the well disposed is the sense of inadequacy because of the interdisciplinary nature of the questions that arise concerning peace and justice as soon as these questions become more immediately practical. Many of us in the humanities have been rather intimidated by technologists and technocrats who keep telling us that we are naïve and should stay out of the public realm and, as a matter of fact, out of history altogether, confining ourselves to the shrouded realms of eternity or the mysteries of inner space.

Actually, no matter how much anyone may try to discourage us, we cannot stay out of the public realm and the affairs of human history because the questions with which both faith and theology professedly deal keep spilling over into that domain. Because we must deal with these questions in any case, we may just as well have a careful plan of attack. That means planning courses explicitly to include questions of social justice and peace, and finding the resources to support the plan. Even more importantly it means careful reflection on the subject matter of the courses to uncover the ways that these issues arise appropriately and inherently, so that they are not simply added on because we have been convinced that we ought to include justice and peace education in all phases of the curriculum.

This essay will attempt to sketch the ways in which questions of social responsibility and public decisions arise appropriately in the various branches of religious studies more commonly taught in Catholic college and university programs for undergraduates. The most obvious context is that of courses in ethics and moral theology. However, because this is being considered at length in the essay by Suzanne Toton on ethical dimensions of world hunger and in that of David Burrell on ethics in philosophy, this area will be mentioned rather briefly here.

The more traditional texts in ethics, and even more so in Catholic moral theology, tended to place heavy emphasis on the actions of individuals in their private lives and in their one-to-one relationships. Public issues tended to appear in the text and the discussion only in relation to performing the duties of one's state in life. The problem in this, as becomes plain at times of crisis such as the Nazi era in Germany, is that it takes the structures and institutions and policies of the society for granted and asks only how the individual should discharge her or his obligations within it. This approach does not provide principles for a critique of the social order as such.

There seems to be an explanation for this in church history and practice. In the early church the concept of sin tended to be formulated for Christians in the context of baptism. Baptism was a turning away from the sinful order of the world to the graced and redemptive order of the community of believers, involving a drastic change in lifestyle and social structure, and constituting a countercultural stance. However, with the establishment and respectability of the churches and the gradual emergence of Christendom, people were more usually baptized as infants and did not experience this strong turning to a countercultural and therefore sociocritical stance. The concept of sin was shaped far more with reference to deviance from established expectations and therefore from the order that obtained. In fact, in the course of the centuries the theology of sin and of moral obligations was worked out largely with reference to the sacrament of penance in the form of individual confession. It is not surprising that the focus of such a moral theology was individualistic, and certainly the privatization of faith brought about by the Enlightenment could only have furthered this tendency.

Today we are aware of the bias expressed by that focus in moral theology. We are the heirs of almost a century of papal encyclical letters taking a very strong stand on issues of social justice and peace. They are a powerful resource in themselves and they also demand further reflection and inquiry. Likewise, recent North American episcopal statements demand a serious educational response—statements such as that on Appalachia and the elaborately researched and prepared paper on nuclear war and armaments.[1] Introductory courses in moral theology are no longer complete without a consideration of such issues. However, there is also sufficient subject matter for special courses dealing specifically with these questions. At Georgetown University, where I now teach, there is a distinctive international character in many programs. We regularly offer courses on "Ethics and International Relations," "Catholic Tradition in Politics," "Protestant Tradition in Politics," "War and Peace," "The Non-Violent Revolution of Peace," "The Bible and Social Justice," "Christian Ethics and Modern Life" (including the political aspects), and "Theology of Social Action." We have also experimented with an interdisciplinary "World Hunger" seminar.

Scripture study, like ethics and moral theology, offers an obvious context for reflection on social justice and peace. It is true, however, that most biblical scholars in modern times have avoided the topic. This does not seem to have been a deliberate choice. The prevailing post-Enlightenment privatization of religious practice and awareness, combined with the lengthy and demanding training in the deciphering and translation of texts in dead languages, seems to have turned the attention of Scripture scholars away from what might otherwise have been obvious in the Bible itself, namely, the inseparability of true worship of God from true relations with other people in all facets of human life.

In consequence of this, it is easier to find the bibliographic resources for a course in Scripture that treats of social justice or peace as a special theme than to find suitable secondary sources to assign to undergraduates in which they may see themes of social justice and peace as integral to the Bible. The Scripture professors at Georgetown University do both, however. Courses that take social justice and peace as specific themes are "Power and Politics in Biblical Tradition" (which deals with questions of human relationships, social organization, conflict, authority, and force in the light of the biblical testimonies on covenant, holy war, prophecy, wisdom, faith versus works, and the teaching and ministry of Jesus); "The Bible and Social Justice" (a critical study of the various ways in which Christians try to apply the Bible to questions of social justice in contemporary society, in particular to world hunger, the poor and oppressed, revolution, pacifism, the role of government, and so forth); "The First Christians and Christianity Today" (a study of Luke and Acts with strong emphasis on lifestyle, community, and social attitudes).

Courses in historical theology seem to offer opportunities and difficulties similar to those in biblical studies. The history of Christian thought is full of reflection on social questions, but the books that have been written on the history of Christian thought more usually concentrate on the Christological controversies, discussions of grace and free will, the more abstract formulations of soteriology and trinitarian theology, and the issues that are at the heart of the great schisms among Christians. Such histories of Christian thought tend to see social issues as peripheral to theology.

It is not, therefore, impossible to reintegrate the social with the rather abstract systematic strand in a course in the history of Christian thought, but it is difficult and time-consuming. It must be done either from the primary sources or from specialized studies running parallel in the time sequence covered. Fortunately, literature that makes this possible is beginning to appear in secondary sources, a number of which are included in the bibliography that follows this essay.

It is, however, particularly in the areas of systematics and of spirituality that the inclusion and integration of themes of social justice and peace are not only opportune but needed for the correction of an existing bias in the more conventional academic approach to the subject matter. The elaboration and systematic explanation of the central themes that express the content of Christian faith should include all aspects of human experience, activity, relationships, and expectations. A brief survey of the main themes of Christian faith may suggest how this integration is to be accomplished.

The principal themes of Christian faith might be reduced to six: revelation, creation, sin and redemption, Christology, ecclesiology, eschatology. The theme of revelation must be related to experience before it is related to authority, formulations, or texts. It is possible to focus on experience in a highly individualized and introspective way, but this is not true to the legacy that we have in our Scriptures. Not only the Hebrew Scriptures but also the Christian testimonies of the New Testament bear witness to the experience of God's creative purpose and saving grace revealed in history; that is, in the interaction of human persons in society.

The principal revelation story of the Hebrew Scriptures is the whole story of Moses—the oppression of his people; his privileged childhood; his conversion to identification with the oppressed; the interpretive vision of the burning bush; the discerning of God's call to the liberation of the people; the experience of freedom and peoplehood as dependent each on the other; the covenant with God, which makes peoplehood and freedom possible by the giving and receiving of the law that shares God's wisdom in the governance of human affairs—all making up a strongly political theme. The principal revelation story of the Christian Scriptures is the whole story of Jesus—the oppression of his people, his own relatively privileged position, his turning in compassion to the oppressed masses, the interpretive vision of the temptations in the wilderness, the discerning of the Father's call to liberate the people from fear and servility to the conquerors and their collaborators, the rediscovering of freedom and peoplehood that is possible in radical acceptance of God's rule in human affairs, and the realization of it in the growing community of the resurrection—all making up an equally political theme, but by a far more radical perception of what it is that transforms human lives and societies from their foundations.

This understanding of revelation is interdependent with the Judeo-Christian theme of creation. The basic thrust of the creation stories and their elaboration in doctrine is that human life is meaningful, purposeful, and happy when all is oriented to God as source, criterion, and destiny. According to God's creative design there is room for all of us, our needs can be met, and we can live together in this world in deep peace and harmony and mutual sustenance and welcome. As guests of God's lavish hospitality we can afford to be generous with one another and live without fear of want and vulnerability. God's providence is all-inclusive, and our stewardship and familial concern should be similarly all-inclusive.

Into this idyllic scene comes the awareness of sin. Sin is not in the first place any specific act but the pervasive state of disorientation from God. This disorientation of human lives centered upon themselves, of human societies whose concerns and stewardship are shaped by protection of self-interest to the exclusion of others, disrupts and destroys the harmony of God's good creating. When God is at the center there is room for all of us without deprivation, violence, or fear; but when the individual or collective self is at the center, there are so many competing and incompetent creations vying for the same space and resources that there can be only chaos and destruction. Sin, in the basic sense of a turning from God-as-center to self-as-center, is never simply a private matter. It has immediate social consequences, which eventually embody themselves in social structures and values and expectations at all levels of complexity in human organization.

In the light of this understanding of sin it is clear that redemption begins with the recognition of what is sin. We tend to take for granted the order of things that we find in the world into which we are born and raised. The power of God's grace works within our freedom, and is in the first instance a gift of illumination of our dim consciousness of what is going on in our history and our world—an illumination through which it is possible to come to a critical awareness both of sin and of God's ever present redemptive mercy. The execution of Jesus is such an illumination for us in history. It shows the ambivalence, in face of God's Word spoken into history, of all the people we think of as good as well as those we generally consider bad. It also shows a certain ineluctable pattern in the structures of society, which leads them to condemn Jesus. Before the crucified Jesus we have to reconsider many of our judgments of right and wrong.

A faithful quest for a fuller understanding of Jesus and his purpose reveals a man living in the politically difficult situation of a conquered and oppressed people in occupied territory, with all the problems and daily decisions that that implies. Much recent scholarship has helped to uncover the facts of that situation and of the stance that Jesus took within it. This is beginning to be a very helpful corrective to the ahistorical, apolitical Jesus of traditional Christology. The recent challenge concerning ascending and descending Christologies has brought us back to the realization that we cannot build a Christology and a soteriology indifferent to what can be known about the historical Jesus. At this stage of scholarly exchanges, a good course in Christology or soteriology cannot be taught without reference to the social, economic, and political context of Jesus and the stance that he took within it.

CHRISTIAN PERSPECTIVES ON WORLD PEACE *(three credits)*

The purpose of this course is to show peacemaking as a positive enter-prise and to discover from Bible, history, and systematic reflections what it involves and why it is integral to the redemption and the Christian life.

OUTLINE

Introduction (two lectures)
  Topic: Why peacemaking is a Christian issue (sketch out what is to be explicated in the course).
  Reading Assignment: Helder Camara. *Spiral of Violence*. Denville, N.J.: Dimension Books, 1971.
Part I: Biblical Foundations (two weeks)
  Topics: The concept of "shalom," peace and justice in prophetic literature, nonviolence in the New Testament.
  Reading Assignment: Excerpts from Scripture; P. Regamey. *Non-Violence and Christian Conscience*. New York: Herder and Herder, 1966.
Part II: History of Christian Understanding (three weeks)
  Topic: Developments from early pacifism to reluctant just-war theor-ies, to crusades, to modern reconsiderations.
  Reading Assignment: Roland Bainton. *Christian Attitudes toward War and Peace*. Nashville, Tenn.: Abingdon, 1960.
Part III: Systematic Reflection (three weeks)
  Topic: Relation of questions of war and peace to central themes of Christian faith.
  Reading Assignment: John XXIII. *Pacem in Terris* ("Peace on Earth," 1963). Paul VI. *Populorum Progressio* ("On the Develop-ment of Peoples," 1967). Both in *The Gospel of Peace and Justice*, ed. Joseph Gremillion. Maryknoll, N.Y.: Orbis Books, 1976.
Part IV: Practical Issues (three weeks)
  Topics: Modern issues of total war, ideological wars, cold war and armaments buildup, wars of liberation, revolution, peace and social justice, nonviolent revolutions.
  Reading Assignment: Richard McSorley. *Kill for Peace?* New York: Corpus Books, 1970; United States Catholic Bishops. "The Chal-lenge of Peace." Washington, D.C.: United States Catholic Con-ference, 1983.
Part V: A Spirituality of Peace (two weeks)
  Topics: Acknowledgment and discernment of pervasive violence in society and international relations; questions raised by discrepan-cies in wealth of nations; possibilities of creative response in life-style and interaction.

Reading Assignment: Thomas Merton. *Faith and Violence*. Notre Dame, Ind.: University of Notre Dame Press, 1968.

BASIS OF EVALUATION

a. Two short reading reports.
b. Midsemester and final examinations on lecture and reading material, testing correct understanding of history and various positions as well as ability to synthesize into own informed position.
c. It is recommended that practicum not be evaluated directly, but be allowed to contribute to understanding of issues raised in lectures and reading.

NOTE: This type of course offers particularly good opportunities for discussion. Students can be asked to come prepared to defend a viewpoint from Scripture, history, and authoritative teachings as well as from their own insights.

The implications of this carry over, of course, into ecclesiology and eschatology. Serious reflection on the content of Christian hope, a return to general as well as individual eschatology, and the challenge to relate this to expectations, private lifestyles, and public action in history necessarily lead to a theology of the world and its problems. The understanding of eschatology bears a direct relationship to the understanding of creation. The outcomes for which we may hope are related to the harmony and purpose we discern in God's design for the universe and for human history within it. The unity, mercy, and power of God logically demand acknowledgment of a unified horizon in our faith and theology, taking in all aspects of public and private life and all dimensions of world and history.

In this context church cannot be thought of as an enclave of salvific processes in an otherwise doomed world. Church can only be seen as a movement among peoples pursuing the vision that Jesus communicated for the redemption of the whole world, with the hope that Jesus inspired, and with the power of his all-embracing compassion and redemptive love. The task of the church at any time, therefore, cannot be understood without reference to the actual and concrete social, economic, and political situations of suffering and oppression of that time, in all their daunting complexity and apparent insolubility. Any course in ecclesiology today must address these, just as pastoral action and Christian life must address them.

The dimensions of the central themes of Christian faith as just sketched suggest the intrinsic connection between doctrinal or systematic theology courses and current issues of peace and justice in the world. They are intended to suggest how a specialized course, such as Christology, soteriology, ecclesiology, or eschatology, might be constructed and presented, but also to suggest a mode of presentation for an introductory course on Christian faith or Catholic theology or the themes of systematic theology. The first outline presented in this chapter is for a course offering "Christian Perspectives on World Peace," and demonstrates how a particular theme might be traced in Christian theology. Authors who have particularly addressed the social justice content of Christian faith in a specialized way are the "liberation theologians." Therefore, the second outline presented below is for a course on "Theologies of Liberation."

THEOLOGIES OF LIBERATION *(three credits)*

The aim of this course is to explore the political dimension of Christian faith and to reflect on the implications this has for an understanding of basic Christian doctrines. To this end the focus of the course is mainly on some of the third-world theologians who have persistently drawn our attention to this political dimension.

OUTLINE

Introduction: What is Liberation Theology? (one lecture)
>   Topics: Explanation of the issue of "de-privatization" of faith and theology; general introduction to the goal and agenda of liberation theology.
>   *Reading Assignment*: Essays of Segundo Galilea and José Comblin. In *The Mystical and Political Dimensions of the Christian Faith*, ed. Claude Geffre and Gustavo Gutiérrez. New York: Herder and Herder, 1974.

Part I: What Is the Gospel of Jesus Christ? (three weeks)
>   Topics: Discussion of what we know of Jesus and his message in the context of the Jewish expectations and of his own historical situation.
>   *Reading Assignment*: Sebastian Kappen. *Jesus and Freedom*. Maryknoll, N.Y.: Orbis Books, 1977.

Part II: The Goods of the Earth by Nature and Grace (three weeks)
>   Topics: Presentation of the doctrines of creation and sin in sociopolitical perspective, with reference to contemporary problems and suffering.
>   *Reading Assignment*: Edward Rogers. *Poverty on a Small Planet*. New York: Macmillan, 1964; Monika Hellwig. *The Eucharist and the Hunger of the World*. New York: Paulist Press, 1976.

Part III: What Is Salvation? (three weeks)
>   Topics: Discussion of redemption, grace, and general eschatology in contemporary practical context, with the sociopolitical implications.
>   *Reading Assignment*: Hugo Assmann. *Theology for a Nomad Church*. Maryknoll, N.Y.: Orbis Books, 1976.

Part IV: The Role of the Church in the Redemption (two weeks)

Topics: Discussion of ecclesiology in the light of all the foregoing, with reference to the church as inevitably a political presence faced with choices as to how to use its leverage.

Reading Assignment: Essays of Enrique Dussel, Gustavo Gutiérrez, and Leonardo Boff. In *The Mystical and Political Dimensions of the Christian Faith* (cited above).

Part V: What Does Redemption Mean in Practice? (two weeks)

Topics: Discussion of the ambiguity of poverty in relation to the gospel; structures of political and economic power in relation to the gospel. Where can anyone begin?

Reading Assignment: Julio de Santa Ana. *Good News to the Poor.* Maryknoll, N.Y.: Orbis Books, 1979; essays by Juan Luis Segundo and Ronaldo Muñoz. In *The Mystical and Political Dimensions of the Christian Faith* (cited above).

BASIS OF EVALUATION

a. Two reading reports.
b. Mid-semester examination (after part II).
c. Final examination demanding synthesis of the material as well as clarity on positions presented in lectures and reading.
d. If there is a practicum, it will certainly contribute to this synthesis, but it is probably best to avoid the insoluble difficulties of trying to grade the practicum.

NOTE: Class discussion of the implications of each author's position will be very helpful, because discussion tends to prevent simple memorization and repetition of the material.

Many professors consider an educational experience more complete if lectures and readings and discussions can be combined with some form of practicum. This depends, of course, on local opportunities. Probably the most helpful approach to this in a single semester, in which the undergraduate students are taking five or six courses and have many demands on their time, is to arrange for them to work with some voluntary organization that already has many contacts and much practical information. Students working in such a setting for about two hours a week can observe a great deal. Examples of such agencies are Amnesty International, Oxfam America, Bread for the World, Campaign for Human Development, Catholic Peace Fellowship, Fellowship of Reconciliation, Catholic Worker Houses, the United Nations Association, American Friends Service Committee, American Civil Liberties Union, and so forth.

Obviously, the possibilities for interdisciplinary courses are many. Peace studies offer a fertile field for cooperation among theologians, political and social scientists, and psychologists, among others. A study of peacemaking can fruitfully place beside the lessons drawn from history and diplomacy, from psychological studies of projection and prejudice, from sociological studies of group behavior and political studies of institutional structures and processes, a profound theological reflection on the Christian understanding of sin and redemption.

Similarly, questions of social justice relating to human rights, world hunger, refugee problems, inequality of bargaining power between rich and poor nations, all have more than one side. There is the need for factual information and for economic and political analysis of the processes and structures involved. But there is also the need for critical reflection on what we may hope and ought to strive for, and on the grounds for such hope and such sense of obligation. This is the role of the theological reflection that must complement the technical analysis.

It is, of course, not only with the social sciences that theologians can and should plan interdisciplinary courses. It may be equally important to consider collaboration with some of the natural sciences, for instance on questions of ecology and stewardship responsibilities for the earth and for future generations. Likewise, a course on responsibility for peacekeeping in the nuclear age might well enlist collaboration of physicians as well as some members of the Union of Concerned Scientists or of scientists on one's own campus who have kept well informed on research and projections related to nuclear war.

What we academics must realize, however reluctantly, is that strict adherence to disciplinary boundaries, maintenance of scholarly neutrality on all subjects and of an open mind on all issues, and a preference for the strictly theoretical and the realms of pure research are no longer helpful to undergraduate students. Students are in quest of a liberal education and a liberating education that equips them both to enjoy the cultural heritage to which we introduce them and to defend its survival and adaptation in a world where the issues are complex, threatening, and immediate. We know and they know that if their college years are not to be a useless postponement of adulthood, their studies must equip them to deal with the great public issues of our time.

NOTE

1. See "Powerlessness in Appalachia," *Origins* 4, no. 34 (Feb. 13, 1975): 529, 531–43; United States Catholic Bishops, "The Challenge of Peace: God's Promise and Our Response" (Washington, D.C.: United States Catholic Conference, 1983), p. 103.

SELECTED READINGS FOR FACULTY

PEACE AND WAR AND NONVIOLENCE

Böckle, Franz, ed. *War, Poverty, Freedom.* New York: Paulist Press, 1966.
Davies, J. G. *Christians, Politics and Violent Revolution.* Maryknoll, N.Y.: Orbis Books, 1976.

Douglass, James. *The Non-Violent Cross*. New York: Macmillan, 1968.

––––. *Resistance and Contemplation*. New York: Dell Publishing Co., 1972.

Gandhi, Mohandas. *Non-Violent Resistance*. New York: Schocken Books, 1951.

Guinan, Edward, ed. *Peace and Non-Violence*. New York: Paulist Press, 1973.

Hauerwas, Stanley. *The Peaceable Kingdom*. Notre Dame, Ind.: University of Notre Dame Press, 1983.

King, Martin Luther, Jr. *Where Do We Go From Here: Chaos or Community?* Boston, Mass.: Beacon Press, 1968.

Lochman, Jan Mili. *Reconciliation and Liberation*. Philadelphia, Pa.: Fortress Press, 1977.

Long, Edward L. *Peace Thinking in a Warring World*. Philadelphia, Pa.: Westminster Press, 1983.

Macquarrie, John. *The Concept of Peace*. New York: Harper & Row, 1973.

Mayer, Peter, ed. *The Pacifist Conscience*. New York: Holt, Rinehart and Winston, 1966.

National Conference of Catholic Bishops. *In the Name of Peace: Collective Statements of the U.S. Catholic Bishops, 1919–1980*. Washington, D.C.: USCC, 1982.

Pontifical Commission, Justitia et Pax, and Commission of Churches on International Affairs. *Peace and Disarmament: Documents of the Roman Catholic Church and the World Council of Churches*. Washington, D.C.: USCC, 1982.

Sheerin, John. *Peace, War and the Young Catholic*. New York: Paulist Press, 1973.

Stotts, Jack L. *Shalom: The Search for a Peaceable City*. Nashville, Tenn.: Abingdon, 1973.

Swift, Louis. *The Early Fathers on War and Military Service*. Wilmington, Del.: Michael Glazier, 1983.

Vanderhaar, Gerard A. *Christians and Nonviolence in the Nuclear Age*. Mystic, Conn.: Twenty Third Publications, 1982.

LIBERATION THEOLOGY

Alves, Rubem. *A Theology of Human Hope*. Washington, D.C.: Corpus Books, 1969.

Ellacuría, Ignacio. *Freedom Made Flesh*. Maryknoll, N.Y.: Orbis Books, 1976.

Fierro, Alfredo. *The Militant Gospel*. Maryknoll, N.Y.: Orbis Books, 1977.

Gutiérrez, Gustavo. *A Theology of Liberation*. Maryknoll, N.Y.: Orbis Books, 1973.

Jones, Major. *Black Awareness*. Nashville, Tenn.: Abington, 1971.

Laurentin, René. *Liberation, Development and Salvation*. Maryknoll, N.Y.: Orbis Books, 1972.

Míguez Bonino, José. *Doing Theology in a Revolutionary Situation*. Philadelphia, Pa.: Fortress Press, 1975.

Miranda, José. *Marx and the Bible*. Maryknoll, N.Y.: Orbis Books, 1974.

SOCIAL JUSTICE IN GENERAL

Böckle, Franz and J. M. Pohier. *Power and the Word of God*. New York: Herder and Herder, 1973.

Campaign for Human Development. *Poverty Profile*. Washington, D.C.: USCC, 1972.

––––. *Sourcebook on Poverty, Development and Justice*. Washington, D.C.: USCC, 1972.

Clark, Henry B. *Escape from the Money Trap*. Valley Forge, Pa.: Judson Press, 1973.

Clarke, Thomas E., ed. *Above Every Name*. New York: Paulist Press, 1980.

Gremillion, Joseph, ed. *The Gospel of Peace and Justice*. Maryknoll, N.Y.: Orbis Books, 1976.

Haughey, John C., ed. *The Faith That Does Justice*. New York: Paulist Press, 1977.

Kee, Alistair, ed. *A Reader in Political Theology*. Philadelphia, Pa.: Westminster Press, 1974.

Kerans, Patrick. *Sinful Social Structures*. New York: Paulist Press, 1974.

Paupert, J. M. *The Politics of the Gospel*. New York: Holt, Rinehart and Winston, 1969.

2

Philosophy

DAVID B. BURRELL, C.S.C.
UNIVERSITY OF NOTRE DAME

Education for justice and peace is a matter of setting the context for teaching rather than deciding a particular content for the courses. Context becomes an especially critical variable for education in the first world—the one we unconsciously and presumptively inhabit—for circumstances have made us the ones who set the context for others. A most unfortunate result of that de facto dominance is that we lack a defined context, since we presume that we live at the center. Do we not, after all, assume our way to be the norm? Let me illustrate.

THE CONTEXT

In the fall semester of 1975, I was fortunate to be teaching in the National Major Seminary in Dacca, Bangladesh: fortunate because my religious congregation (Holy Cross Fathers) made the trip possible, as a small contribution to its long-term presence in that land, and fortunate to be able to spend three months with Bengalis in the company of expatriate sisters and brothers who could introduce me effectively to the people and to their culture. I have subsequently contributed to the Holy Cross Fathers' work in Latin America, served for two years in Israel, and I am writing this in Egypt where I am studying Islamic philosophy—yet everything goes back to those three months in Bangladesh. The resolve to go to Bangladesh stemmed from a remark made by the University of Notre Dame's president, Theodore Hesburgh, C.S.C., a year or so earlier. No one, he said, should be teaching students in Western Europe or North America who has not spent some time in the third world, if at all possible. Teachers should be preparing students for an interdependent

27

world, and not simply allow them to perpetuate the current sets of unbalanced attitudes and exploitative practices.

I am always chary in reporting that remark, however apposite it may be, for I am acutely aware how few faculty members would be able to respond to such a challenge. Few enough enjoy the network of a worldwide religious community or can take advantage of a vow of celibacy as it facilitates such displacement. Nor are they likely to find an encouraging response from their respective institutions. (Indeed an academic officer at Notre Dame contested my request for leave, querying how teaching in Dacca would "contribute to his academic furtherance.") Thus, unsurprisingly, do the institutions and attitudes in place further the attitudes and practices that Fr. Hesburgh deplored—unless we shake them up a bit.

That is what I mean by the power of context. The need for some form of displacement, for faculty as well as students, is to allow them a vantage point from which to put their world in its place; to recognize, in short, the context in which one truly lives, and of which one can remain quite unconscious. This is all the more true because we normally presume ourselves to be at the center of a universe and hence naturally relegate everyone and everything else to the periphery. That presumption, moreover, leaves us little imagination for alternatives, and hence without a coherent context ourselves. One has only to compare the proportion of global to local news in an ordinary American newspaper with dailies anywhere else in the world, or to consider the average English-speaking person's linguistic ineptitude in order to realize how *deprived* an upbringing in the dominant society can be. As shocking as it is when put that way, the shock can be a salutary one if it manages to fix attention on what members of the dominant society are missing.

Just such a focus is imperative to meet the concerns that at once motivate justice education and call it into question. Those who demand it and will be attracted to courses with a justice dimension are normally those concerned to "do something about the world," those who have been touched by compassion for the plight of the poor and want to find out how to ameliorate such conditions. Those who call it into question, on the other hand, consider such concerns alien to academe and its proper disciplines, having at best to do only with their applications. Applications, they say, have little place in the classroom. Thus faculty members who do pursue such questions are engaged in academically questionable pursuits, though church-related colleges and universities may have to tolerate them as having something to do with the institutions' wider mission.

What is worth noting about the critique and the enthusiasm is that both stem from the same presumption—that it is a matter of *our* doing something for *them*. What each overlooks, however, are the considerations of context just elaborated. Few faculty members reflect on the manner in which their topics, orientations, and research agenda are set by their situation in the first world; and students in first-world countries are not accustomed to thinking of themselves as deprived—though those who have spent even one semester abroad have begun to have some second thoughts. In a milieu that considers itself to be critical *ex professo*, we offer little criticism of accepted standards and criteria, even when these embody and promote attitudes and practices we might deplore.

This, I submit, is the situation in which we find ourselves, and which justice education in each discipline should be designed to address. In that respect, to raise questions of justice will be to raise critical questions about our work and the context in which we work. It will direct itself not so much to "helping others" as to overcoming our myopia, for that very ignorance of our context impedes us from altering things in the world, by allowing us to continue unconsciously contributing to a system whose very presumptions we fail to test. Justice education, then, offers a dimension to every discipline whereby it can become critically self-conscious, and offers faculty and students alike an opportunity to ask themselves what it is they are about.

IN THE DISCIPLINE OF PHILOSOPHY

Since my initial reflections on our context were clearly philosophical in tone, one might think philosophy to be a natural discipline for raising such questions. Moreover, philosophy, unlike literature or engineering, can count "justice" as a natural topic. On the other hand, it would be unlikely if philosophy did not share the myopia just exposed, so that considerations of justice would be constrained to fit a certain mold to be respectable. Thus philosophy turns out to be the best and the worst of disciplines for exploring justice issues. Exposing the reasons for that requires a bit of philosophical therapy, though it may prove useful for other fields as well.

We need to keep reminding ourselves that a discipline offers a way of understanding the world. One teaches a discipline appropriately when one presents it as a perspective on reality, a way of relating to the world. A central concern about the world is its order, and a crucial question about its order is the extent to which it is (or is not) a just ordering. So far, so good; yet at this point, at the point where one must become specific, philosophy experiences a peculiar temptation. Lacking a subject matter it can call its own, it can easily feel the need to appropriate certain topics—say, justice. The temptation then becomes to lose sight of the original concern, and to treat justice *within* philosophy. The strategy of teaching will be to canvas "philosophers" on the issue and to become fascinated by the analysis of this topic. Students other than those captured by a like fascination will be left wondering what it was they were concerned about.

Fortunately, attention to the essentials can correct this penchant of philosophers to "capture" a topic. One strategy would be to use the justice-focus as a prism through which one could attempt to understand worldly issues: development, distribution of goods, affirmative action, corporate policies, and the like. Especially with a class of students who are themselves primarily interested in one or another such area, one can set about analyzing current writing on the subject, trying to understand it in the light of a just ordering, and ask as well how one might influence these affairs. Such a course introduces students to characteristically philosophical ways of dealing with issues, yet also shows how this issue will in turn modify the way one treats it.

In Aristotle's terms, we would be dealing with human practices, and so need to attend to their practical as well as their speculative dimensions. The study of justice, then, would not turn justice into a topic "inside" philosophy, but would itself become an opportunity to learn how one might relate to a world marked by disorder: critically, so as to recognize injustice for what it is (and why it must be so called); constructively, to ascertain what sorts of steps would be required to render a situation less unjust. In fact, one result of such a strategy is to learn that one is better off to use the comparative ("more/less just") construction, then to attempt to speak of a "just society" *tout court*. These are subtle yet far-reaching lessons in the branch of practical philosophy that Aristotle called "ethics."

ISSUES IN JUSTICE (three credits)

DESCRIPTION

This course endeavors to test proposals for understanding human justice against the complexities of actual situations, and to bring about a particular and personal synthesis of that exploration by imagining alternative ways of organizing a sector of society. To that end, we first read standard classics as well as modern and contemporary writers on the subject, then we divide the class into smaller groups to lay out particular practical issues, and finally we invite each participant to imagine how that sector of society in which he or she may be most interested could be altered in the direction of greater justice. The final examination can profitably be planned as a critique of a current public document, to let students realize how their capacities for analysis and for negotiating complexities can be brought to bear on a particular official proposal.

READINGS (listed in order of assignment)

Plato. *Republic*. Baltimore, Md.: Penguin Books, 1975.
Aristotle. *Ethics* (from Feinberg, ed., *Justice*; see below).
Thomas Aquinas. In Pieper, Josef. *Four Cardinal Virtues*. Notre Dame, Ind.: University of Notre Dame Press, 1966. Section on "Justice."
Feinberg, Joel, ed. *Justice*. Belmont, Calif.: Dickenson Publishing Co., 1977. Selections from David Hume, John Stuart Mill, John Rawls, and Robert Nozick.
Illich, Ivan. *Towards a History of Needs*. New York: Bantam Books, 1980.

Wilber, Charles, and Mary Evelyn Jegen, eds. *Growth with Equity*. New York: Paulist Press, 1979.

Holland, Joseph, and Peter Henriot. *Social Analysis*. New York: Paulist Press, 1983.

COURSE OUTLINE

I. Weeks One–Seven: Readings in classical, modern, and contemporary figures (Plato, Aristotle, Thomas Aquinas, Hume, Mill, Rawls, Nozick), followed by midterm examination on these readings.

II. Weeks Eight–Ten: Presentation, by groups, of practical issues chosen early in the semester, organized and researched by the groups with assistance of other faculty members, community resources, and so forth.

Week Eleven: Transition to part III—implications of complexity.

III. Weeks Twelve–Fourteen: Exploring alternative structures for society. A selection among the sources noted (Illich, Wilber and Jegen, Holland and Henriot), followed by a final paper outlining an alternative way of structuring one sector of society.

Final examination: Critique of a public-policy document.

NOTE: One might consider the three sections of the course to correspond to theory (I), practice (II), and imagination (III). Most of us are least prepared in the third area; students do remarkably well in the second.

A NOTE ON ASSESSMENT

If one-page responses to the readings are solicited in order to help structure class discussion and direct the development of analytic skills, the rest of the course provides ample material for assessment of student performance. The quality of individual participation in the group projects is clear enough, and the final paper, together with the examination, offers sufficiently varied responses to allow the instructor to come to a fair assessment of student performance in meeting the goals of the course.

ORGANIZING THE COURSE

A course in "Ethics" (mine is titled "Issues in Justice") properly considers practical as well as speculative matters, and can profit from what contemporaries call "theories of justice," for here one acquires habits of analysis. It should not begin with contemporary or even modern ways of posing the question, however, since history helps us to establish the context as effectively as cross-cultural experience.

The practical side poses difficulties of its own, especially with a young and relatively homogeneous student body from the first world. All the unconscious presumptions noted earlier will conspire to block insight, and class discussion will amount to trading prejudices. Where the student body is of mixed age and background, the opportunity is richer, yet it will need to be brought to an effective focus. At this point what usually falters is the imagination of the teacher, as well as his or her tolerance for opening the class beyond one's "control." Experiential learning of some sort is clearly called for, but how is it to be done?

I have found it useful to give a portion of the course over to the students, encouraging them early in the semester to settle upon two or three topics of interest to them. With minimal assistance from the teacher, they have followed leads to approach other faculty members or community organizations for help, organized the analysis of the situations themselves, and made presentations to the rest of the class. (Using three topics allows one-third of the class to address the rest.) Their very clarity of presentation helps to make them, as well as those whom they address, aware of the complexities of the issues involved.

Careful analysis of the various notions of justice elaborated through history usually produces bewilderment. It is not a simple question of which one is right, but a more profound consideration of how to order the ideas so as to discover which would be more properly evoked in what situations. The detailed study and presentation of specific issues, moreover, can leave one with a hopeless feeling of complexity—and we all know how easily "complexity" becomes an excuse for inaction. Something else is needed to bring the issues closer to home, and to pinpoint ways in which we might be able to affect them. I call this final step "imagining alternatives."

One result of the peculiar context of privilege is that the students' least developed capacity is imagination. (Indeed, this is probably true of teachers also.) Trained to analyze and successful in the measure to which they can organize, their range of experience is nonetheless limited. Hence one must carefully determine an *alternative* situation in which one (or more—but at least one) significant feature has been altered. The test for significance will reflect, of course, how well students have assimilated the speculative treatments of justice. The choice of features that we might stand a chance of changing will test the students' feel for the complexity of our world. Two works come to mind as particularly provocative and mind-stretching for reading at this point: E. F. Schumacher's *Small Is Beautiful*, and Ivan Illich's *Towards a History of Needs*. A final paper in which each student focuses on a sector of society that he or she anticipates entering, and sketches how one's presence might contribute to an alternative way of ordering it, affords a useful way of exercising the student's imagination and of pinpointing the two earlier sections of the course.

Examination offers little difficulty in such a course. A midterm exam on the reading in the history of analysis allows students to show how well they have sorted out that history and assimilated it. Participation in the group presentation of a specific issue lets them display their capacity for concrete analysis.

One can usually find a quasi-official document to offer for criticism at the end of the course, thereby contributing to their own sense of having learned from the course by their ability to place such a document in context, assess its arguments, and indicate its shortcomings. (In 1979 we used the United States paper for the United Nations meeting on appropriate technologies; in 1983, the Canadian Catholic Bishops' statement on the economy.)

IMAGINATION FOR ALTERNATIVES

I have so far sketched the structure of a course in philosophy that utilizes questions of justice to develop students' skills in practical philosophy. The threefold pattern of theory, practice, and imagination has proved particularly adaptable to that goal. I am most intrigued with the third step—imagination— not only because it represents the single advance beyond Aristotle in the course, but also because it locates a lacuna in the students' educational background and seeks to correct it. Utilizing some literary, especially dramatic materials in the theoretical portion (selected from materials ranging from Sophocles' *Antigone* to Brecht's *Mother Courage*) would assist in this endeavor. The challenge now is to think of topics other than "justice" as a way of raising the questions germane to a just ordering of the world.

One such issue, certainly, is "violence." An advantage of focusing on violence is that it has not been the subject of much philosophical analysis. Hence one is forced to exploit the analysis of other disciplines, thus displaying that justice issues cannot be contained as a topic *within* philosophy. Moreover, the varied cultural perceptions of violence invite collaboration with anthropologists, at least one of whom (Rodney Needham) has argued eloquently for the relevance of anthropological research to philosophical reflection on such shaping human issues as faith and friendship, love and death.

The second course outline, presented below, deals with "Roots of Violence," and is organized on a pattern paralleling the "Issues in Justice" course described above. It is a team-taught course, my co-teacher being Patrick Gaffney, C.S.C., an anthropologist colleague at Notre Dame. Through the readings selected, and especially through the interaction of these two teachers, a healthy respect for the ways in which violence, like injustice, is indeed a fact of life (even though its ethical valence is prima facie negative) can be generated. Something of the perspectives peculiar to one trained as an anthropologist and to one trained in philosophy prove especially illuminating on a subject as central to human life, yet so elusive of analysis, as violence.

We move rather quickly in the course to considerations of nonviolence as *the* outstanding alternative presented to our time, notably by Mohandas K. Gandhi. A careful study of his arguments helps one to overcome the commonplace character of violence as it appears through media today. However one might locate the subject in the spectrum of philosophical subdisciplines, the salient feature of this course lies in its interdisciplinary character. In fact, as the extant philosophical literature testifies, it would be foolish to undertake an exploration of violence without assistance from anthropology.

ROOTS OF VIOLENCE (three credits)

DESCRIPTION

This course explores the senses of violence through philosophical and literary works, as well as in Mohandas K. Gandhi's notable alternative of "nonviolence"; it considers actual situations in the world about us, and focuses on a particular conflict as an extended case study. To that end, we read two political theorists and two creative writers, then divide the class into smaller groups to present specifics on situations of violence, and complete the course with a close analysis of the Arab-Israeli conflict over the Holy Land. Each student participates in the group research of zones or dimensions of violence in our society, and is asked to write a final paper on how things could be altered to alleviate violence in those areas. The final examination tests the student's ability to organize the factors operative in the final conflict studied in order to appreciate the relative intractability of violence in our world, and to offer practicable suggestions for containing or alleviating it.

READINGS

Aeschylus. *Oresteian Trilogy*. Baltimore, Md.: Penguin Books, 1959.
American Friends Service Committee. *A Compassionate Peace*. New York: Hill & Wang, 1982.
Arendt, Hannah. *On Violence*. New York: Harcourt Brace Jovanovich, 1969.
Bondurant, Joan. *Conquest of Violence*. Berkeley, Calif.: University of California Press, 1969.
Burgess, Anthony. *Clockwork Orange*. New York: W. W. Norton, 1963.
Shehadeh, Rajah. *The Third Way*. New York: Quartet Books, 1982.

COURSE OUTLINE

I. Weeks One–Seven: Readings in political analysis and in literature (Arendt, Bondurant, Aeschylus, Burgess), followed by midterm examination on these readings.
II. Weeks Eight–Ten: Presentation, by groups, of their analyses of violence in areas classified as (1) interpersonal, (2) situational, (3) structural. The first envisages familial conflicts; the second views those circumstances that create unusual conditions, such as prisons, crowding, alcohol and drug cultures; the third probes those respectable façades that systematically relegate particular groups to unfavorable circumstances.

III. Weeks Eleven–Fourteen: An extended case study—the Arab-Israeli conflict. Background on the historical situation of the Jewish people in the West, leading up to the strategy of Zionism, and the resulting transformations of the Syro-Palestinian territory, regarded by each religious group as the Holy Land. The AFSC report offers a balanced presentation of the issues at once uniting and dividing all contenders, and selections from more personal statements (e.g., Rajah Shehadeh's journal) and current articles supplement this presentation.

Final Examination: Reappraisal of the Arab-Israeli conflict, in the light of works studied and local alternatives proposed.

A NOTE ON ASSESSMENT

One-page responses, by each student, to the readings in the first portion of the course, plus the midterm examination; followed by individual participation in the group research projects, capped by the group's paper; and then the final examination, offer abundant material for assessment of students in relation to the goals of the course. The most difficult feature of this course is for the students to gain a perspective of relative neutrality and cool comprehension of violence, for its initial valence is invariably negative, and prevailing causal explanations prove of little practical worth.

SOME SUBSTANTIVE ISSUES

The matter of sources in philosophy is too complex to be dealt with in a course outline alone. We live in an age of fragmented moral discourse, with fragmentation elevated to a matter of principle in the liberal ethos we all share, and embodied in anthologies of short readings. The fragmented image has been exploited admirably by Alasdair MacIntyre in *After Virtue*, and anyone teaching practical philosophy should assimilate his argument. That one is hardly *allowed*, as it were, to argue a single normative viewpoint should not, however, reduce a teacher simply to sampling various views.

In presenting the course on justice, we devoted the first three weeks to a close reading of Plato's *Republic*. This provides an extended framework (and one that shows interrelationship of individual and social structure) that can be used as a baseline for other readings. The disadvantage of this procedure is to weight the course decidedly in favor of more classical renderings of justice (Plato, Aristotle, Thomas Aquinas) in such a way as to make the more characteristically modern (or liberal) treatments (Hume, Mill, Rawls, Nozick) appear somewhat thin by comparison. The sole justification for such an approach is to offset the inbuilt bias of students, who are often liberal-leaning in their unspoken social philosophy, and firm believers in a social contract. Hence the point that I wish to make here is that some larger framework for analysis ought to attend the presentation of the diverse views of justice available from the philosophical tradition. Having MacIntyre's thesis in mind, as an analytic tool in presenting each thinker, might well fill that need.

Regarding student acceptance and participation, courses such as these are more effective with students in their final two years of college, for they are already pursuing their major field of study and may well have had the enriching experience of study abroad. The presence of students majoring in economics or business or science or engineering is an obvious plus when the class is considering specific issues. The bonus of overseas experience contributes markedly to the students' capacity for imagining alternatives, for such students have begun the process of placing their life in this portion of the world into a larger context. Consequently, the aim of each course to establish such a context for assessment will be helped by these students, and they in turn will challenge others to enlarge their perspectives.

Finally, it cannot be overemphasized that teaching of this sort will challenge a teacher's presumptions as much as those of the student. Undertaking to explore, through one's discipline, the justice dimensions of the world in which we live is a radical endeavor in that it demands that we become as self-critical as academe celebrates being critical. Yet it is one thing to extoll critical thinking, and another to turn it on one's own discipline or institution. We can expect the results of such an inquiry to be unsettling. Yet philosophy, rooted as it is in Socrates' quest for performative consistency, cannot avoid inquiry of this sort. Moreover, the students of today, who are sensitive to the ominous clouds over their future, need clear and compassionate analysis to help them chart a path for their lives. Courses like these, in as many disciplines as possible, may well help them to do so. Let us never forget that such explorations are always joint ventures, with rewards for both teacher and student.

SELECTED READINGS FOR FACULTY

STANDARD CLASSICS

Aristotle. *Ethics*. Indianapolis, Ind.: Bobbs-Merrill, 1962. Book 5.
Hume, David. *Inquiry Concerning the Principle of Morals*. Indianapolis, Ind.: Bobbs-Merrill, 1957.
Mill, John Stuart. *On Liberty*. Indianapolis, Ind.: Bobbs-Merrill, 1956.
Plato. *Republic*. Baltimore, Md.: Penguin Books, 1975.
Thomas Aquinas. In Josef Pieper. *Four Cardinal Virtues*. Notre Dame, Ind.: University of Notre Dame Press, 1966. Section on "Justice."

CONTEMPORARY WRITINGS

MacIntyre, Alasdair. *After Virtue*. Notre Dame, Ind.: University of Notre Dame Press, 1981.

Nozick, Robert. *Anarchy, State, and Utopia*. New York: Harper & Row, 1974.

Rawls, John. *Theory of Justice*. Cambridge, Mass.: Harvard University Press, 1971.

Walzer, Michael. *Spheres of Justice: A Defense of Pluralism and Equality*. New York: Basic Books, 1983.

Wolff, Robert Paul. *Understanding Rawls*. Princeton, N.J.: Princeton University Press, 1977.

ANTHOLOGIES

Feinberg, Joel, ed. *Justice*. Belmont, Calif.: Dickenson Publishing Co., 1977. Selections from Aristotle, David Hume, John Stuart Mill, John Rawls, and Robert Nozick.

Sterba, James. *The Demands of Justice*. Notre Dame, Ind.: University of Notre Dame Press, 1981.

ALTERNATIVES

Holland, Joseph, and Peter Henriot. *Social Analysis*.Maryknoll, N.Y.: Orbis Books, 1983.

Illich, Ivan. *Towards a History of Needs*. New York: Bantam Books, 1980.

Schumacher, E. F. *Small Is Beautiful*. New York: Harper & Row, 1976.

3

Literature

DON FORAN
CENTRALIA COLLEGE

Teachers of the humanities and arts have a distinct advantage in addressing issues of justice and peace in the college classroom. Theirs is the province of the imagination: they peddle metaphors as skillfully as sociologists disseminate information and biologists dissect frogs. Professors of literature have a unique opportunity to highlight issues involving human solidarity and oppression, peace and war, because the writers whose works they analyze are often tapping into the rich vein of universal values implicit in imaginative choosing. Often literary figures—William Faulkner comes immediately to mind—"argue from absence"; that is, they portray the horror caused by the failure to choose the common good and they suggest that things might have been different. However they argue, writers present the complexities and subtleties of human interactions. Once exposed to those subtleties of interaction through an author's skillful characterization, students come to see that every person struggles against the limitations of understanding, imagination, and personal power to create something of value. This quest to scratch one's "Kilroy was here" on the wall of life can be fulfilling or tragically fruitless.

The skillful teacher provides access to a literary text and facilitates the student's understanding of the ultimate truth or truths that a poem, short story, play, essay, or novel conveys. In order to accomplish this task, the teacher of literature frequently focuses on structural devices, repeated images, and dominant themes in the works at hand as the student becomes immersed in the fictional world the writer has created.

Finally, the teacher elicits insights from the students, both in discussions and by means of essay tests and compositions. He or she offers opportunities for the student to explore the surface and symbolic levels of the work in order to discover the truth about life and value that has been distilled by the writer into a poem, parable, imaginative re-creation, or vignette. Shakespeare has suggested that the play is a mirror held up to nature, and Joseph Conrad insisted that the artist holds a fragment of the truth up to the light; but perhaps American poet William Carlos Williams says it best:

> It is difficult
> to get the news from poems
> yet men die miserably every day
> for lack
> of what is found there.[1]

In great literature—the type that outlives popular interest and narrow concerns—writers often capture ideas or portray events or reveal characters in such a way that we learn to live life more compassionately. We see people choosing wisely or unwisely; we recognize situations we know from experience. Sometimes we understand our radical interdependence with the rest of humankind. Occasionally we are inspired to act with integrity or to affirm life rather than deny its possibilities. When antiheroes are presented—isolated protagonists caught up in their own egos—we weigh the dangers of self-deception and note, with Melville's Ahab, that the howling infinite where conscience is formed is not necessarily more hazardous than the "lee shore" where the comforts of hearth and home can also sink us.

At its best, literature motivates us to think relationally, to be imaginative in our choosing. In a sense it appeals to the eye of the eye, speaks to the heart of the heart.

ALLOWING IDEOLOGY TO SURFACE

Certain works of literature are particularly conducive to helping the student learn that he or she wears, as every human does, a unique ideological lens. Because of our socialization, we see things the way we see them and not some other way. This understanding is important when we speak of justice issues and contemporary events because, unless we confront the degree to which our perspective is influenced by our own socialization, we find it very difficult to see another point of view. When we do grasp how ideology works, we are more open to the excitement that learning is about. We suddenly find that when we begin to "unlearn" we find room to learn anew. We sense the power each of us has to "own" our experience, to succeed and perhaps to survive no matter how limited or limiting our past education has been. We want to know more and know better.

In a literature class a teacher might ask whether Rivkeh Lev, the wife of Aryeh Lev in *My Name Is Asher Lev,*[2] is submissive or not, or whether the behavior of her husband is appropriate or inappropriate, but during such a discussion it would be important for students to know and articulate their own attitudes toward male-female relationships. To stimulate this kind of sharing, the teacher might introduce a news clipping on Bureau of Labor Statistics figures comparing weekly earnings of men and women in comparable full-time jobs. If Stephen Crane's *The Red Badge of Courage*[3] is read, the Reagan administration's "build-down" concept of arms reduction might be discussed in comparison with the movement for a bilateral, mutually verifiable freeze. Many people do not realize that they have a personalized ideology, a lens through which they view reality and shape reality to their view. Literature helps individuals to regard others acting on their unique perceptions, and enables each student to assess the degree to which a particularized worldview influences the choices one makes.

The powerful interaction between Blanche Dubois and Stanley Kowalsky in *A Streetcar Named Desire*[4] succeeds dramatically because the playwright understands—and helps the viewer to understand—the fact of ideology.

Ideology, the manner or content of thinking that characterizes a group or individual, is perfectly natural. One cannot be human and not have it. The Scholastic philosophers used to say, "Quidquid recipitur ad modum recipientis recipitur" ("Whatever is received is received according to the mode of the one receiving it"). Gerard Manley Hopkins's poems, for example, are always infused with God's presence, whether he is singing praise of God in nature or feeling the pain of God's absence:

> And all is seared with trade; bleared, smeared with toil;
>   And wears man's smudge and shares man's smell: the soil
> Is bare now, nor can foot feel being shod.
>
> And for all this, nature is never spent;
>   There lives the dearest freshness deep down things;
> And though the last lights off the black West went
>   Oh, morning, at the brown brink eastward, springs—
> Because the Holy Ghost over the bent
>   World broods with warm breast and with ah! bright wings.[5]
>
> . . . birds build—but not I build; no but strain,
> Time's eunuch, and not breed one work that wakes.
> Mine, O thou lord of life, send my roots rain.[6]

A perhaps more compelling example of ideology is found in Howard Nemerov's "Santa Claus," a poem that insists that the apparent innocuousness of Santa Claus may hide, from many, a fundamental perversion:

> Somewhere on his travels the strange Child
> Picked up with this overstuffed confidence man,
> Affection's inverted thief, who climbs at night
> Down chimneys, into dreams, with this world's goods,
> Bringing all the benevolence of money.

He teaches the innocent to want, thus keeps
Our fat world rolling. His prescribed costume,
White flannel beard, red belly of cotton waste,
Conceals the thinness of essential hunger,
An appetite that feeds on satisfaction;
Or, pregnant with possessions, he brings forth
Vanity and the void. His name itself
Is corrupted, and even Saint Nicholas, in his turn,
Gives off a faint and reminiscent stench,
The merest soupçon of brimstone and the pit.

Now, at the season when the child is born
To suffer for the world, suffer the world,
His bloated Other, jovial satellite
And sycophant, makes his appearance also
In a glitter of goodies, in a rock candy glare.
Played at the better stores by bums, for money.
This annual savior of the economy
Speaks in the parables of the dollar sign:
Suffer the little children to come to Him.

At Easter, he's anonymous again,
Just one of the crowd lunching on Calvary.[7]

Santa's rotundity conceals "the thinness of essential hunger," and his sterile "pregnancy" brings forth "Vanity and the void." It is clear that the ideology of retail merchants dictates that they use this "jovial satellite/And sycophant" to save the economy and dispense "the parables of the dollar sign." It is equally clear that consumers find Santa "cute," while the poet sees him as an "over-stuffed confidence man," an obscene substitute for the Child who was born and died to alert humankind to a less worldly salvation. Discussions of varying ideologies and perceptions can and should introduce questions of economic justice and action for the common good.

Both the Hopkins poems and the Nemerov piece portray events applicable to contemporary experience. Though Hopkins noted a world "seared with trade; bleared, smeared with toil," he made his observations over 100 years ago. Are things better or worse today? Is Nemerov's Santa Claus and the rampant consumerism he epitomizes less in evidence or more in evidence today?

These poets present the teacher with several avenues of literary analysis, but surely the most exciting classes are those that reveal the justice themes derived from the content of the literary works. Each of us looks at reality expecting to find what we are expecting to find. We come with what T. S. Eliot calls "our certain certainties." But the truth about reality mediated by the literary artist is usually deeper or richer or more complex than we expected. "Art is a lie," says Picasso, "which makes us realize the truth."[8]

Most of our college and university students are members of one or more dominant cultures. Each of them comes to college with unique experiences and a certain amount of critical judgment. It is quite likely that most students are unquestionably nationalistic and are culturally underdeveloped. They might not see things as narrowly as did President Lyndon Johnson when he told Eric Servareid, "There's not a person out there who doesn't want to be an American . . . it's the natural way of being human."[9] But, as many educators have observed, our students are handicapped by inadequate intercultural learning. Literature "broadens personal moral vision through exploring character, circumstance and choice; it makes human solidarity across boundaries possible."[10]

By carefully explicating poems like those of Hopkins and Nemerov, teachers can begin to elicit students' perceptions, and even build classroom discussions around the universal ideas of the poets. This does not do violence to the discipline of literature but, rather, enhances it by bringing literature to life. Such teaching makes of it a springboard to discuss the "news" that is in poems, news for lack of which the world is literally dying. News items expressing facts that counter official governmental policy can and should be cited in classroom discussions of literature. A student whose mind is reaching out for the truth can be encouraged to read more widely—a lifelong habit that has to begin somewhere—by a teacher who is role-modeling by his or her own broad interest in society's perceptions.

Not to comment on events like the invasions of Afghanistan and Grenada, disasters like the bombing of marine barracks in Lebanon, or on Watergate-like illegalities when one is dealing with illusion and reality in literature is to betray either a moral timidity verging on cowardice or a cynicism about learning and grappling with the truth, which is even more disturbing. The following quotations (and many more like them) can touch off excitement about current events and justice issues even as they deepen one's appreciation for the power of literature to expand our capacity for critical judgment:

A U.S.-funded study on El Salvador's land-reform program contradicts Washington's claims that the Salvadorean government has curbed evictions from redistributed land.

The report by the U.S. Agency for International Development said between 4,700 and 8,000 peasant farmers had been evicted from land they acquired under the land program. Last week the Reagan Administration told Congress 995 farmers had been evicted.[11]

The issue of the Cuban death toll has become one more point of contention in a growing dispute between the international press and the U.S. Government over both the accuracy of U.S. statistics and their role in the Reagan Administration's justification for the Grenada intervention.[12]

I spent 33 years . . . being a highclass muscle man for Big Business, for Wall Street and the Bankers. I was a racketeer for capitalism. . . . I helped purify Nicaragua for the international banking house of Brown

Brothers. . . . I helped in the rape of half a dozen Central American republics for the benefit of Wall Street [Maj. Gen. Smedley Butler, USMC, 1881–1940].[13]

We have grasped the mystery of the atom and rejected the Sermon on the Mount. Ours is a world of nuclear giants and ethical infants. We know more about war than we know about peace, more about killing than we know about living [Gen. Omar Bradley].[14]

A great deal of intellectual excitement can be generated by this kind of relational thinking.

JUSTICE METHODOLOGIES IN SEMESTER-LONG COURSES

What one can do in a lower-division course differs from what the same teacher might accomplish in a special-topics course, a senior seminar, or a study of one author or period. Clearly, an upper-division study of Thoreau or Faulkner or Joyce, or an in-depth exploration of humanistic themes in black poets or women writers or utopian authors can yield excellent results for those interested in infusing justice and peace issues into the college curriculum. But part of the problem that academics have experienced in addressing social issues in an integrative, developmental way has stemmed precisely from the sequestering of justice themes from the daily teaching of literature on all levels. What we must counter is the elitism that the discipline consciously and unconsciously fosters. There is little virtue in teaching Shakespeare or Milton or Woolf or Kafka if the students do not know how a characterization or event in the play or novel speaks of what Faulkner insisted "is the only thing worth writing about," "the human heart in conflict with itself."[15] That English teachers could show students fictional archetypes and artistic mimesis and themselves miss the meaning is an irony worthy of some of literature's more thoroughly self-deceived protagonists and narrators.

Even though a source book of this kind can further freeze our notions of what is possible in literature courses into one or two models—lulling us into believing, perhaps, that these are the *only* places infusion of justice themes into the curriculum can take place—it is necessary, as Prospero says in *The Tempest,* to "give to airy nothings a local habitation and a name." We shall therefore outline in some detail the rich themes embedded in the material most teachers impart in American literature survey classes, and then shall show how an upper-division seminar can build upon an awareness of peace and justice themes—including small-group learning situations outside of class. Finally, we shall suggest ways to evaluate the learning that takes place.

American Literature Survey Classes

These classes, often entitled "American Literature," are usually taken by freshmen and a few other students who either didn't get around to taking

AMERICAN LITERATURE SURVEY *(three credits)*

Two texts are required: the one-volume fifth edition of the Bradley, Beatty, Long, and Perkins text, *The American Tradition in Literature,*[16] and John Updike's novel, *Rabbit, Run.*[17]

This course is an introduction to authors and themes in the American literary tradition from the beginnings to contemporary times. About three-fifths of the anthology *The American Tradition in Literature* will be assigned. Approximately thirty pages of reading per night is required. Classroom participation and alternating essay tests and two-page focus papers are required. There will be a total of five tests and six two-page papers.

Tests will last one hour and will have three questions. There is no midterm exam. A "minimal-adequate" answer proving the student's familiarity with both texts and class discussions will yield a "B" (ninety points). (Thirty points are given for each adequate response, slightly fewer points for less adequate ones. More points are earned for greater insights and greater familiarity with texts and discussions.) Papers with a limited focus (exploring or explicating a theme or structural device or symbol or strand of imagery or aspect of characterization) will be graded for both form and content. Active participation and consistent attendance in class constitutes about one-fifth of the final grade.

The course (a sixteen-week, forty-eight class semester based on the Bradley, Beatty, Long and Perkins volume) will cover:

    Puritan Culture (three classes)
    Reason and Revolution (two classes)
    Romantic Rediscovery (two classes)
    Symbolic and Ethical Idealism (four classes)
    Transcendental Idealism (four classes)
    Humanitarian and Critical Temper (one class)
    Pioneers of a New Poetry (three classes)
    Regional Realists (two classes)
    Masters of Critical Realism (three classes)
    The Turn of the Century (two classes)
    Introduction to *Rabbit, Run* (one class)
    American Reevaluations (two classes)
    Poets in Waste Land (one class)
    The Attack on Convention (two classes)
    Fiction in Search of Reality (two classes)
    Poetry of Idea and Order (one class)
    Expression of Social Thought in the 1930s and 1940s (two classes)
    Twentieth-Century Writers (six classes; the Updike novel introduced earlier is also considered in this segment)
    Tests (five classes)

literature their freshman year or who transferred into the college or who are, as seniors, able at last to "spend electives" on something they would enjoy outside their major.

The syllabus that accompanies this essay assumes that there are approximately forty students in a class, a somewhat unwieldy but not untypical classroom situation. The course is one semester long and includes everything in the American literary tradition, from the Puritans to contemporary authors. It is designed as an introduction to writers and themes that might be grappled with more intensively in upper-division courses dealing with American novelists or the Transcendentalists or American poets. A teacher might, of course, choose to emphasize some writers and underplay a Cooper or a Poe or a Malamud. Any universal literature has human themes, and therefore justice and peace possibilities. What makes a difference is the teacher's ability to lead students to reflect on unfolding events with attention to the common good.

Some of my colleagues prefer to begin the course at 1850 and skip the Puritan period altogether. I think this is a mistake, yet I do not dwell on the Puritan writers overmuch because, as writers, most were more English than American. We usually sample a short section of William Bradford's diary and a few poems of Anne Bradstreet or Edward Taylor. It is Jonathan Edwards upon whom I invite the class to focus. He is, in his personal life, humble, even ingenuous ("Personal Narrative") and deeply religious, even mystical ("A Divine and Supernatural Light"). But in the pulpit, he, like Cotton Mather and other religious orators, preaches hellfire and damnation. This public posture and private conduct are worth noting. Do such dichotomies exist today? Why do they exist in religion and in government? Does the Calvinistic idea of election contribute to an American certainty that the accumulation of property is a sign of God's blessing? Is wealth a sign of God's pleasure and poverty a sure indicator of evil and curse? If anyone in the class has seen Arthur Miller's *The Crucible*,[18] that person might describe how Edwards, sincere though he may be, might be faulted for the kind of hypocrisy that the judges in the witch trials of Salem epitomized.

A teacher might also read a section from Richard Tawney's *Religion and the Rise of Capitalism*[19] or from the Reverend Jerry Falwell's speeches[20] for comparison and additional insight.

Jonathan Edwards stands in high contrast to the Deist, Benjamin Franklin, who, as D. H. Lawrence has suggested in *Studies in Classic American Literature*,[21] views the human being as a moral machine. God is far in the background, and Franklin's propensity to do, to invent, to act—but not to reflect—is the other side of Jonathan Edwards's anguished soul-searching. Together, these two strands come together in one of America's most important writers, Nathaniel Hawthorne. By the time students encounter the arrogant "Young Goodman Brown," who is clearly out of his depth in dealing with the blandishments of the devil, or "Ethan Brand," or Robin in "My Kinsman, Major Molineux," they have become adept at unearthing the theme of self-deception, a fascination for American writers from Hawthorne and Herman Melville to Faulkner and Flannery O'Connor. Hawthorne is an antiquarian psychologist, a man who knew the dangers of isolation from human community and the costs of repression.

Before departing the Puritan era, I always assign "Cases of Conscience" by John Woolman, the Quaker shopowner and statesman whose journals reveal a religious and ethical person who seems to avoid both the sheer activism and pridefulness in his own virtue exemplified by Franklin and the brooding introspection and angry pulpit fundamentalism of Edwards. Woolman's ability to communicate his personal experience of the goodness of God and "leadings of the truth" is both refreshing and instructive. His decision to scale down his business in order not to profit at the expense of others, his refusal to notarize slave dealings, and his openness to learning from the Indians are indications that, as a culture, we need not have followed Edwards and Franklin, as I believe we have, but could have found in the more modest and ethically motivated Woolman a fine role model. He is a man who in the 1750s had intimations of a way of acting appropriately, which the late E. F. Schumacher further elaborated in *Small Is Beautiful.*[22] Schumacher, like Woolman, believed that most citizens are "only too ready to believe that ethics is a field where thinking does no good."[23] Woolman's reverence for life seems to have generated an ethics of appropriate action, another topic worth pursuing with students.

Edwards, Franklin, Hawthorne, and Woolman are the nucleus for a survey of American writers from 1600 to 1800. One could surely take a sidetrip here into Thomas Paine's revolutionary rhetoric and Thomas Jefferson's delineation of democracy or could consider the surprising obliviousness of contemporary America to the radical roots of its relatively conservative culture. This unit anticipates the American renaissance and Henry David Thoreau's conviction that "for everyone who is striking at the root there are ten thousand hacking at the branches."

The period from 1800 to 1860 is perhaps the most exciting one in American literature, and the writings of Ralph Waldo Emerson, Henry David Thoreau, Herman Melville, and Walt Whitman are treasure troves of powerful themes, which the teacher of English can help students to discover.

Ralph Waldo Emerson not only propounded theories of self-reliance, the wonders of the natural environment, and the genius of "representative men" (his ideology was such that a book on "representative women," sadly, would not occur to him), but also had the unique experience of being banned from Harvard Divinity School after delivering his stunning commencement address of 1838.

As I do when we study Jonathan Edwards's sermon, I ask students to imagine themselves as divinity students trained in traditional religion. I then "play Emerson" in order to allow the force of his insights to register. The speech, frequently one of the favorite selections in the survey once it is understood, is about "the moral sentiment," an extolling of "the laws of the soul" over formalities and conventions. This sentiment is "divine and deifying"; those who follow their intuition become themselves "newborn bards of the Holy Spirit." "Men have come to speak of . . . revelations as somewhat long ago given and done, as if God were dead," Emerson says. He insists that this is a great mistake. The pulpits have been "usurped by formalists." To "convert life into truth they have not learned." He says he has listened to many a preacher who gave no word "intimating that he had sighed or wept, was married or in love, had been commended or cheated, or chagrined. If he had ever lived and acted, we were none the wiser for it." This raises the important justice question of *witness*—a perfect place in which to discuss Archbishop Oscar Romero, Dorothy Day, Jean Vanier, or Mother Teresa of Calcutta.[24] "The true preacher" Emerson says, "can always be known by this, that he deals out to the people his life—life passed through the fire of thought."

This can be, as it was in 1838, heady stuff. The Harvard Divinity School faculty was not amused when Emerson suggested that the graduating ministers cast behind themselves "all conformity and acquaint men at first hand with Deity." He intimates that to be "a man" is to hold "fashion, comfort, authority, pleasure, and money" as "nothing to you." Further, he looks for the hour when truth, "that supreme Beauty which ravished the souls of those Eastern men, and chiefly of those Hebrews . . . shall speak in the West also." Finally, Emerson drew the wrath of church theologians when he said that historical Christianity "dwells, with noxious exaggeration about the *person* of Jesus," making of him "a demigod, as the Orientals or the Greeks would describe Osiris or Apollo." Emerson is a committed admirer of Christ, but feels that "that which shows God in me fortifies me." He is afraid that traditional religion has robbed its adherents of their self-motivation and individual conscience by urging people to put on Christ's nature rather than fulfill their own.

This one essay inspires discussion of religious ideology, personal action and witness, courageous advocacy of unpopular positions, and authentic Christianity. It prepares students to wrestle with Thoreau's and Whitman's iconoclastic dissent and affirmation, and leads very well into such intellectually challenging works as Melville's "Billy Budd" and "Bartleby the Scrivener," and Henry James's "The Beast in the Jungle."

Emerson and Thoreau, but much more so Melville and Whitman, were consciously forging an *American* literature. Melville declared literary independence from British standards at the end of *Mardi*,[25] and by the time he wrote *Moby Dick*[26] he was joining popular romance to metaphysical musings in a way never done before. His "Billy Budd: Sailor" is a classic study of the need for goodness *and* experience, discipline *and* compassion. Whitman was, at this same time, writing *Leaves of Grass*.[27] In it, particularly in "Song of Myself," he is consciously naming the world anew from the American Edenic perspective. He, like Adam, absorbs and translates every unfolding experience. He extolls the beauty of all bodies, and all parts of all bodies. He sounds his "barbaric yawp" over the rooftops of America, shaking people awake to the promises of a new way of being, an interdependent compassionation with all of society.

Thoreau's essay "Civil Disobedience" and the correlative "Life without

Principle" raise questions about involvement in foreign wars, about the silliness of doing "anything by which you earned money merely" and the necessity of acting on principle so that we might not become "all husk and shell, with no tender and living kernel to us." The application of these terms, the cogency of nonviolent action, and the appropriateness of considering "the way we live our lives" is, for the teacher, a great opportunity to inculcate values and work toward solutions with students whose imaginations are often engaged by these works. Whether it is *Walden*,[28] with its love of nature and challenge to live simply, which inspires, or the more radical "Civil Disobedience," which exhorts one to let his or her life "be a counter-friction to stop the machine," it is clear that "action from principle" will occur if the writings of Thoreau are internalized.

It has been my experience that students become more excited about literature through the writers of the American renaissance than through modern and contemporary poets and storytellers. The relevance of Whitman's antiwar poetry like "A Sight in Camp" and his compassionate "The Wound-Dresser" or Melville's anguished parables of the conflict between innocence and evil, experience and authority, seems to capture the imagination of many young adults. In some ways they seem to envy the integrity of an Emerson, a Thoreau, a Whitman, and a Melville, and yet not know how to live with integrity in today's violent and security-conscious world. Sadly, they will not find in the literature of the twentieth century many answers, only darker questions. It is up to the teacher to provide hope by witnessing to action in the face of complexity. It is the teacher who must draw upon the literature of America, suggest the dilemmas it so often reveals, and explain how integrity and positive action for justice have occurred in even the most dangerous and oppressive situations and continue to occur whenever women and men of conscience refuse to capitulate to evil and death. Edmund Burke once said the surest way for the forces of evil to win out in the world is for enough good people to do nothing. An excellent resource for augmenting the literature of the American renaissance is the anthology *The Power of the People: Active Nonviolence in the United States.*[29] Helen Caldicott's positive pleas to end nuclear madness by positive action are also helpful.[30]

The "schoolroom poets"—Longfellow, Whittier, Holmes, and Lowell—are dull and uninspiring. Occasionally a student will argue against this opinion of mine—a valuable exercise in itself—but most can see that alongside Walt Whitman or Emily Dickinson, Whittier, for instance, seems to be more a versifier than a poet.

The authors whose works I choose to emphasize in midsemester are Henry James, Emily Dickinson, Henry Adams, Mark Twain, Sherwood Anderson, and Stephen Crane. These turn-of-the-century writers are much more diverse than the Transcendentalists, a fact that is perfectly understandable given the immense changes in America in the late 1800s and early 1900s. One writer who was insulated from change by wealth and position in society nevertheless became one of the most proficient practitioners of the art of fiction: Henry James.

Henry James's writing style is convoluted and difficult. With a little patience, however, students can respond to the intricacies of his moral elaborations. "The Beast in the Jungle" has left college students close to tears. It is about John Marcher's failure to choose to love, a failure tragic both for himself and for May Bartman. The great destiny that Marcher always felt he would achieve was to become, ultimately, the one person "to whom nothing on earth was to have happened." His obtuseness and incapacitating passivity in the face of life's possibilities presents the class with a fine opportunity to discuss the price of inaction in society. Often I bring in at this point the fine half-hour film *Peege*,[31] written and directed by Randal Kleiser, to focus on the importance of memory and the need for touch. The context is a family visit to a rest home at Christmas. The contrasting metaphor is the choice to act with affection made by Peege's grandson Greg, who is the sensitive person he is because his grandmother is the loving person she has always been. Greg is the antitype to Marcher, a person who understands what is necessary, and acts with compassion. Another film, *Close Harmony*,[32] works well in this context or as a summary statement of human potential.

Emily Dickinson, a rather passive and reclusive person, nonetheless has many insights into the human condition that can be capitalized upon in a course designed to raise value questions. In simple, almost offhand phrases, she holds truth up to the light, which can stimulate much discussion:

> . . . Liberty
>
> Left inactive on the Stalk
> all its Purple fled
> Revolution shakes it for
> Test if it be dead.

Dickinson also questions the meaning of madness, normalcy, death, and conscience.

Henry Adams's essay "The Virgin and the Dynamo" discusses the power of the new technology that supplanted but perhaps never equaled the force generated by moral fervor that caused cathedrals to be built in honor of Mary centuries before. Students confronting the motivating forces of other ages will discuss the values and motivations of their own time and place.

In "The Man That Corrupted Hadleyburg" Mark Twain tells a subversive tale of a smug town's moment of truth. It thought of itself as honest until its untried virtue was tested and it fell like a card castle. The lessons of Vietnam, Watergate, and other revelatory defeats of what William Fulbright has called "the arrogance of power"[33] can be profitably discussed. Mark Twain is a regional humorist with an uncanny knack for universal questions.

Sherwood Anderson's story "I Want to Know Why," often sparks wide-ranging discussions about growing up, the pain and the value of disillusionments, the subtlety of racism, and the loss of innocence.

Stephen Crane's "A Man Said to the Universe" and two of his stories not in the assigned text, "The Open Boat" and "The Monster," address the possibility that nature goes on no matter what we do, and ultimately shows our actions to be worthless. Given the tendency of people to feel that they can do little or nothing to dismantle the structures of injustice, Crane's naturalism should be confronted head-on. Examples of how individual action *has* made a difference can be elicited from the class, and positive approaches like that of Helen Caldicott, quoted below, should be extolled. Never has it been more important to counter despair:

> I really beg you . . . as a citizen of the planet, and as a resident of this wonderful country, that you now change the priorities of your lives. Make sure that you grow up knowing that this is the single most important issue that we have ever faced in the three million years. This is the ultimate medical issue because a nuclear war will create the final medical epidemic; this is the ultimate parental issue, because what is the use of looking out for children, if they are not going to grow up; and this is the ultimate religious issue. What is our responsibility towards God? To continue his wonderful process of evolution.[34]

The twentieth-century American writers are quite accessible to most students, and their work often touches upon value-laden considerations that move students to act compassionately.

Edwin Arlington Robinson, Robert Frost, Theodore Dreiser, Ezra Pound, T. S. Eliot, H. L. Mencken, F. Scott Fitzgerald, William Faulkner, Thomas Wolfe, and Ernest Hemingway present bold modern themes with many implications for modern students' lives and continuing education. Poets William Carlos Williams and Wallace Stevens, both of whom, like Emily Dickinson and Harte Crane, carry forward the Whitmanian tradition of poetry, should not be neglected. E. E. Cummings's defense of conscientious objection in "I Sing of Olaf Glad and Big" should be assigned for discussion. It is a tribute to the authors of the text I use for this course that poems like "Olaf," celebrating dissent, have been included in their anthology.

Black writers Richard Ellison and Imamu Baraka present powerful metaphors for dehumanization. Wright's "Big Black Good Man" is a very successful presentation of a black man using power and humor to turn the tables on a bigoted desk clerk. The fact that the bigot does not know what to expect increases the leverage—as it does in all power struggles—that the big black good man has over him. Many significant discussions of social mores have stemmed from this story. This might be a good time to bring Martin Luther King, Jr.'s "Letter from Birmingham Jail"[35] into class, and perhaps hark back to Frederick Douglass's narrative written in the time of slavery. The race issue should, of course, be addressed on its own merits, but teachers miss a rich opportunity for humanistic education when they fail to relate racial injustice to other kinds of oppression. Virtually every student has felt at some time oppressed, and frank discussion of the rights of women, the poor, Native Americans, children, the aged, South Africans, Central Americans, Filipinos, Cambodians, Palestinians, Jews, gays, and other relatively powerless minorities can bring the literature to life and break through some of the ideology of the dominant culture. Encouraging students to walk a mile in the moccasins of another is vitally important to education.

Sometimes a creative teacher can bring into class a news item or a newly discovered quotation from a public figure that suggests a reevaluation or a surprising stance, and solicit student response on the basis of literature that the class is currently reading. If I were introducing Hemingway depicting the "lost generation" in *The Sun Also Rises* or dealing with "The Short Happy Life of Francis Macomber," I might ask if Hemingway's characters would be likely to act for changes that they perceived as necessary. When Dwight David Eisenhower said, "I think that people want peace so much that one of these days governments had better get out of the way and let them have it,"[36] he probably realized that the very despair that keeps people from acting also traps governments into destructive postures of hostility, and everyone loses. The following news item would presumably be of interest to students participating in a discussion of priorities: "In 1982, every major group queried in a Gallup poll agreed that America's strength in the future will depend more on developing the finest educational system in the world than on developing the best industrial system or the strongest military force."[37]

Most teachers will want to deal with humanistic moral themes in a Faulkner or a Flannery O'Connor story. "That Evening Sun" and "Good Country People" reveal to the reader layers of self-deception in carefully crafted characterizations that can be tragic or comic by turns. The more adventurous academic may tackle T. S. Eliot's "The Waste Land" or Allen Ginsberg's "Howl" or the potent poems of Sylvia Plath and Anne Sexton, to discuss where contemporary life leads for those who have lost the desire to find meaning or seek healing in mainstream society.

I have found it very helpful to assign *Rabbit, Run* by John Updike along with selections in the anthology, because a novel is a broad canvas, and Updike paints the selfish perennial adolescent Harry Angstrom so well. Discussions on his injustice toward Janice and Ruth and Nelson and Rebecca are easily entered into. The egotism, clichés, chauvinism, rootlessness, faithlessness, and manipulations of Rabbit, Eccles, Tothero, and others in the novel repel most students, yet they are instructive and perhaps all too familiar.

Finally, a teacher should help the class to think relationally, and more importantly he or she should bear witness to active involvement in human, life-enhancing action. The teacher should be a resource person for at least some of the issues brought up in class. Explicit reference to "The Challenge of Peace," the United States Catholic Bishops' pastoral letter on the arms race,[38] or to legislative issues supported by Bread for the World[39] or Physicians for Social Responsibility[40] can and should be related to human situations described in literature, or metaphorically suggested. Reference books like *Toward a More Human World Order* [41] should be made known to students.

An American literature survey course is indeed an appropriate place to point out historical facts that are relevant to current global crises. For example, seven years elapsed between the British Cabinet recognition of United States independence in 1782 and America's government by constitution in 1789. The Sandinista government of Nicaragua publicly announced in 1980, after gaining liberation from the brutal United States-backed Somoza dictatorship, that elections would be held in 1985, yet the United States has continually objected to Managua's "undemocratic" delay of voting. Even were we not conspicuously tolerant of martial law in places like the Philippines, where it allegedly "serves our interests," might not discussion of such issues clarify what Emerson or Ellison or Plath or William H. Gass say of double standards in a variety of circumstances?

We must respect our students enough to challenge them and yet be open to differences of opinion about what is said in a text or what values can be derived from a given theme. I have found that a good rule of thumb is to accept any competently presented interpretation or alternative opinion so long as it is defensible with careful reference to the literary text. Academic freedom cuts both ways, and is best guaranteed where dissent is honored. Literature can help students to understand that the common good is in everyone's self-interest, but only involved and caring teachers can reveal the importance of action that goes beyond comfortable theorizing.

A Semester-Long Upper-Division Seminar

A course that I created, which has proved extremely successful for more focused justice and peace topics, is "Human Solidarity Themes." Designed for about 16 students, the course combines literature and public policy, and includes an action component called "praxis groups." After studying Paulo Freire's *Pedagogy of the Oppressed* (a fine study of oppressive structures and the need to move beyond critical thinking to acts of solidarity and hope),[42] a dozen or so news articles from the *Christian Science Monitor,* Sojourners materials, *Bread for the World Background Papers,* and so forth, students begin Albert Camus's thesis novel, *The Plague.*[43] Special attention is paid to limit-situations, true healings, pestilences and victims, simple decency, and other thematic considerations. Juan Luis Segundo's *The Community Called Church*[44] is the next text, followed by *Identifying a Food Policy Agenda for the 1980's,* a working paper on hunger issues.[45] The Segundo volume introduces theology-of-liberation topics, and the *Food Policy Agenda* applies steps toward liberation to the situation of the desperately poor and malnourished.

A fine African novel, which has a lot of impact on students in a dominant culture, is now introduced: Chingali Achebe's classic, *Things Fall Apart*.[46] The final text, *The Tenants of Moonbloom*,[47] is Edward Lewis Wallant's powerful novel about a man totally disengaged from the tenants he collects rent from for his brother, until he becomes "infected" by the lives of the people he serves, and begins to act, to do what is necessary despite the personal cost.

Moonbloom's struggle for integrity in contemporary Brooklyn brings home to students the choice before each of them: safe accommodation to the status quo or risky action for the common good. At about the seventh or eighth week I assign four "praxis groups" (Freire's term means action/reflection) to study a limit-situation in the city—a home for battered women, displacement of elderly citizens by condominiumization, closure of a local halfway house for mental patients, and so forth. Each group chooses its own topic and researches it independently. During the last week of class each group must give a presentation including data from interviews on both sides of the issue chosen by the students, and possible steps to remedy a bad situation in a humane way, or to appeal or change an outcome. Sometimes reevaluations occur midway. Occasionally the group chooses to lobby the legislature or to become in some other way actively involved in a solution to the problem investigated. The best presentation thus far has been from a group of four seniors who elected to role-play two scenes exemplifying the "battered-woman syndrome" and the difficulty the victim has in leaving the situation and seeking help.

The student evaluations of the "Human Solidarity Themes" seminars have been more than gratifying. Several students insisted that the class was by far the best they had in college—usually because their learning was relevant to the world in which they lived, their eyes were opened to issues they simply had not thought about seriously before, or because the blend of literature, theology, public policy, and personal education was a powerful amalgam that would continue to motivate them to new learning and further action.

In all classes and seminars I insist that acting locally is not enough and working for global justice is not enough. One must be involved in local issues in order to know how power operates, and *also* must be aware of global issues and active in lobbying for good policies and in opposing bad ones—because, if one is limited to local action, the major structural inequities will continue to plague the mass of humankind. Just as there is no way *to* peace (peace *is* the way), so there is no path to justice apart from acting justly. The just person, says Gerard Manley Hopkins, "justices."[48] Pope Paul VI, speaking to members of the Council of Laity in 1974, best summarized this point: "Modern man listens more willingly to witnesses than to teachers, and if he does listen to teachers, it is because they are witnesses."[49]

Literature teachers are uniquely qualified to witness to the dignity of every individual person. The texts they explicate have the power to touch the hearts and minds of students. Both the literature and the teacher's passion for justice can inspire the moral imagination of the young men and women committed to the care of educators. Fr. Zossima says, in *The Brothers Karamazov,* that "a touch in one place sets up movement at the other end of the earth,"[50] and as Alyosha Karamasov knows, sometimes a good memory, preserved from childhood, has made us "better perhaps than we are."[51] Acts of human solidarity allow us to transcend our conventional way of being. For literature teachers committed to the common good of their students, such truths are important to remember.

NOTES

1. William Carlos Williams, *Pictures from Breughel* (New York: New Directions Books, 1962), p. 161.

2. Chaim Potok, *My Name Is Asher Lev* (Greenwich, Conn.: Fawcett-Crest Books, 1972).

3. Stephen Crane, *The Red Badge of Courage* (New York: W. W. Norton, 1962).

4. Tennessee Williams, *A Streetcar Named Desire* (New York: New Directions Books, 1980).

5. Gerard Manley Hopkins, *Gerard Manley Hopkins: Poems and Prose,* ed. W. H. Gardner (Middlesex, England: Penguin Books, 1963), p. 27.

6. Ibid., p. 67.

7. Howard Nemerov, "Santa Claus," *The Collected Poems of Howard Nemerov* (Chicago, Ill.: University of Chicago Press, 1977). Reprinted by permission of the author.

8. Pablo Picasso, quoted as the epigraph for Chaim Potok's *My Name Is Asher Lev,* cited above.

9. Langdon Gilkey told this anecdote in a seminar at Saint Martin's College, June 24, 1983.

10. Commission on the Humanities, *The Humanities in American Life* (Berkeley, Calif.: University of California Press, 1980), p. 70.

11. News item in *Christian Science Monitor,* July 28, 1983.

12. Quoted by Michael Layton, *Seattle Post-Intelligencer,* July 17, 1983.

13. Smedley Butler, quoted in *Seattle Post-Intelligencer,* July 17, 1983.

14. Omar Bradley, quoted in *Service News,* a publication of Church World Service Education Department, Washington, D. C.

15. William Faulkner, "Address upon Receiving the Nobel Prize for Literature" (Dec. 10, 1950), in *Essays, Speeches and Public Letters* (New York: Random House, 1965), p. 119.

16. Bradley, Beatty, Long, Perkins, eds., *The American Tradition in Literature,* 5th ed. (New York: Random House, 1981). All references not mentioned here in Notes are included in this text.

17. John Updike, *Rabbit, Run* (New York: Fawcett-Crest Books, 1960).

18. Arthur Miller, *The Crucible* (New York: Viking Press, 1967).

19. Richard Tawney, *Religion and the Rise of Capitalism* (New York: Penguin Books, 1947; republished 1954).

20. Jerry Falwell, *Listen America* (Garden City, N.Y.: Doubleday, 1980).

21. D. H. Lawrence, *Studies in Classic American Literature* (New York: Viking Press, 1961).

22. E. F. Schumacher, *Small Is Beautiful: Economics as if People Mattered* (New York: Perennial Library, 1975).

23. E. F. Schumacher, *Good Work* (New York: Harper Colophon Books, 1979), p. 34.

24. Jim Wallis, ed., *Peacemakers: Christian Voices from the New Abolitionist Movement* (New York: Harper & Row, 1983).

25. Herman Melville, *Mardi: And a Voyage Thither* (New York: Signet Classics, 1967).

26. Herman Melville, *Moby Dick* (New York: W. W. Norton, 1967).

27. Walt Whitman, *Leaves of Grass* (New York: W. W. Norton, 1973).

28. Henry David Thoreau, *"Walden" and "Civil Disobedience"* (New York: W. W. Norton, 1965).

29. Robert Cooney and Helen Michaelowski, eds., *The Power of the People: Active Nonviolence in the United States* (Culver City, Calif.: Peace Press, 1977).

30. Helen Caldicott, *Nuclear Madness—What You Can Do* (New York: Bantam Books, 1980).

31. *Peege,* Kleiser/Knapp Productions, 1973 (available from Phoenix Films/Video, 468 Park Ave. S., New York, NY 10016).

32. *Close Harmony,* Arlene Symons (available from Learning Corporation of America, 1350 Avenue of the Americas, New York, NY 10019).

33. William Fulbright, *The Arrogance of Power* (New York: Random House, 1967).

34. Helen Caldicott, "Modern Consequences of Nuclear War," *New Catholic World* 226 (November/December 1983): 281.

35. Martin Luther King., Jr., "Letter from Birmingham Jail," in *A World of Ideas,* ed. Lee A. Jacobus (New York: St. Martin's Press, 1983), pp. 181-99.

36. Ken Keyes, Jr., *The Hundredth Monkey* (Coos Bay, Ore.: Vision Books, 1982), p. 83.

37. Ernest L. Boyer, *High School: A Report on Secondary Education in America* (New York: Harper & Row, 1983), p. 33.

38. United States Catholic Bishops, "The Challenge of Peace: God's Promise and Our Response, " in *Origins,* May 19, 1983 (National Catholic News Service, 1312 Massachusetts Ave., N.W., Washington, DC 20005).

39. Bread for the World: A Christian Citizens' Movement, 802 Rhode Island Ave., N.E., Washington, DC 20018.

40. Physicians for Social Responsibility, 639 Massachusetts Ave., Cambridge, MA 02139.

41. Gerald and Patricia Mische, *Toward a More Human World Order* (New York: Paulist Press, 1977).

42. Paulo Freire, *Pedagogy of the Oppressed* (New York: Seabury Press,1973).

43. Albert Camus, *The Plague* (New York: Vintage Books, 1972).

44. Juan Luis Segundo, S.J., *The Community Called Church* (Maryknoll, N.Y., Orbis Books, 1973).

45. *Identifying a Food Policy Agenda for the 1980s,* Interreligious Task Force on U. S. Food Policy, 110 Maryland Avenue, N.E., Washington, DC 20002.

46. Chingali Achebe, *Things Fall Apart* (Greenwich, Conn.: Fawcett Publications, 1959).

47. Edward Lewis Wallant, *The Tenants of Moonbloom* (New York: Harcourt Brace Jovanovich, 1963).

48. Hopkins, "As Kingfishers Catch Fire, Dragonflies Draw Flame," *Poems and Prose,* p. 51.

49. Pope Paul VI, "Address to Members of the Concilium de Laicis," Oct. 2, 1974.

50. Fyodor Dostoyevsky, *The Brothers Karamasov* (New York: Modern Library, 1950), p. 384.

51. Ibid., p. 938.

SELECTED READINGS FOR FACULTY

Achebe, Chingali. *Things Fall Apart.* Greenwich, Conn.: Fawcett Publications, 1959.

Bennett, William J. " 'To Reclaim a Legacy': Text of Report on Humanities in Education, National Endowment for the Humanities." *The Chronicle of Higher Education,* Nov. 28, 1984.

Bradley, Sculley; Richmond Beatty; E. Hudson Long; George Perkins, eds. *American Tradition in Literature,* 5th ed. New York: Random House, 1981. All references not mentioned in Notes for the present essay are included in this text.

Caldicott, Helen. "Medical Consequences of Nuclear War." *New Catholic World* 226 (November/December 1983).

———. *Nuclear Madness—What You Can Do.* New York: Vintage Books, 1972.

Camus, Albert. *The Plague.* New York: Vintage Books, 1972.

"Catholic Social Teaching and the U.S. Economy." *Origins* 14 (Nov. 15, 1984).

"Challenge of Peace: God's Promise and Our Response." Statement by the United States Catholic Bishops, in *Origins,* May 19, 1983. National Catholic News Service, 1312 Massachusetts Ave., N. W., Washington, D C 20005.

Cooney, Robert, and Helen Michalowski, eds. *Power of the People: Active Nonviolence in the United States.* Culver City, Calif.: Peace Press, 1977.

Crane, Stephen. *The Red Badge of Courage.* New York: W. W. Norton, 1962.

Dostoyevsky, Fyodor. *The Brothers Karamazov.* New York: Modern Library, 1950.

Faulkner, William. "Address upon Receiving the Nobel Prize for Literature" (Dec. 10, 1950). *Essays, Speeches and Public Letters.* New York: Random House, 1965.

Foran, Don. "The Moral Force of Nonviolent Direct Action." *The Progress* (Seattle archdiocesan newspaper), June 9, 1983.

Freire, Paulo. *Pedagogy of the Oppressed.* New York: Seabury Press, 1973.

Fulbright, William. *The Arrogance of Power.* New York: Random House, 1967.

Hopkins, Gerard Manley. *Gerard Manley Hopkins: Poems and Prose,* ed. W. H. Gardner. Middlesex, England: Penguin Books, 1963; p. 27.

Identifying a Food Policy Agenda for the 1980s. Interreligious Task Force on U. S. Food Policy, 110 Maryland Avenue N. E., Washington, D C 20002.

Kidder, Rushworth M. "Why Should the Humanities Matter?" *Christian Science Monitor,* Dec. 3, 1984, p. 45.

King, Martin Luther, Jr. "Beyond Vietnam: A Prophecy for the 80s" (Riverside Church, New York, N.Y., Apr. 4, 1967). Available from Clergy and Laity Concerned, 198 Broadway, New York, N Y 10038.

———. "Letter from Birmingham Jail." *A World of Ideas,* ed. Lee A. Jacobus. New York: St. Martin's Press, 1983.

Lawrence, D. H. *Studies in Classic American Literature.* New York: Viking Press, 1961.

Melville, Herman. *Moby Dick.* New York: W. W. Norton, 1967.

Miglen, Helene. "Erosion in the Humanities: Blowing the Dust From Our Eyes." *Profession 83* (1983). Annual, Modern Language Association of America.

Miller, Arthur. *The Crucible.* New York: Viking Press, 1967.

Mische, Gerald and Patricia. *Toward a More Human World Order.* New York: Paulist Press, 1977.

Potok, Chaim. *My Name Is Asher Lev.* Greenwich, Conn.: Fawcett-Crest Books, 1972.

Schumacher, E. F. *Good Work.* New York: Harper Colophon Books, 1979.

———. *Small Is Beautiful: Economics as if People Mattered.* New York: Perennial Library, 1975.

Segundo, Juan Luis, S.J. *The Community Called Church.* Maryknoll, N.Y.: Orbis Books, 1973.

Thoreau, Henry David. *"Walden" and "Civil Disobedience."* New York: W. W. Norton, 1965.

Updike, John. *Rabbit, Run.* New York: Fawcett-Crest Books, 1960.

Wallant, Edward Lewis. *The Tenants of Moonbloom.* New York: Harcourt Brace Jovanovich, 1963.

Wallis, Jim, ed. *Peacemakers: Christian Voices from the New Abolitionist Movement.* New York: Harper & Row, 1983.

Whitman, Walt. *Leaves of Grass.* New York: W. W. Norton, 1973.

Williams, Tennessee. *A Streetcar Named Desire.* New York: New Directions Books, 1980.

Williams, William Carlos. *Pictures from Breughel and Other Poems.* New York: New Directions Books, 1962.

4

Composition

JANE F. MORRISSEY, S.S.J.
COLLEGE OF OUR LADY OF THE ELMS

The teaching of writing often confounds teachers of writing. Caught between Scylla and Charybdis, deans and duties, we are obligated to teach "Freshman Composition." So we ennoble the course by considering it the keystone of the college curriculum, but we simultaneously demean it by considering it a course without content. We turn to handbooks, readers, grammars. What if we change our approach? What if we see composition as the course that has the world as its content? Words do, after all, give us control over our world. What if we enter the composition classroom to make the world more just? Justice implies that we choose the words that honestly reflect what our world is and what was created to be.

Experience convinces me that when students and teachers cooperate in "teaching unto justice," everyone is quick to see that a choice of words is a value judgment. They recognize that "the old man" is distinct from "my grandfather," that "busing" differs from "equal educational opportunity," and that "war" is different from "pacification" or "nuclear exchange." Taking words seriously brings the class to discuss values; discussing values causes students to find their own voice, and an articulate one at that; and finding one's voice often initiates students into a commitment to justice and peace.

It takes a little ingenuity and effort on the teacher's part to fashion such a course. We begin, as Paulo Freire suggests in *Pedagogy of the Oppressed*, by "owning" our words.[1] Dylan Thomas once explained his love of the English language by telling how he, as a child, felt about nursery rhymes. He wrote, "I had come to love just the words of them, the words alone."[2] We shall own our words if we love them, when we realize that they are things, real things.

Anne Sexton's poem "Words" can help students to find words real, by alerting them to the need to be concrete. Her metaphors and personifications can demonstrate the power of the concrete to fix the attention of a reader. She writes:

> Yet I am in love with words.
> They are doves falling out of the ceiling.
> They are six holy oranges sitting in my lap.
> They are the trees, the legs of summer,
> And the sun, its passionate face.[3]

However much students love words, they struggle above all to find something to say, to feel assured that they have something worth writing about. Like Joseph Conrad they know well "the terror of the blank page," but lack the craft to say so. Responding to this dilemma, trained rhetoricians and teachers of communication may hold the key. In an article entitled "The Primacy of Substance and Ideas in the Teaching of Practical Discourse," Karl Wallace points out that all people believe certain things are desirable, obligatory, and admirable (or undesirable, optional, and loathsome) and can think and talk about these subjects in interesting and sometimes compelling ways.[4] The task of the teacher is to lead students to realize the worth of their own ideas.

The writing course should be designed to bring students to discover and articulate what they really do value. Here the questions become the text: What do you consider desirable? Why are you in college? Why this college? Why this class? Even the student who can go no further in probing motives than saying "Because my parents sent me" or "Because the course is required," can be brought to realize that he or she values the will of a parent or the judgments of a school, and so sort out premises, values, and their consequences.

The course that has the teaching of justice and peace as an objective should thus begin with the personal and the worth of the personal before approaching global concerns. Particularly when students in their own development are emerging from the narcissism of youth, they need opportunities to see the worth of their own experience before studying the effects of the arms race, or America's foreign aid, or the plight of the Native American. Therefore, we design the context in which we probe questions of value to begin with the personal and move toward the global.

I begin my "Composition" course by assigning personal narratives. Several questions of value can stir students' thoughts for this essay. The teacher need only consider the students and the standard rhetorical categories—what is desirable, obligatory, or admirable—and put the two together. Some questions that cause students to reflect on and relish their own experiences are: Whom do I most trust? What fear or remorse robbed me of a good night's sleep? The question that follows is "Why?" The "why" both engenders the narrative and gives it a purpose, at best the semblance of a thesis.

My second assignment is designed to bring students to describe in a comparative essay the world they come from—home, high school, neighborhood, city, or state—and their college world. Whereas the first guideline of the course

COMPOSITION (Three Credits)

DESCRIPTION

A course designed to help students to write clear, concise, coherent expository prose.

OBJECTIVES

1. To educate thoughtful, articulate persons, conversant in the issues of their times.
2. To improve expository writing by examining substantive issues.
3. To consider such subjects as grammar, syntax, and style insofar as they facilitate or interfere with clear communication.
4. To develop basic tools of investigation, research, critiquing, and rewriting.

TEXT

New York Times (Monday through Friday)

REQUIREMENTS

Students are to write eight essays of approximately 500 to 750 words. The essays are due on Fridays of the first and third weeks of the month. The third and seventh essays are written in class.

GRADING POLICY

The student's grade will be based on improvement, rather than the average of eight marks received on essays, i.e., the students who are doing "B" work on their last three essays will receive a "B" for the course, even if they started the course with "D" work.

OUTLINE

Unit I: An Introduction (four weeks). The forms of personal narrative, description, and comparison.

Unit II: Exposition (eight weeks). An introduction to writing on social issues; an analysis of language and an introduction to argument; writing as a social process: from outline to text.

Unit III: Argumentation (four weeks). Research; taking a stand on a controversial issue.

is to be concrete, the second is to be specific. The student who compares Virginia to Massachusetts may not prove so successful as the one who compares Alexandria to Chicopee or her neighborhood to her floor in Rose William Dormitory. The objective of the assignment is to bring students to take their world seriously and to realize their own ability to remember, to analyze, and once again to evaluate. At the same time, because they work with new forms, description and comparison, they need to organize material more carefully.

By the end of the first month of class, my students have written the first two essays on themselves and their world, and I have corrected, prodded, encouraged, and very probably disheartened them. They begin to get uneasy and to wonder how I can expect them to "love the words" when I seem to "red-line" more extensively than the most biased banker or realtor. Just as they feel uneasy and are motivated to improve, I want to enlarge their frame of consideration, to invite them not only to approach the use of words more critically, but also to be willing to alter the way they perceive themselves and their world.

This stage in teaching writing deals more explicitly with peace and justice. It is best introduced by a film or pair of films. I would suggest *Journalism: Mirror, Mirror on the World,* [5] which in forty-five minutes provides students with a detailed comparative analysis of several journalists' handling of the Jeanette Rankin Brigade, a women's antiwar march on Washington, D.C., in the late 1960s. It brings to consciousness questions of belief, questions that are timely for students whose self-doubt and skepticism are the offspring of education and adolescence. This film takes language seriously, approaches it critically, and relates its use to a significant social issue.

Journalism: Mirror, Mirror on the World is best used with a companion piece, a film that analyzes a contemporary problem. I would suggest *Last Grave at Dimbaza,* [6] a documentary on South Africa's apartheid system. The second film should lead students to examine their own lives in relation to the world's poor, to consider the causes and consequences of injustice. Both are chosen to create the consciousness that the word and the world are inseparable, that if we are to change reality, to create a more just social order, we must change our rhetoric. Jerome Wiesner, of the Massachusetts Institute of Technology, paid equal attention to the arms race and its rhetoric in a letter to the *New York Times.* His letter, written in 1983, implies that the nuclear freeze necessitates not only a change in arms policy, but also a change in use of language. He writes, "The risks in a freeze are incalculably smaller than the risks inherent in the continued escalation of weapons *and polemics* into the next century."[7] I want my students to care about words while writing on social issues as does Anne Sexton, who closes her poem "Words" this way:

> But I try to take care
> And be gentle with them.
> Words and eggs must be handled with care.
> Once broken they are impossible
> Things to repair.[8]

Next I concentrate on teaching students how to deal with social issues, how to learn both sides of the issue, how to take a stand, and how to construct a solid argument with different kinds of evidence for support. "These are the times that try our souls," for in addition to knowing how a reporter or essayist reports an issue, we must know what we believe. In these violent times, I feel that it is essential to instruct students in nonviolence by introducing them to the life and work of Gandhi, Thomas Merton, Dorothy Day, and Martin Luther King, Jr. They might be encouraged to see the film *Gandhi*, to read Merton's pamphlet "Blessed Are the Peacemakers," and King's "The Greatest Priority." Charles McCarthy's (Fr. Emmanuel's) writings also present a well-reasoned explanation of the need for, and implications of, Christian nonviolence.[9]

A good newspaper that includes the texts of significant press conferences and speeches or a book of readings on social issues provides us with resource materials and models for writing. Some teachers like the security and order of the collection of essays; others enjoy learning about the immediately relevant through the news. I do find it exciting, if unpredictable and unwieldy on occasion, to teach with the *New York Times*.

Students often find global concerns a labyrinth in which they feel the fate of the earthbound Icarus. Lest they be destined for his early death as well, after a week of readings students need an opportunity to name issues they consider important: ecology; the arms race; some international trouble spot; the plight of the alien, the hungry, the homeless, the sick, the imprisoned, the aging, the young. Any one of these issues is likely to have related readings, in the newspaper or reader, as well as related experiences in which students can become involved. One student can read Mark Twain's "War Prayer" and interview a local draft counselor. Another can read in the *New York Times* about the plight of Central Americans and volunteer with a center of the Sanctuary movement.

Such experiences influence students' vocabulary, syntax, and communication by modifying their experience. Jonathan Swift's "A Modest Proposal" and a night of service at the local soup kitchen can instruct anyone in human inhumanity and dignity in a way that alters and invariably improves expression from the inside out. The permutations and combinations of readings and experiences relevant to instruction in justice issues are endless: local centers for justice and peace education and organizations like the American Friends Service Committee can supply the teacher readily with fresh ideas. Students also have their own ideas as to what they might do to become more involved in their social scene and should be encouraged to follow their inclinations. If their involvement is recommended rather than required, the spirit generated is contagious.

The remaining essays should be written on issues that the students have identified as important to them. I know of no magic formula for organizing these writing assignments. Yet I do think that generally each essay should be written on a different issue, should include a clear thesis, and at least two arguments of different kinds in defense of that thesis. And I do know that the standard rhetorical formula of refutation followed by confirmation opens students' minds to both sides of an issue and teaches them to honor decisions clearly based on informed thinking.

The exploration of local and global issues naturally evolves into the final assignments in which students must do more thorough research and take a stand on a controversial contemporary issue. About two months into the course, they choose the issue on which they will concentrate in the final weeks. They read carefully on both sides of the question, untangle their premises, organize their argument, and write a persuasive essay. As a model for the final essays, I find that the Op-Ed pieces in the *New York Times* serves students well. Their length, style, and often their point-of-view are within the reach, if not the grasp, of the student. The clear, coherent, concise persuasive essay is the final response to a question of value within the course, the culmination of the cooperative attempt to find the statement that represents the person.

Just as the content of the "Composition" course is justice, so too its pedagogy must be just. In his *Short Course in Writing,* Kenneth Bruffee describes in detail a classroom model and process for making the teaching of writing a community endeavor.[10] He has two premises: writing is social and writing is a process. In short, writing is a social process. For Bruffee the model appropriate for teaching writing is collaborative learning. A class unit involves prewriting or research, followed by several stages in which a draft of a paper is written and critiqued and rewritten a few times before the final draft is composed. After seven years of struggling with "Freshman Composition," I have found Bruffee's model useful and effective.

For example, suppose my students express an interest in ecology. For research, I might assign Michael McLaverty's *The Wild Duck's Nest* or an Op-Ed piece from the *New York Times* on Greenpeace. I would suggest a visit to the local Audubon Society, an interview with an environmentalist, or a visit to Warren, Massachusetts, a small neighboring milltown where for several years a furor has raged over the possible use of the Quaboag River for the disposal of hazardous wastes. Students elsewhere will themselves be able to suggest appropriate sources for research—and research must be done. For the next class, students prepare a tentative thesis statement. The class will work in pairs for a short exercise of paired interviews to refine the thesis. Two students will look at one another's thesis; each will tell the other both what she knows about the thesis and what she wants to know. Each student will then inform the whole group how she will proceed, if she needs to do further research, how she will organize her essay, and what types of support she will supply for the thesis. She may indeed ask for help, and it is likely that both students and teacher will offer assistance.

For the next class, a first draft of the essay is due; it is to be submitted with a descriptive outline, that is, an outline that specifies the essay's thesis, what each paragraph says, and what it does. The draft is to be as finished as possible. Once again the students will pair off, with someone other than the person with whom interviews were traded. Papers will be exchanged, and the students will write their first critique. They will write their descriptive outline of the other person's essay: state the thesis, paraphrase each paragraph, and explain its function in relation to the thesis and preceding paragraph. A simple comparision of the writer's and the reader's descriptive outlines usually reveals if the author has communicated what she wanted to say. A revision is often in order.

The second critique of the essay begins with the descriptive outline. The second critique goes further, however, to examine the essay's strengths and weaknesses and how it might be improved. It includes comments on unity, coherence, development, style, and mechanics. A third critique evaluates the essay in the same ways but includes comments on content.

Bruffee's process can become quite complex: it includes authorial responses to critics, mediation between critic and author, and the teacher's critique of the peer criticism.[11] It needs to be modified in accordance with the needs and talents of the students. Nevertheless, it is helpful for at least two reasons: it creates several vehicles for collaboration during the writing process, and it gives students the tools they need in order to analyze and evaluate their own and others' writing.

This curriculum can easily be modified for interdisciplinary courses. Many colleges are now offering courses such as "Writing about the Natural Sciences," "Writing about History," "Writing about Film." In such courses, the writing teacher can easily organize the course so that students face the moral questions raised by such matter as genetic engineering or nuclear disarmament. In fact, colleges might well develop such courses for juniors and seniors in particular so that we might graduate young men and women who are more articulate about the highly complex issues of our day.

Some colleges have tried different models. In schools that have adopted "writing across the curriculum," the "English Composition" faculty works with all teachers in what may be misnamed "content areas." In others, "Composition" is integrated into another traditional freshman-year course. An English teacher might be team-teaching with a history teacher, helping students to analyze and write about the Lincoln-Douglas debates or a decree of Elizabeth I. At the Elms College for instance, all freshmen now take a year-long rhetoric course, which is team-taught by the departments of English and Speech. Imagine what could happen in a college that infused all its courses with the respect for language that leads one to justice.

In teaching justice while teaching writing, the teacher's role remains what it has always been. Students need to know how to formulate a proposition and defend it adequately with different kinds of support. They need to know how to organize material, how to justify a conclusion. They need to know what is desirable, obligatory, or admirable, and their contraries; they need to know what is just. Even more, they need to know that they do know such things and to modify their knowledge in intelligent discourse with masters of writing as well as with their peers. The writing teacher who believes in the student, who cares about matters of consequence, who is willing to engage in mature dialogue about a class's personal experience and beliefs, who encourages dissent and its defense will inevitably teach a course in which members instruct themselves and one another in justice.

NOTES

1. Paulo Freire, *Pedagogy of the Oppressed* (New York: Seabury Press, 1970). Freire's book is based on the premise that lasting liberation is rooted in mastery of language.

2. Quoted in *Dylan Thomas's Choice: An Anthology of Verse Spoken by Dylan Thomas,* ed. Ralph Maud and Aneirin Talfan Davies (New York: New Directions, 1963), p. xxi.

3. Anne Sexton, "Words," *The Awful Rowing Towards God* (Boston, Mass.: Houghton Mifflin, 1975) p. 71 (II. 11–14).

4. *English Journal* (January 1964), p. 5.

5. Available from the Audio-Visual Center, Office for Learning Resources, Indiana University, Bloomington, IN 47401.

6. Available from Instructional Media Services, Film Department, University of Washington, Seattle, WA 98195.

7. Text of letter included in the *Congressional Record,* July 11, 1983, p. S9596. Italics added by present writer.

8. Sexton, "Words," II. 22–26.

9. Among McCarthy's writing are "St. Maximus, the Confessor," *Nonviolence—Central to Christian Spirituality,* ed. Joseph T. Culleton, C.S.B. (New York: Edwin Mellen Press, 1982), pp. 63–87; and *Epistle to the Church of the 20th Century: Christian Nonviolence, the Great Future, the Only Hope* (Brockton, Mass.: Agape Center for the Study and Practice of Christian Nonviolence, 1982). McCarthy's works on videotape include *The Theology of Christian Nonviolence* and *The Spirituality of Christian Nonviolence* (Catholic Education Center, 328 W. 6th St., St. Paul, MN 55102).

10. Kenneth Bruffee, *A Short Course in Writing* (Boston, Mass.: Little, Brown, 1980).

11. Ibid., p. 124.

SELECTED READINGS FOR FACULTY

Booth, Wayne C. *Modern Dogma and the Rhetoric of Assent.* Chicago, Ill.: University of Chicago Press, 1974.

———. *The Rhetoric of Fiction.* Chicago, Ill.: University of Chicago Press, 1961.

Brufee, Kenneth. *A Short Course in Writing.* Boston, Mass.: Little, Brown, 1980.

Burke, Kenneth. *Grammar of Motives.* Berkeley, Calif.: University of California Press, 1969.

———. *Language as Symbolic Action.* Berkeley, Calif.: University of California Press, 1966.

———. *A Rhetoric of Motives.* Berkeley, Calif.: University of California Press, 1969.

———. *The Rhetoric of Religion.* Berkeley, Calif.: University of California Press, 1970.

Burks, Don M., ed. *Rhetoric, Philosophy and Literature: An Exploration.* West Lafayette, Ind.: Purdue University Press, 1978.

Campbell, Karlyn, *The Rhetorical Act.* Belmont, Calif.: Wadsworth, 1982.

Corbett, E. P. J. *Classical Rhetoric for the Modern Student.* London: Oxford University Press, 1971.

Edleman, Murray. *Political Language: Words that Succeed and Policies that Fail.* Santa Clara, Calif.: Academy Press, 1977.

Ellul, Jacques. *Propaganda: The Formation of Men's Attitudes.* New York: Random House, 1959.

Freire, Paulo, *Pedagogy of the Oppressed.* New York: Seabury Press, 1970.

Golden, James.; Goodwin F. Berquist; and William Coleman. *The Rhetoric of Western Thought.* Dubuque, Iowa: Kendall/Hunt Publishers, 1976.

Grassi, Ernesto. *Rhetoric as Philosophy: The Humanistic Tradition.* University Park, Pa.: Pennsylvania State University Press, 1980.

Guinan, Edward. *Peace and Nonviolence.* New York: Paulist Press, 1973.

Hairston, Maxine. *A Contemporary Rhetoric.* Boston, Mass.: Houghton Mifflin, 1982.

Merton, Thomas. *Thomas Merton on Peace,* ed. Gordon Zahn. New York: McCall, 1971.

Orwell, George. "Politics and the English Language." In *Themes for Writers,* ed. Joyce Steward. Glenview, Ill.: Scott Foresman, 1983, pp. 58–72.

Pereleman, Chaim. *The New Rhetoric: A Treatise on Argumentation.* Notre Dame, Ind.: University of Notre Dame Press, 1969.

Richards, I. A. *The Philosophy of Rhetoric.* New York: Oxford University Press, 1965.

Searle, John R. *Speech Act: An Essay on the Philosophy of Language.* Cambridge, England: University Press, 1969.

Wallace, Karl R. "The Primacy of Substance and Ideas in the Teaching of Practical Discourse." *English Journal,* January 1964, pp. 1–9.

Weaver, Richard. *The Ethics of Rhetoric.* Chicago, Ill.: Regnery Gateway, 1953.

White, Eugene E., ed. *Rhetoric in Transition: Studies in the Nature and Uses of Rhetoric.* University Park, Pa.: Pennsylvania State University Press, 1980.

PART II

THE SOCIAL SCIENCES

5

Economics

WILLIAM J. BYRON, S.J.
THE CATHOLIC UNIVERSITY OF AMERICA

In the teaching-learning transaction that is the business of the economics classroom, the objective is to come to an understanding of economic behavior and the impact of structure on behavior, as well as the importance of theory for the explanation of economic reality.[1]

I recall my own experience as a graduate student in economics in recognizing for the first time (thanks to an etymological reference in an essay by Milton Friedman) that the words "theory" and "theater" are related. Each is constructed to focus the attention of the viewer. My earlier exposure to the study of the Greek language should have made that connection obvious to me, but it had not. In any case, and particularly in the case of classroom economics, it is important to make the point early with students that theory is a way of looking at reality, and without a theory the student will miss seeing important parts of reality.

The complex reality of the world economy is one of uneven production and distribution. Is that uneven reality fundamentally unjust? The professor of economics cannot set that question aside as irrelevant, unanswerable, or inappropriate to the discipline. Theories appropriate for the discipline of economics require an infusion of the idea of justice if the discipline is to meet the classroom demand for an explanation of economic reality. Why? Because the discipline deals with human choice, not impersonal forces, and human persons individually and collectively are the "responsible selves" whose economic choices can produce results that are not simply uneven but are unjust.

A view of economic reality must be enhanced by a range finder capable of including the dimension of justice. Otherwise, the reality—the product of free choice—will remain unexplained. Every professor of economics should have at hand an image of justice expressive of a sound idea of justice. The two most ancient images of justice that come to mind remain useful today. They involve measurement and in that sense are normative. They, or images like them, can and should be routinely applied to economic reality in the teaching of economics.

The famous plumb-line image used by the prophet Amos is one of them. Whereas a philosopher like Plato deals with justice as a concept, a prophet like Amos treats justice as a command. Professors of political economy should possess more than a bit of both.

> This is what the Lord Yahweh showed me:
> a man standing by a wall,
> plumb-line in hand.
> "What do you see, Amos?" Yahweh asked me.
> "A plumb-line," I said.
> Then the Lord said to me,
> "Look, I am going to measure my people Israel by plumb-line;
> no longer will I overlook their offenses" [Amos 7:7–8].

The nation will be inspected. It will be measured for its uprightness, its integrity. Just as a wall that is "out of plumb" will collapse, so a society that is unjust is going to topple. The plumb bob falls toward the exact center of the earth. The string between hand and bob is therefore "upright," an image of justice. Human relationships are subject to measurement for proper balance. Are they on the "up and up," or "on the level," or "fair and square"? Economic relationships can be measured in the same way.[2]

Similarly, the familiar trays in balance on a scale provide an image of justice. As Barbara Ward has written:

> To illustrate the degree to which philosophers have long recognized the consequences of unbalanced power, one has only to recall Thucydides, the great Greek historian's account of Athens and Melos. "The human spirit is so constituted that what is just is examined only if there is equal necessity on both sides. But if one is strong and the other weak, that which is possible is imposed by the first, accepted by the second." That is why, since antiquity, the symbol of justice has been a figure holding equally balanced scales.[3]

The scales of justice are more readily associated with lawyers than with economists. But economic reality admits of division on the trays; the image of the scales of justice can help to infuse a justice dimension into economic analysis.

What we experience in economic relationships as uneven is not necessarily unfair or unjust. To establish injustice, one must first establish relatedness between the trays. Not every imbalance is wrong. An imbalance is also an injustice when one side's advantage (the down tray) has been taken at the expense of the other side. Related to a downside gain is an upside injury *(injure)*. Is the holder of the downside gain the active perpetrator of the injury? If so, the relatedness is quite direct. If the advantaged down tray represents a passive benefit derived from an injury inflicted by another (even by impersonal social forces), the question of relatedness must be examined carefully. The closer the relatedness, the deeper the implication in the injustice and the larger the obligation to work to bring the trays into balance.

If an imbalance is evident, the question to be asked is: Has one side's gain been taken unfairly at the expense of the other? Is one side up precisely *because* the other is down? The important thing is to raise these questions in the context of economic problems. No one can answer without first reflecting on the issue of relatedness. If there is no relatedness, there is no question of justice. Few if any economic problems will survive scrutiny through the framework of the scales of justice without revealing some trace of a line of relatedness.

Students of economics should be encouraged to look at the world through the framework of the scales of justice. Do the imbalances they will see represent acceptable unevenness or unacceptable injustice? In economic analysis, the question of relatedness of down-tray gain to up-tray loss must take account of the freedom, or lack of it, that the losers brought to the transaction.

Whatever the student's image of justice, his or her idea of justice is likely to touch upon the notion of equity, of fair shares. There will probably be a recognition that justice does not necessarily mean prosperity, and an admission that it will always mean something related to decency and human dignity. The student's idea of justice will ordinarily apply the notion of equity first to the distribution of material goods, to the distribution of wealth and income. Only secondarily is the notion of justice likely to include considerations in the realm of spirit—human rights relating to freedom of speech, religion, conscience, and, of particular significance in economic matters, self-determination. There can be violations of human rights both in the distribution of material goods and in the exercise of self-determination. Such violations are often discernible behind the economic problems a student encounters in the classroom. If the justice issue is overlooked, the economic analysis will be incomplete. Disagreement will often arise over the presence and extent of relatedness. Such differences of perception need not be reconciled in the economics classroom. My point, of course, is that they should not go unnoticed there.

EXPERIENTIAL LEARNING

To say that the infusion of the idea of justice into economic analysis begins with theory could be misleading. One of the ongoing debates in academe touches the interesting question of whether it is preferable to act one's way into new ways of thinking or to think one's way into new ways of acting. The classroom approach to learning tends to favor the second alternative. There is nothing so practical as a good theory, it is said. Learn the theory first and then put it into practice. A solid pedagogical argument can be made, however, that runs in exactly the opposite direction. Experience first, reflection later. Just as students may have been unaware that they were speaking prose long before they "saw" prose for the first time in the classroom, so all of them were economic decision-makers long before they ever heard of Adam Smith. The pedagogical task is to help them to see, to understand. Experience and reflection upon experience prepare the way for understanding. There is much to be said for experiential learning.

I was teaching economics at Loyola College in Baltimore, Maryland, when the riots following the assassination of Martin Luther King, Jr., put parts of nearby Washington, D.C., in flames. Within a day, the burning and looting came to Baltimore. The city was stunned. For Baltimore, in those anxious days in 1968, nothing was more real than the so-called civil disorders. I invited my students to examine this reality from several perspectives—sociological, historical, psychological, ethical, political, and economic. Each angle revealed more of the reality. The economic perspective gave us the opportunity to turn the telescope around and examine various economic theories in themselves. To the extent that the troubled reality had economic causes, the uses of economics might contribute to a solution. Meanwhile, people were hurting and the city was burning. We put faces on the unemployment statistics and noticed how labor markets can malfunction. We also looked with great interest at the distribution of wealth and income in Baltimore and noted that those maldistributions were not unrelated to the complicated phenomenon we were trying to understand.

This experience carried over next semester into my labor economics course, in which each student had to write a term paper derived from nonlibrary sources. They went to the Bureau of Employment Security, to the Chamber of Commerce, private employment agencies, skill training centers, and similar agencies and organizations, private and public. As part of the term project, experience in the local labor market counted a lot: for example, the experience of presenting oneself for a day's employment at one of the "rent-a-man" offices that broker the services of unskilled, marginal labor to match the temporary heavy-duty needs of port-city businesses. To ensure, however, that the library did not recede to a position of irrelevance in the minds of those same students, all were expected to follow a reading list and each was called upon in the classroom for an oral presentation of a preassigned journal article. Experience of inner-city labor markets was important in that class; so was the experience of public speaking gained through oral summaries of the assigned journal articles. Reflection on both kinds of experience proved beneficial to the students.

INTERDISCIPLINARY POSSIBILITIES

At Loyola University of New Orleans, Louisiana, where I served as dean of arts and sciences from 1973 to 1975 and did a small amount of teaching, certain courses were presented in the mode-of-thought (MT) format. The MT design at Loyola was consciously interdisciplinary. Normally, MT courses were given only in twice-weekly, seventy-five minute sessions. The MT design focused on the front of the classroom, on the interaction of the disciplines. Each participating professor (there were normally two or three) represented a different discipline. Each professor was committed to attendance at all classes. MT courses were not team-taught in the sense that professors came and went in sequential fashion; interaction between the professors (and hence the disciplines) was expected at every class session. If three professors taught an MT course, each was credited with three hours on a normal teaching load. Enrollments for MT courses were planned on a ratio of twenty-five students to each participating faculty member. Loyola had a sufficient number of large classrooms to accommodate the large enrollments. It also had a policy guideline that limited students to one MT course per semester, in order to guarantee that most of their instruction would be received in much smaller classes. The MT experience was offered by way of exception precisely to provide an opportunity for interdisciplinary instruction.

In designing a mode-of-thought course, faculty members had first to select a truly significant problem area around which the disciplines could interact. Next came the division of labor—assigning segments of the course to the appropriate discipline. Perhaps an example will be helpful.

As dean, I decided to teach one of these courses myself in hopes of stimulating wider interest among the faculty. I (an economist) invited a historian and a professor of American literature to join me for a course on the Great Depression. It was the spring semester of 1975. We opened the course with a newsreel, a "March of Time" film documentary on the depression. Students began their reading from a list that included novels, historical accounts, journalistic essays, records of oral history, and a simplified textbook on macroeconomic theory (Robert Heilbroner's *Understanding Macroeconomics*).

The first third of the course was turned over to the historian, who lectured for the first fifty minutes of each seventy-five-minute period. Comments on his lectures (somewhat in the fashion of reactors at a professional meeting) came from both the economist and the literateur. American literature (John Steinbeck's *In Dubious Battle,* James Agee's *Let Us Now Praise Famous Men,* Richard Wright's *Native Son,* and several other selections) occupied the middle third of the course along with the film version of John Steinbeck's *The Grapes of Wrath.* Economic theory and policy filled the third segment. Macroeconomic theory, as we now know it, was in fact a response to the problem of widespread unemployment and economic depression. An interest in the problem, cultivated by the experience of the first two-thirds of the course, prepared the students for a better understanding of the theory. It also prepared them for a better understanding of the public-policy debates over the relative merits of tax cuts and public spending as economic-stimulus mechanisms. Daily newspaper stories of macroeconomic interest (President Gerald Ford was wearing his WIN button then, urging citizens to "whip inflation now") became a regular part of classroom discussion.

We attracted 158 students to this course. We succeeded in holding their interest, and most of them evaluated the experience positively. I enjoyed it and learned a lot. Colleague ties were strengthened. All three of us who shared the teaching responsibility agreed that interdisciplinary work of this kind is an effective device for on-the-job faculty development.

IMAGING THE FUTURE

If you believe, with René Dubos, that "the logical future, determined by past and present conditions, is less important than the willed future, which is largely brought about by deliberate choice," you will acknowledge a place for literary imagination in the formation of students of economics and business. Let me explain.

It is important for students to imagine what the future might be like for them in the United States business system. I encourage them to "image" themselves in the setting that is likely to evolve from the deliberate choice of the career path that will begin where the graduation procession ends. To set one's mind only on "getting a job" is to close one's mind to the "willed future." But how can a professor encourage this recommended and desirable forward thinking? I suggest the use of fiction to activate the imagination.

The following note appeared on the syllabus of the last course I taught— "Business and Society," at the University of Scranton (I have since had to drop teaching for full-time administrative responsibilities):

> Each student will select, read and report on a novelist's portrayal of the business person in the United States. Appended to this syllabus is a list containing the novels and directions on how to approach the project.

This assignment represents parallel reading, a supplement to the regular reading list. The assignment also requires a short but important written essay. All of this is explained in a special assignment instruction attached to the syllabus.

BUSINESS AND SOCIETY

Special Assignment: Business in Fiction

The novels listed here are selected less for their literary merits (some represent fine literature, some do not) than for their potential to provide a window on the past or present world of business.

The first books of this type were written by William Dean Howells and H. E. Hamblen in the 1880's and 1890's; but a real deluge of such books appeared after the "muckrakers" of the Progressive Era had shown the corrupting influence and undemocratic methods of American Business. In the 1920's the attitude toward business was often satirical, as in Sinclair Lewis, and in the 1930's it was generally antagonistic, but numerous books in the 1950's are neutrally realistic or down-right compassionate portrayals of businessmen—who are shown as realizing too late that man does not live by commercial values alone. Most novels about businessmen are antidotes for the Horatio Alger tradition and the success-story myth [Otis W. Coan and Richard G. Lillard, *America in Fiction* (Stanford, Calif.: Stanford University Press, 1956,) p. 80; note that this was first published in 1956].

In his essay "The Major Novelists View the American Businessman," excerpted from the *Wharton Quarterly* and published in the *New York Times* on June 29, 1975, Dr. Robert F. Lucid, chairman of the graduate group in the University of Pennsylvania's Department of English, reminds us that it is possible to envision a society in a microcosmic way, and the microcosm used by many novelists—Ernest Hemingway, for example—to symbolize all of our social institutions is the military: "For him [Hemingway] the military is a perfect symbol, revealing the essence of institutionality, for it acknowledges candidly what most institutions—including industry, of course—often cover up. It acknowledges that, by comparison with the welfare of the institution, the welfare of the individual doesn't matter." Is this also applicable to the institution known as American business?

Not all the writers listed below are major writers, nor do all these novels envision society in a microcosmic way. Some do. All deal with human persons in a business context, often within the institution known as the business corporation. The student's assignment is to read one of these novels; then, from the perspective of the protagonist or the narrator of the story, to write an essay entitled "On the Possibility of a Full Human Life in the United States Business System." Use the "My Turn" feature in *Newsweek* magazine as a model for length and style.

BUSINESS IN FICTION

1. Jeffrey Archer, *Kane and Abel* (1980)
2. Marcia Davenport, *The Valley of Decision* (1942)
3. John Dos Passos, *The 42nd Parallel* (1930)
4. ———, *The Big Money* (1936)
5. Theodore Dreiser, *The Financier* (1912)
6. ———, *The Titan* (1914)
7. ———, *The Stoic* (1947)
8. Ralph Ellison, *Invisible Man* (1952)
9. Edna Ferber, *Come and Get It* (1935)
10. F. Scott Fitzgerald, *The Last Tycoon* (1941)

11. Martin Flavin, *Journey in the Dark* 1943)
12. Gene Fowler, *Timber Line* (1933)
13. Arthur Hailey, *Hotel* (1965)
14. ———, *Wheels* (1971)
15. ———, *The Money-Changers* (1975)
16. Cameron Hawley, *Executive Suite* (1952)
17. ———, *Cash McCall* (1955)
18. Joseph Hergesheimer, *The Three Black Pennys* (1917)
19. Robert Herrick, *The Memoirs of an American Citizen* (1905)
20. William Dean Howells, *The Rise of Silas Lapham* (1885)
21. ———, *A Hazard of New Fortunes* (1890)
22. ———, *A Traveler from Altruria* (1894)
23. Sinclair Lewis, *Babbitt* (1922)
24. ———, *Dodsworth* (1929)
25. ———, *Work of Art* (1934)
26. ———, *Gideon Planish* (1943)
27. Jack London, *The Iron Heel* (1908)
28. John P. Marquand, *Point of No Return* (1949)
29. ———, *Sincerely, Willis Wayde* (1954)
30. Frank Norris, *The Octopus* (1901)
31. ———, *The Pit* (1903)
32. John O'Hara, *From the Terrace* (1958)
33. ———, *The Lockwood Concern* (1965)
34. David Phillips, *The Great God Success* (1901)
35. ———, *The Master Rogue* (1903)
36. ———, *Light-Fingered Gentry* (1907)
37. Ayn Rand, *Atlas Shrugged* (1957)
38. Upton Sinclair, *A Captain of Industry* (1906)
39. ———, *The Jungle* (1906)
40. ———, *The Money Changers* (1908)
41. ———, *King Coal* (1917)
42. ———, *Oil!* (1927)
43. ———, *Boston* (1928)
44. ———, *Co-op* (1936)
45. Harvey Sivados, *On the Line* (1960)
46. Booth Tarkington, *The Magnificent Ambersons* (1935)
47. Frederick Wakeman, *The Hucksters* (1946)
48. Edward Westcott, *David Harum* (1898)
49. Sloan Wilson, *The Man in the Gray Flannel Suit* (1955)
50. Herman Wouk, *Aurora Dawn* (1947)

The point of this assignment is to bring the student to see the United States business system through eyes of another—the protagonist or narrator in the novel selected by the student. The literary portrayal provides the window on the business world. It is the protagonist or narrator who speaks to the assigned essay topic, "On the Possibility of a Full Human Life in the United States Business System." In writing the essay, the student can begin to see himself or herself inside another's skin, within the business system, in a future world of work. Each student can then ask: Is this the "willed future" I really want? Is there anything in this world I want to change?

Justice themes can be located more easily in some novels than in others. Some novels are clearly pro-business, others hostile, still others neutral in their portrayal. A work by Emily Stipes Watts, *The Businessman in American Literature* (1982) will help the interested professor to become acquainted with the literature. A novel about the pharmaceutical industry, Arthur Herzog's curiously titled *L*S*I*T*T** (1983), although not on the reading list, is an example of a return on the part of novelists to the corporation as the setting for works of fiction.

THE INTRODUCTORY COURSE IN ECONOMICS

I have not taught a course on principles of economics for many years. I would like, however, to suggest that professors of economics could employ the scales-of-justice framework for presentation of topics throughout a course on economic principles. A final judgment on a given situation is not expected, of course, but an indication that the complex reality under examination does have a justice dimension is desirable.

For a principles course, any one of the basic textbooks available could be used. I have selected William J. Baumol and Alan S. Binder, *Economics: Principles and Policy* (New York: Harcourt Brace Jovanovich, 1979) for purposes of this essay. The table of contents of this text constitutes a satisfactory syllabus outline. The professor should divide the matter into manageable time blocks, schedule examination dates, and assign term-paper topics, supplementary readings, oral reports, and special events, if there are to be any.

PRINCIPLES OF ECONOMICS

Here is a summary of the eleven-page Baumol-Binder table of contents. It is suggestive of the structure of a syllabus of topics to be covered in any "Principles of Economics" course.

PART I: GENERAL

1. What Is Economics? (concepts, theories, models, tools, values)
2. The Use and Misuse of Graphs (functions, relationships, measurement, interpretation)

At the beginning of their book, Baumol and Binder present twelve "Ideas for beyond the Final Exam." In summary they are: (1) the illusion of high interest rates; (2) economic principles to protect the environment; (3) inflation and unemployment; (4) increasing equality and the sacrifice of output; (5) the crisis in urban services; (6) interferences with the "laws" of supply and demand; (7) a new way to measure costs; (8) the surprising principle of comparative advantage; (9) the importance of marginal analysis; (10) stabilizing the economy without "big government"; (11) the consequences of budget deficits; (12) why speculation can be a good thing. Each idea is outlined briefly in the opening pages of the text and reference is made to a subsequent chapter where the idea receives fuller treatment. Wherever the idea appears later in the text, it is accompanied by a small, boxed imprint of the book's logo in order to alert the reader to the presence of a fundamental idea to be carried "beyond the final exam," wrapped—if the course is successful—in a better understanding of the economic principle involved.

Several of these ideas involve "trade-offs" (the expression invites application of the scales of justice) that economists are fond of discussing. For example, Idea No. 2 involves the "costly trade-off between the size of a nation's production and the degree of equality with which the products are divided among the nation's families." The authors assert: "The more equal we force incomes to be, the smaller the products of the economy will become." This is the trade-off between equality and efficiency. Students should be invited to examine this idea within the framework of the scales of justice.

Another trade-off is the much debated relationship between inflation and unemployment (Idea No. 3). How does the weight of inflation, borne by all who have to pay the rising prices, balance off on the scales against the weight of unemployment borne by a relative few (even though a small percentage of the labor force represents a large absolute number of unemployed persons)?

Idea No. 6 opens the door to discussion of farm price supports and the difficult issue of reconciling the conflicting interests of farmers, consumers, and taxpayers. The scales of justice might serve as a useful framework for classroom reaction to, for example, a *Washington Post* writer's argument (Robert J. Samuelson, Aug. 23, 1983) that "a legitimate public purpose exists in continuing government-maintained grain reserves. Supply and demand conditions fluctuate, and an adequate reserve ought to temper the resulting swings. But the further effort to sustain farmers' incomes—through price supports of various sorts—seems an increasingly costly, ineffective and unjustifiable anachronism."

The examples could be multiplied; the issues seem endless. As blue-collar workers lose their jobs to steel-collar robots, as government tries now to "control," now to "decontrol" prices and output; as the one face of the only earth we have shows simultaneous signs of feast and famine, those who attempt to explain economic activity cannot ignore the justice dimensions of the problems under analysis. Neither can they ignore the assumptions and presuppositions upon which their analysis (and that of the textbook) rests.

CONCLUSION

There are three basic models of social change: fatalism, reform, and revolution. Fatalism ill becomes anyone alive in mind and heart (not to mention faith, hope, and love). Revolution need not be violent; it can involve an attitudinal "turnaround" and, subsequently, new and better choices. Reform is always, of course, a matter of degree, and should not be attempted without an antecedent judgment concerning the essential soundness of the foundations of the system to be reformed. Students should be encouraged to face up to these issues as they look at the national economy and its place in the world.

It has been suggested that an economist is a person who sees something working in practice and then tries to find out if it will work in theory. Surely, professors of economics would serve their profession (and their students) well if they first determine how justice is supposed to work in theory, and then seek out what it may have to do, in practice, with what they are teaching.

A final note on the teaching-learning transaction itself. In economics, as in any discipline, this should be a relationship marked by justice. The student voice should be heard; the person of the student should be fully respected. Why should students not be invited to participate in course-opening discussions of the "terms of trade" that will affect them—number of assignments, dates for tests, deadlines for papers, absentee policy? All that some students need to do in order to understand the domination-dependency relationship that characterizes the economic relationships between powerful and weak nations is to reflect on their own experience at the feet of domineering professors.

The tuition dollar should command full value in lectures delivered, assignments and tests marked and returned, advice and encouragement provided, office hours kept, and professional growth maintained. One professor whom I know assigns, as a required text, a book that he authored; but he refunds to the student-purchaser the amount of the royalty he receives from that sale of the book. He explains that he does this because he has not left the student free not to purchase that particular book.

Inevitably, a professor's own sense of justice (or insensitivity to considerations of justice) will be communicated with what he or she presents from the professorial side of the teaching-learning transaction. As that transaction goes, so goes education for justice.

NOTES

1. Several paragraphs of my own previously published material have been included in this essay. Readers may be interested in seeing my "Institutional Purpose and Classroom Teaching: The Case of Economics," *Occasional Papers on Catholic Higher Education* 3, no. 2 (Winter 1977): 12–16. This is a publication of the College and University Department (now Association of Catholic Colleges and Universities) of the

National Catholic Educational Association. Another article from which I have drawn material for this chapter is my "Ideas and Images of Justice," *Loyola Law Review* 26, no. 3 (1980): 439–52.

2. Chrysler president Lee Iacocca began his Aug. 2, 1983, *Washington Post* Op-Ed article on "World Trade: What U.S. Firms Are Up Against," with the following lines: "The playing field in world trade is not level; it is blatantly tilted against the United States. . . . And unless the field can be made level, we will rapidly slip from the major leagues to the minors—with small chance of a comeback." He concludes his discussion of exchange rates, value-added taxes, cyclical downturns, protectionism, and preservation of market share with this paragraph: "A level field means a fair game—a game in which all players go by equivalent rules. A level playing field in international trade is necessary to put the biggest game in the world back on the level."

Other observers will have different conclusions, but the plumb-line perspective will serve to initiate a productive argument with or without the additional mixture of metaphors.

3. Barbara Ward, "Looking Back at *Populorum Progressio,*" *Catholic Mind* 76, no. 1327 (November 1978): 9–25; quotation from n. 1.

SELECTED READINGS FOR FACULTY

Bird, Otto A. *The Idea of Justice.* New York: Frederick A. Praeger, 1967.

Byron, William J., S. J. "Christianity and Capitalism: Three Concepts from the Tradition, Three Challenges to the System." *Review of Social Economy,* 40, no. 3 (December 1982): 311–22.

———. "The Machine and the Workbench." *Santa Clara Magazine* 26, no. 3 (January 1984): 12–13.

Gurley, John G. *Challenges to Capitalism: Marx, Lenin and Mao.* San Francisco, Calif.: San Francisco Book Company, 1976.

Hirsch, Fred. *Social Limits to Growth.* Cambridge, Mass.: Harvard University Press, 1978.

John Paul II. *Laborem Exercens* ["On Human Work"]. Washington, D.C.: United States Catholic Conference, 1981.

Lewis, W. Arthur. *The Evolution of the International Economic Order.* Princeton, N.J.: Princeton University Press, 1978.

Wien, Barbara, ed. *Peace and World Order Studies: A Curriculum Guide.* 4th ed. New York: World Policy Institute, 1984.

6

History

DAVID J. O'BRIEN
COLLEGE OF THE HOLY CROSS

Over the years since Vatican II much has been written about education for justice and peace in the Catholic community. Indeed there is now a small library of books and articles, and many justice and peace centers have well-stocked rooms of films, filmstrips, slides, and tapes, and boxes upon boxes of study guides, case studies, and other educational materials. Religious communities have led the way in rededicating themselves to the poor and powerless, defining their apostolates in terms of the struggle to make peace and build justice. Because so many of these religious orders are involved in higher education, it is hardly surprising that many colleges and universities are now deeply involved in the surprisingly difficult task of rethinking how teaching and research can be made more directly relevant to the pressing issues of our times. The pastoral letters of the United States Catholic Bishops on higher education, on nuclear arms, and on the economy give strong support to this effort, as do Pope John Paul II's powerful statements on the arms race as it affects scholars, especially in the sciences and the social sciences.

While this exciting discussion goes on in higher education, there has so far, unfortunately, been little success in developing approaches to curriculum that are proportionate to the challenge. Peace studies and education for justice programs remain somewhat marginal in most schools. Often they provide optional programs of study, which draw some response from the more religiously motivated students and the more activist members of the faculty and sponsoring religious community. Only rarely are they creative centers for innovation that spark controversy and response in the core curriculum, or in departments and schools, leading to changes that touch directly on the central work of students and faculty. As a report on priorities at the University of

Notre Dame suggests, justice and peace are surely important values, worthy of extended discussion, but the central work of the university remains solidly within the prevailing standards of excellence as defined by the bureaucratic systems that dominate American higher education.[1]

All this is understandable, for the obstacles confronting those who would bring education for justice and peace more directly into the curriculum and into the research agenda of the faculty are enormous. They are administrative, political, and most of all cultural, and they operate in every discipline from business and engineering to languages and classics. The education for justice and peace conversation invariably begins around a current issue like race, women's rights, or nuclear arms, but it quickly becomes another conversation about values, about general education and the core curriculum, or about language itself: Can people in one discipline talk to people in another discipline without extended training in the language and methods of the discipline they wish to address? If the answer is No, then justice and peace are best left to ethics or moral theology, and may the students make what sense of things they can.

Once this is understood, advocates of education for justice and peace settle in for a long cultural struggle, as significant in its way as that of their colleagues in North American ghettos, or resistance communities, or Latin American barrios. The long process of finding a discourse at once independent of prevailing culture, yet not so independent as to marginalize the argument, is a work of tremendous importance, which is in fact going on. Meanwhile, the immediate problem remains: those students who show up in our classes each day. So individuals and groups of faculty search for ways to bring political and moral concerns to bear on their teaching, some in separate institutes and extracurricular programs, others in their own departments and courses, both options more easily taken by senior than junior faculty and by people in the humanities and social sciences than by their peers in sciences and the career-oriented schools of engineering, business, law, and medicine.

History should be one of those disciplines in which the second option is more easily followed, if for no other reason than that students and faculty expect history courses to deal with controversial subjects and with social change. Yet history, like all the other disciplines, has its peculiar obstacles to serious discussion of politics and social justice. Despite the fact that the great American historians—George Bancroft, Frederick Jackson Turner, Charles Beard, Carl Becker—were deeply committed men who wrote history with a very clear political commitment, contemporary American historiography continues to labor under a professional ethic of detachment and objectivity, expressed too often in ways suggesting that the historical process itself is so powerful that human actions and ideas have little real significance. Historical knowledge easily becomes therapeutic, inducing a sense that the best one can do is to adapt to the conditions created by vast forces over which people have little control. Having written previously on this subject,[2] I need not belabor the point here, beyond a reminder of Paul Valéry's famous statement that "history is the most dangerous product distilled by the chemistry of the intellect" because it ends in suggesting that the world is chaos, without human meaning, or that it is ordered in such a way that people simply make no difference. In either case, the world is out of control and we had best, willy-nilly, make what peace we can with it.

Of course, as the example of the great United States historians suggests, history can do better than that. Those men were important, not simply because they offered new insights into the American past, but because they engaged in the ongoing effort to shape American public culture in ways that would affirm and advance the values of reason and freedom they believed central to the American experiment in democracy. Today, United States historiography remains an exciting cultural battleground where contending factions struggle to define the heart of the American experience and help to shape the images through which publics understand and interpret experience.

The historian need make no great departure from traditional materials or methods to incorporate consideration of justice and peace themes into his or her teaching. Indeed, some of the central developments in history teaching fit very well with these concerns, though that may not always be evident.[3] In elementary and secondary school education, for example, the major developments are to replace the traditional preoccupation with national events with creative efforts to engage local experience. Community-studies themes in the literature of American history have an educational payoff in programs designed to train teachers of elementary school children in techniques to help them introduce their students to their own neighborhoods, cities, and rural communities, to learn through original documents and pictures. Visits to historical restorations, walking trips through city streets, "reading old houses" and hands-on experiences of wearing old-style clothes, using tools of a bygone era, cooking in old-fashioned kitchens, and singing old-time hymns—all help children to learn that in their community once were people like themselves who made lives and built families and institutions, who pursued values and contributed to making the world that is now theirs. We need not say, as one youngster did to Jonathan Kozol, "History always happens to somebody else." As they once did, so we can do; such experiences enable the child to claim this neighborhood, this town, as his or her own, to begin to see it as a world that people have made and remade, and which he or she can make and remake again. Once gaining that sense of responsibility in and for this community, a sense of responsibility for larger worlds may seem possible, surely more possible than when one is presented with a huge world of war, hunger, and oppression in a context in which the local world remains mysterious, even threatening and hostile.

The new social history that informs such work is having an equally valuable impact on college and university teaching. Courses in family history, urban studies, immigrant history, and a variety of other fields are focusing attention today on small-scale experiences of definable groups, some of whose members even have names. They worshiped in these churches, drank in these bars, lived in these houses, and worked in these factories. In the setting of this specific web of daily life, they heard and spoke of God, America, freedom, and justice. They experienced capitalism and socialism, oppression and opportunity, not as philosophical abstractions but as words and symbols filtered through a variety of very concrete relationships. In such studies we learn that the world in which they lived was the way it was because of the kind of people they were, and they were the kind of people they were because of the kind of world they lived in and were constantly making for themselves. They were both subjects and objects in the historical dramas of immigration, urbanization, and industrialization. They made their own lives, but in settings not always of their choosing. So it is for us: the world of American society of the late twentieth century is our world; it is making us as a certain kind of people at the very moment we are making it by our actions and decisions. Social action, if you will, is not something that we might or might not choose to engage in; we are already engaged in social action, like it or not. There is not an "in here" world of personal or group consciousness, say as Christians, and an "out there" world of capitalism, consumerism, or imperialism. The out there is already in here, shaping the kind of Christians we are; the in here is already out there, shaping the symbols and cultural constructs that give power and legitimacy to social structures. We are already engaged, we are already involved, as our parents and grandparents were before us.

Historical study at its best can thus encourage development of what C. Wright Mills once called "the sociological imagination," the ability to understand the interaction of biography and society, of personal troubles and social issues. It is a power to locate ourselves in a specific social setting and understand ourselves at once as persons, unique and possessed of our own consciousness, and social beings, intimately bound up in a way of life that is part and parcel of who we are.[4] Such an attitude and disposition is a far better basis for serious political and moral discussion (it seems to me) than the Protestant and all too American sense of personal autonomy, which makes of social engagement a matter of personal choice and decision. We have the capability, as Mills insisted, to direct our lives by the values of reason and freedom, and to enlarge the sphere of democracy in which all of us share in the collective decisions that shape our common life, but the existence of a common life, the movement of history, and our responsibility, perhaps complicity, is not a matter of our choice.

To take but one example of a historical episode that can illustrate all this, we need only think of William Styron's *Confessions of Nat Turner*, a book that professes to be fiction based on historical fact.[5] Styron's Turner is created from the slim evidence of Turner's own testimony expanded by the artist's imagination, informed and disciplined by immersion in the historical literature of slavery. Turner is a unique individual, but one whose personality, whose language and emotions, instincts and thoughts, spring from the concrete experience of being a slave, and being a certain kind of slave. Through Turner the reader is enabled to enter inside the experience of slavery, to taste something of the feelings engendered by oppression within a near total system of control, to appreciate slavery as a human problem as well as a black-white problem. Reading that book, along with the short text of Turner's own confession, a sampling of black writers responding critically to the text[6] and, perhaps, Eugene Genovese defending Styron against the black critics,[7] one can come to appreciate the interaction of past and present, the dangers and opportunities available to all of us through historical study, and the profound interrelationship between person and society, individual experience and shared culture.

It would be hard to think of a course in American history into which justice and peace themes could not be inserted. Standard courses, including surveys of United States history as a whole, social and intellectual or diplomatic history, period courses from colonial times to the twentieth century, or thematic courses on literature, political theory, or constitutional law—all lend themselves to consideration of profoundly significant issues of social justice, human rights, and peace. Indeed, in many ways they are more useful settings for raising issues of contemporary significance than courses directly focused on current problems. One is reminded of the wisdom of the staff of the United States Catholic Conference Office of International Justice and Peace who, during the Vietnam War, prepared a useful study guide on the Spanish American War considered according to the principles of just-war teaching.

For those who wish to consider such problems more directly, a few general reminders might be useful.

1. Many students are initially uncomfortable with discussion of values in history courses. A brief discussion of the value assumptions involved in various approaches to history can provide a helpful introduction during the first week of class. One way to do this is to read a general essay, such as Max Weber's "Politics as a Vocation," or one that I have found very stimulating, Hayden V. White's "The Burden of History." Another possibility is to take a general interpretive essay on American history and indicate how its pretension to objectivity and neutrality masks a strong political bias. For example, I have often used Thomas C. Cochran's 1973 presidential address to the American Historical Association, "History and Cultural Crisis," which argues the need for Americans to revise their commitment to equality in order to restore harmony in a society inevitably dominated by massive bureaucratic institutions.[8]

2. Obviously, in taking up a problem for study, care should be taken to present a variety of viewpoints that indicate varying political or moral orientations. At the same time, every effort should be made to overcome the tendency of students to conclude that evaluation depends upon subjective moral judgments that are simply personal and idiosyncratic. Conflicting views should be debated and evaluated, and the instructor should not be shy about expressing his or her own sympathies and the reasons for them.

3. Every effort should be made to avoid simplistic moralism or a simply negative revisionism. The personal and political shortcomings of reformers as well as conservatives should be faced directly; one thinks of C. Van Woodward's critique of John Brown or Aileen Kraditor's sympathetic but rigorous evaluation of William Lloyd Garrison. Similarly, while retrieving the

memory of history's outsiders—blacks, women, abolitionists, pacifists, social-
ists, anti-imperialists—one should not present American history as a one-
dimensional morality play in which truth and justice are always the sole
possession of outsiders. If contemporary concern for justice and peace has as
its ultimate goal to help solve the problems facing the human community, and
not simply to hold forth the correct moral standard, then the moral struggles of
insiders deserve equal time. Eugene Genovese's sophisticated Marxist approach to the culture of slavery, David Brody's effort to locate labor history in
the setting of an industrial society in which employers as well as workers were
attempting to build more efficient, stable, and orderly structures and procedures, and William Appleman Williams creative effort to explain the ideology
of foreign-policy elites are all helpful in this regard.[9] Far from dulling the
critical edge of committed scholarship, these studies help us to understand the
complexity of moral issues and the interplay of cultural, economic, and
political considerations in any sophisticated social analysis.

4. In short, education for justice in the setting of American studies of any
sort must be something more than muckraking. If all that is involved is
examination of social/economic conditions and their evaluation in light of the
Christian gospel or one or another political ideology, then neither the United
States nor any other society is going to come off very well. It is not difficult to
show that American society is not now and never has been all that just or
peaceful. Given a normal selection of students and given a reasonable exposure
to the injustices and inequities of American life, one might well be able to
convince some that they should cut themselves off as much as possible from
"normal" processes and institutions and seek their integrity through a church
or a political movement. But the line between alienation and creative engagement is a thin one, as is the line between a social analysis designed to encourage
intelligent commitment to social change and one designed to enhance the
morale of a church or a political party. The goal, it should be remembered, is
not to show how bad America or any other country is, but to understand how
societies and cultures work, and how men and women live their lives in specific
historical settings, so that one can more honestly and intelligently make
decisions about one's own life and work.

If it turns out that things are so bad that decent people should not want to
live and work in the United States, for example, then few of us are going to
make much of a dent on the country. We may stir up protest and expose
hypocrisy, but we shall not contribute to public understanding of how things
can be made more just and more peaceful. Noam Chomsky once wrote that the
responsibility of the intellectual was to tell the truth and expose lies; too often
we act as if the exposure of lies and the telling of truth were one and the same.
Historical research and teaching in particular tend to identify the two, for
history is a marvelous device for puncturing the pretensions of all who claim to
act from pure motives and for showing that things were not and are not the way
they are supposed to be. In an age when serious commitment to decent public
values is regarded with cynicism, a historical effort that stops there runs the
risk of deepening despair and fatalism. To overcome that tendency it is neces-

sary to seek out the positive and constructive dimensions of human actions, to observe how oppressed and oppressor alike struggle to reconcile their values and their actions in order to make a world fit for what they regard as decent human habitation. Only in that way can we promote a style of learning that has the spirit of engagement in order to remake the world, to find means of making human rights more than rhetoric, justice an operative factor in human interaction, and peace a spirit of mutuality and a willingness to submit to alternative procedures for resolving human conflict.

One course that I have taught, which illustrates some of the potential of ordinary history teaching to develop a greater awareness of social issues and social responsibility, is "The United States in the 1930s." There are some obvious reasons why such a course is helpful. It is (as of this writing) a period recent enough to have personal connections for the students. Their grandparents recall those days, there are a variety of people around to whom they can talk whose memory encompasses a period when poverty and social dislocation were widespread American experiences. Also, it is a period when some of the basic structures and symbols that still define public life and policy took shape. For better or worse we live with the legacy of the New Deal's compensatory state as the basic framework of social policy, while the memory of isolationism and appeasement still shapes understandings of international affairs both for the foreign-policy elites and for broad segments of the public. The very limited "great debate" over American response to World War II was the last public debate about the foundations of American foreign policy. The hundred days at the start of the New Deal was probably the last time the public was open to radical suggestions for changes in the political economy. It was one of those periods when Americans rediscovered the paradox of want-in-the-midst-of-plenty that is American poverty, but it was a unique episode in that history because many of the middle-class were poor as well and shared an anger and frustration before the irrationality of a highly productive economic system that could not meet the needs of huge portions of the people.

THE UNITED STATES IN THE 1930s (three credits)

This course examines society, politics, literature, religion, and people in the United States during the years of the Great Depression. We shall read books and articles, watch films, listen to lectures, and engage each other in discussion—all in the hope that we can learn something more about our country and ourselves.

REQUIREMENTS

1. Students will be expected to attend every class and to have completed the assigned readings.
2. There will be a midterm examination and a final examination.

3. Every student will complete a class project. Students are encouraged to study subjects in which they are interested. In the past people have studied radio, advertising, music, sports, religion, the arts, architecture, and poetry as well as political and economic subjects. Many have attempted to explore the experience of their own families or local communities during the depression. While most projects end up in written papers (for which detailed guidelines will be provided later in the term), some are suited to alternative presentations through films, slides, tapes, or other media. Serious and practical proposals for such presentations will be considered.

READINGS

Agee, James. *Let Us Now Praise Famous Men*. New York: Ballantine Books, 1974.

Brody, David. *Workers in Industrial America*. New York: Oxford University Press, 1980.

Burns, James M. *Roosevelt: The Lion and the Fox*. New York: Harcourt, Brace, 1956.

Day, Dorothy. *The Long Loneliness*. New York: Harper & Row, 1980.

Galbraith, John Kenneth. *The Great Crash*. Boston, Mass.: Houghton Mifflin, 1980.

Kazin, Alfred. *Starting Out in the Thirties*. New York: Random House, 1980.

Lippmann, Walter. *The Good Society*. New York: Scribners, 1948.

Niebuhr, Reinhold. *Moral Man and Immoral Society*. New York: Scribners, 1932.

Pells, Richard. *Radical Visions and American Dreams*. New York: Harper & Row, 1974.

Steinbeck, John. *In Dubious Battle*. New York: New American Library, 1979.

Terkel, Studs. *Hard Times*. New York: Avon Books, 1971.

Wiltz, J. E. *From Isolation to War*. Arlington Heights, Ill.: AHM Publishing Corp., 1968.

COURSE OUTLINE

Week One: The Crash
    Read: Galbraith; Pells, pp. 1–76; Terkel, book 1.
Weeks Two–Five: The New Deal
    Read: Burns, pp. 1–382; Terkel, book 3; Pells, chap. 2.
Week Six: Social Thought in the 1930s
    Read: Lippmann; Pells, chaps. 3–7.
Week Seven: Labor Organizing in the 1930s
    Read: Brody; Terkel, books 4–5.

Weeks Eight–Nine: Religion in the 1930s
  Read: Niebuhr; Day.
Week Ten: Literature in the 1930s
  Read: Steinbeck.
Week Eleven: The Search for America
  Read: Agee.
Weeks Twelve–Thirteen: New Deal Foreign Policy
  Read: Wiltz; Burns, pp. 382–487; Pells, chap. 8.

Films shown during the semester include newsreels available at the local
  public library; *Grapes of Wrath*; and *The River*, Pare Lorentz's famous documentary. (Additional films used depend upon my persuasive powers with local film committees.)

Some thoughts on the accompanying syllabus: First, because of my own
interests the focus of the course remains political. The New Deal also gives a
concrete organization to the decade, which seems to alleviate student anxiety.
Second, the course is an opportunity for students to explore things in which
they are interested and, sometimes, to learn that even matters that at first
appear trivial can provide insight into society and culture. Movies and magazines, musical comedies and a fascination with the grotesque, the 1936 Olym-
pics and a decade of Holy Cross football are some of the topics students have
found interesting and sometimes surprisingly revelatory about the attitudes
and experiences of significant groups of Americans. Oral history and family
histories are favorites. There are now some good aids to both, including Willa
K. Baum, *Oral History for the Local Historical Society* (rev. ed., 1971;
published by the American Association for State and Local History); David
Kyvig, *Your Family History: A Handbook for Research and Writing*
(Arlington Heights, Ill.: AHM Publishing Corp., 1978); and J. F. Watts and
Allen F. Davis, *Generations: Your Family in Modern American History* (New
York: Alfred A. Knopf, 1983). The latter includes an excellent section on the
depression. These family histories have often been most exciting, as students
discover experiences of poverty and heroic sacrifice of which they had seldom
heard anything from their parents. Finally, everyone will have their own ideas
about selections for class reading. For myself, I like Pell's book for the insight it
provides into the formation of what might be called mainstream or establishment liberalism in the postwar years. Such information is more useful for
students, I think, than better-known studies of literary radicalism during the
decade, about which they can learn a bit from Alfred Kazin. I like Steinbeck
for similar reasons. The popular appeal of his work reveals something about
widespread attitudes and emotions in the society, while the confusion of his
own philosophic and political position reflects something of the tendency
toward both determinism and sentimentality in American literary consciousness. Agee's *Let Us Now Praise Famous Men* has always seemed to me a

classic, which combines a powerful evocation of the lives of the rural southern poor with an almost embarrassing exposé of the dilemmas of self-consciousness that beset the American intellectual and artist, indeed all educated and moral persons, in modern society. The tediousness of Agee's detailed descriptions of every minute element of the lives of his subjects is deliberate, intended to aid an almost mystical communion between the poor and the reader; some students are fascinated, others very frustrated. For me it is the indispensable book for the course.

I have made many variations in the schedule in the course of teaching this material. In some terms I have included more time for student reports. In others I have stressed case studies rather than comprehensive approaches; for example, spending a week with texts, poems, and films about the Spanish Civil War and little time with the isolationist-internationalist debate or the details of New Deal foreign economic policy. I have added more on religion some terms, and once spent three weeks on ethnicity. I also have sometimes added a week of historiography, emphasizing the work of Carl Becker and of Charles and Mary Beard and the debate over relativism in the historical profession. One year I used Robert Lynd's *Knowledge for What?* (Princeton, N.J.: Princeton University Press, 1939) to discuss academic culture and the rise of the social sciences, but found the students unresponsive. The present syllabus has little on blacks and women; I have sometimes done a week on the former—obviously not enough. I plan to develop a week's materials on women and the depression. A last word: this "1930s" course is the only one wherein I have preserved a little of my youthful idealism about teaching. I still do believe that students learn and are not taught, and that papers and projects should grow out of student interests. In other courses I have been persuaded by student attitudes and my own middle-aged insecurity to become more structured and to define the demands of my courses in more detail. In the "1930s" course, like one of the tired radicals of that decade, I cling to the hope that, through their own initiative, students will embark upon a modest voyage of discovery and in the process learn something of themselves and of America, which I truly believe lives in them as much as they live in it. Once in a while it happens, and I feel vindicated. It does not happen often enough, I'm afraid.

NOTES

1. "A Report on Priorities and Commitments for Excellence," University of Notre Dame, Nov. 30, 1982.

2. David O'Brien, "History and Renewal," *Occasional Papers on Catholic Higher Education* 4, no. 1 (Summer 1978).

3. For an exciting sampling of developments in the teaching of United States history, see Stephen Botein, et al., eds., *Experiments in History Teaching* (Cambridge, Mass.: Danforth Center for Teaching and Learning, 1977).

4. C. Wright Mills, *The Sociological Imagination* (New York: Grove Press, 1959), especially chaps. 8–10.

5. William Styron, *The Confessions of Nat Turner* (New York: New American Library, 1967).

6. John Henrik Clark, *William Styron's Nat Turner: Ten Black Writers Respond* (Boston: Beacon Press, 1968).

7. Eugene Genovese, "The Nat Turner Case," *New York Review of Books*, Sept. 12, 1968, pp. 34–37.

8. Max Weber, "Politics as a Vocation," in *From Max Weber: Essays in Sociology,* ed. H. H. Gerth and C. Wright Mills (New York: Oxford University Press, 1958), pp. 77–128; Hayden V. White, "The Burden of History," *History and Theory* 5 (Spring 1966): 111–34; Thomas C. Cochran, "History and Cultural Crisis," *American Historical Review* 77 (January 1973): 1–10.

9. Eugene Genovese, *The World the Slaveholders Made* (New York: Pantheon Books, 1969), and *Roll, Jordan, Roll: The World the Slaves Made* (New York: Pantheon Books, 1972); David Brody, *Steelworkers in America: The Nonunion Era* (New York: Harper Torchbooks, 1969), and *Workers in Industrial America* (New York: Oxford University Press, 1981); William Appleman Williams, *The Tragedy of American Diplomacy* (New York: Delta Books, 1972).

SELECTED READINGS FOR FACULTY

The literature of the 1930s, primary and secondary, is so vast and the bibliographies so accessible that a list of further readings here will seem either redundant or too selective. Accordingly, I shall note only a few items I have found helpful. Alonzo L. Hamby's collection *The New Deal: Analysis and Interpretation*, 2nd ed. (New York and London: Longmans, 1981), gives a wide range of opinions of Roosevelt and the New Deal. Harvey Swados, ed., *The American Writer and the Great Depression*, published in the American Heritage Series (New York: Bobbs-Merrill, 1966), is an equally useful collection of literary texts. For those who have access to a film library, Andrew Bergman's *We're in the Money: Depression America and Its Films* (New York: Harper Colophon Books, 1972), is an excellent introduction. Richard D. McKinzie, *The New Deal for Artists* (Princeton, N.J.: Princeton University Press, 1973), is a large and somewhat expensive paperback, but its well-written text and voluminous photographs make it a tremendously stimulating book for class use. Less easily available for student purchase, but nice to pass around, is Roy Emerson Stryker and Nancy Wood, *In This Proud Land: America 1935–1943 as Seen in the FSA Photographs* (New York: Galahad Books, 1973). Stryker's introductory essay is very moving, providing one of the best short texts to convey the energetic, humane hopes of the New Dealers, rolling up their sleeves to make America over. A somewhat specialized text, but beautifully written and illustrated, is Donald Worster, *Dust Bowl: The Southern Plains in the 1930s* (New York: Oxford University Press, 1979). Finally, ranking along with the autobiographies of Dorothy Day, Woody Guthrie, and Alfred Kazin is Malcolm Cowley's memoir, *The Dream of the Golden Mountains: Remembering the 1930s* (New York: Penguin Books, 1981).

7

Political Science

DANIEL T. REGAN
VILLANOVA UNIVERSITY

Political wisdom in Western culture has sided consistently with the notion that "that government is best which governs least." This idea is at least as old as Plato's *Republic* and Aristotle's *Politics*. In varying forms it can be traced through Augustine, Thomas Aquinas, and Bellarmine. In America, Henry David Thoreau echoed Thomas Jefferson with the corollary inference to this idea, in *Essay on the Duty of Civil Disobedience,* that "that government is the best which governs not at all." This tradition represents the finest political perspective. Moreover, reflecting on it can be a useful starting point for establishing the essential role of justice in the discipline of political science. To see why this is the case let me make clear the options that follow from this position.

First, if the role of government is not to force the people into a certain type of action, then political authority is not identified with might or with political "authorities." Once this point is made, the possible sources for political authority are three: a supernatural being; human nature; or some contractual agreement by the governed themselves. In each of these options the concept of justice plays a crucial role in understanding government.

To claim that justice education is part and parcel of political science may seem to many an exercise in belaboring the obvious. Nonetheless, two points, obvious or not, must be made. First, in any large political science department with a graduate program, the positivistic school is sure to be represented. Certain colleagues will look upon normative political science as political theology or political philosophy but not as political *science.* Second, students today are staggering under a barrage of challenges to traditional values. These challenges are not attempts to replace one moral absolute with another. They are, rather, dressed in the garb of amorality. Value-free positions are "scientific" and intellectually acceptable. All value-laden concepts—and justice is surely one of them—are products of a particular intellectual prejudice, subjective and nonscientific. Students may tolerate value claims in the humanities, religion, and philosophy. They are less receptive to these perspectives in the social sciences. Thus my preference for asking students to articulate for themselves the meaning of government as the first step in their study of political science.

Thoreau denies in his essay that he is an anarchist when he tells us, "I am as anxious to be a good neighbor as I am to be a bad subject." If we accept that he is not a "no-government man," if we agree with Augustine when he claims in the first part of his essay "On the Free Choice of the Will" that "an unjust law is not a law," and if we recognize the Socratic wisdom in Plato's *Gorgias* that "it is better to suffer than to do an injustice," then the meaning and relationship of the terms "government," "law," and "justice" come into clearer focus. Political science begins and ends with these concerns.

Political scientists by the very force of their concern for the human species as political are, de facto, persons involved in many disciplines. Economics plays a large part in every body politic. Religions and moral beliefs manifest themselves in the political actions and nonactions of every state and of all peoples. These conditions make clear the plurality of topics that can be properly included in any introductory course in political science. They also suggest the inherently subjective selection process in deciding what is to be excluded and what is to be emphasized.

There is, of course, a need in every discipline to gather the data of that study. Political science, like all wisdoms, is "90 percent perspiration and 10 percent inspiration." A political institution differs from a merely social institution, although often the two can be interchanged. Political systems and their various structures, methodologies, machinations, and ideologies must be understood in the elements they share and in the manner by which they can be differentiated. Equally important to the political scientist is an understanding of human social and economic interactions. Admitting all of this, we can readily appreciate the difficulty encountered when one is trying to devise an introductory course in political science. That professors have agonized over this task from the inception of the university is of small comfort. The syllabus that follows is, therefore, intended only to be a guideline for a great number of variables. It is but a start.

The model for this outline came from Paul M. Dietterich, who suggested several years ago a useful four-part breakdown of values education, namely, inclusion, perception, values, and influence.[1] The syllabus that follows, therefore, has four sections. The "Inclusion" section exposes students to the global neighborhood in which we live. The "Perception" section helps students to reflect upon the relative narrowness of any exclusive vision. The "Values" section aids students in the difficult task of articulating with clarity the nature of certain things they do, and the causes for their acting or refusing to act in certain other ways. The "Influence" section presents a number of readily available options for action. Teachers and students should freely substitute their own preferences, since each of the approaches here is clearly a personal favorite. Specific topics and questions pertain to each of these areas, and will be elaborated upon in some detail following the syllabus.

INTRODUCTION TO POLITICAL SCIENCE *(three credits)*

COURSE DESCRIPTION

Students are introduced to political theory, international relations, organization, law, and political behavior. Emphasis will be placed on the interdisciplinary aspect of all political science. Working definitions from various systems of political economy, political philosophy, and human rights will be analyzed. Parochial and global perspectives and ideologies will be contrasted. Students will be introduced to the actual machinery of our body politic.

REQUIRED READING:

Hollenbach, David. *Claims in Conflict.* New York: Paulist Press, 1979.
———. *Nuclear Ethics: A Christian Moral Argument.* New York: Paulist Press, 1983.
Lindblom, Charles E. *The Intelligence of Democracy.* New York: Free Press, 1965.
———. *The Policy-Making Process.* Englewood Cliffs, N.J.: Prentice-Hall, 1980.
Regan, Daniel T. "Maritain's Distinction between Person and Individual." Unpublished Master's thesis, Villanova University, 1962. Mimeographed.
Thomas Aquinas. *Summa Theologiae.* 61 vols. London: Eyre and Spottiswoode, 1981.
United States Catholic Bishops. "The Challenge of Peace: God's Promise and Our Response." Washington, D.C.: United States Catholic Conference, 1983.

COURSE OUTLINE

Part I: "Inclusion" (three weeks). Readings for this section: "The Challenge of Peace"; Lindblom, *The Policy-Making Process,* chaps. 1–5.
　　Week One: Reflections on the nature of government and the role of political-policy formation of the citizen.
　　Week Two: Pre-test on students' general knowledge of relative

economic, social, political standards in first-, second-, and third-world countries. In-class essay and discussion of family ethnic trees back to grandparents. "Who is included in my world?"

Week Three: Guest lecturer representing socially, politically, economically disadvantaged in United States (American Indian, urban black, Appalachia, etc.). Class discussion on possible relationship between disfranchised and well-off in United States. Class assignment on third-world social, political, economic status of a given country is read and discussed.

Part II: "Perception" (four weeks). Readings: Hollenbach, *Nuclear Ethics: A Christian Moral Argument,* part I, chaps. 1–3; class notes (mimeographed pages from Regan thesis, distributed to class members) on "Maritain's Distinction between Person and Individual" and Thomas Aquinas' treatise on law (*Summa Theologiae* I–IIae, q. 90–94).

Week Four: Film: *Faces of My Brother* (1973) and *Gods of Metal* (1983), both available from Maryknoll Media Relations, Maryknoll, NY 10545. The work of the Maryknoll order around the world is discussed. How do we perceive our world? Lecture and discussion on global vs. more narrow perspectives. Discussion based on Hollenbach, *Nuclear Ethics,* part I.

Week Five: Slide show and commentary: *Guess Who Is Coming to Breakfast* (1978; available from Maryknoll Justice and Peace Office, Maryknoll, NY 10545). Discussion of transnational corporations and how we perceive them.

Week Six: Film: *Night and Fog,* (1955; available from SUNY at Buffalo, Media Library, 1 Foster Annex, Buffalo, NY 14214). How do we now perceive the fact of the Holocaust? Who is to blame for such an event? How do we perceive racism? Can it happen again?

Week Seven: How do we perceive the common good? Analysis of students' perceptions of the "national interest." Discussion of Maritain's *Person and the Common Good,* found in class notes. Midterm exam.

Part III: "Values" (four weeks). Readings: Lindblom, *The Intelligence of Democracy,* part 5, chaps. 15–16; Hollenbach, *Claims in Conflict,* part 2, chaps. 2–3; United States Catholic Bishops, "The Challenge of Peace"; Hollenbach, *Nuclear Ethics,* part 2, chaps. 4–6.

Weeks Eight-Nine: Students take part in practice lobbying session. Each student serves as politician and lobbyist at one time or another. Letters from congresspersons and senators confirming each student's appointment on lobbying day are required. Students should be well read on their specific topic by this time.

Week Ten: Lecture on classical Marxist rejection of "distributive justice" as bourgeois invention. Analysis of Lindblom's clash-of-values section and Hollenbach's description of human rights.

Week Eleven: Class discussions on the necessary application of rights and values in political action. Test on "Values" section.

Part IV: "Influence" (three to four weeks). Readings: Lindblom, *The Intelligence of Democracy,* part 3, chaps. 6–8; and *The Policy-Making Process,* chaps. 6–13; Hollenbach, *Claims in conflict,* part 3, chaps. 4–5.

Weeks Twelve-Thirteen: Description and available literature of selected organizations that are actively involved in influencing public policy; for example, Bread for the World, Catholic Peace Fellowship, Common Cause, Network, Pax Christi. Where possible, in-class presentations from representatives of these groups are preferred.

Week Fourteen: Class lobbying day and reports on this experience.

Week Fifteen: Written evaluation from each student about his or her lobbying topic, readings, and personal experience is due. Summary of course and final examination.

GRADE EVALUATION

Class participation counts for 20 percent of the grade. The three tests count for 60 percent of the grade. The paper on the lobbying topic and the critique of this experience count for the final 20 percent.

The first area of the course is the "Inclusion" section. The basic question for the students is "Who is included in my world?" For the most part excellent results have been achieved by requiring every student to write an essay in class and then read it to the class. The students are asked to trace their familial ethnic roots and to describe any ethnic-flavored family events that they can remember or that still take place. In broad terms the undergraduate population of Villanova University, where I teach at this writing, is largely gleaned from upper-middle-class, white Roman Catholics from the northeast corridor of the United States. Nevertheless, recent semesters have produced a young woman whose Lebanese Christian mother and nonpracticing-Jewish father raised in Finland have kept a number of family traditions alive. She and a fifty-year-old ex-convict from the State Penitentiary at Graterford, Pennsylvania, whose grandfather was a slave, made clear to their respective classmates that a great part of the world beyond their immediate sphere can become more real to each of them.

Another highly recommended tool for this section is a "pre-test" on available data that highlights global issues. Many students have heard of the first-, second-, and third-world countries. Yet many are unaware of the categories that delineate these notions, such as the average yearly wage, the percentage of illiteracy in a country, and the number of medical doctors and hospitals per 1,000 people. Although this type of test more properly belongs in the "Perception" section of the course, an early date for the pre-test is recommended because it generates a global awareness helpful in overcoming any entrenched myopia.

If time allows, each student can be instructed to pick a different second- or third-world country and gather the pertinent social, political, and economic data on that country. The economic status, the health care available, the degree of political freedom, and the rate of literacy provide interesting comparisons with that which too many American students take for granted in the United States.

When possible, it is also beneficial to have a representative of one of the socially, politically, or economically disfranchised groups in the United States lecture to the class. This helps to break through any final barriers to expansion beyond one's parochial perspectives.

The second area of the course is closely related to the first section. The term "perception" is used for this section in order to emphasize the need to understand why and how we look at the issues of world peace and social justice. The inclusion question has the familiar ring of the parable in which Christ asked the assemblage, "Who is your neighbor?" Although the students function nicely as contemporary Samaritans to the people of the third world, they are strangers to these people socially, economically, and culturally. Yet they realize that, in some way, all of us are part of the "spaceship" earth. In the "Perception" section we attempt to focus on the need or folly of a global perspective. In order to do this students are asked to reflect on how they perceive two contemporary issues, the arms race and the international economic order. It is a cruel irony that we are spending millions of dollars on computers to gather, store, and process data to facilitate the obvious shrinking of the planet, or the expanding of our neighborhood, if you will, while we are spending billions building walls of military machines and nuclear weapons with which to isolate neighbor from neighbor.

Such folly fosters distrust and confirms the very worst of international suspicions. It acts against human caring for those who are less fortunate than we. It engenders isolationism and perpetuates the extreme forms of nationalism or misguided patriotism. It creates the blinders that allow legalists—the modern-day scribes of the parable mentioned earlier—to remain blind to those who suffer. We help to create a generation of educated men and women whose conscious concerns never admit thoughtful reflection upon the social, political, and economic relationship between their own living styles and those of their neighbors in "far-off," "exotic" Harlem, Appalachia, Mexico, or the subcontinent of Africa. We do this when we fail to challenge students with questions that force them to perceive the interrelatedness of the peoples of the world.

Current problems of perception are heightened by the fact that we live in an age of increasing specialization, which tends to narrow one's focus. Academicians are often particularly vulnerable. Consider the sincere critiques of the United States Catholic Bishops' pastoral letter on war and peace, which are based almost entirely on the premise that the bishops fail to grasp the complexities and nuances of political reality today, because it is not their area of expertise. They offer, we are told, simplistic remedies for problems that continue to baffle our most brilliant political thinkers. Thus, we are assured, this pastoral letter can be only counterproductive. One is reminded of Churchill's definition of an expert as "one who knows more and more about less and less until one knows everything about nothing." For one's perception, too much knowledge of one area can be as dangerous as too little knowledge. The pastoral letter on war and peace is, therefore, required reading for the "Perception" section.

Two visual aids from the Maryknoll Justice and Peace Office have proved most helpful in this section. The first is a slide presentation with commentary, entitled *Guess Who Is Coming to Breakfast,* and presents a view of Gulf and Western's presence in the Dominican Republic. The second is the film *Gods of Metal,* which makes an excellent case for a Christian perspective on the arms race. Both shows are sources for data and perspectives that impose themselves forcefully on the (more sheltered) students.

The third section concerns values clarification. The process has already begun with the first two parts of the course. However, in the "Values" section we endeavor to demonstrate how one's political stance on one or more issues should reflect a consistent value system. Certainly, a return to the text of the United States Catholic Bishops' "The Challenge of Peace" can help us in this regard. There is no exclusive Catholic answer on most political issues. Yet there is a Catholic tradition of accepted moral principles that can be elucidated, reflected upon, and applied in a consistent fashion to concrete social, economic, and political issues of every age. The bishops have demonstrated this in their pastoral letter on the arms race.

Political scientists cannot discuss the arms race merely in terms of megatons, delivery systems, payloads, warheads, and first-strike capabilities. To do so is to remain mute on Dwight D. Eisenhower's claim that every dollar spent on such endeavors constitutes, in the final analysis, a theft from the poor and the socially disadvantaged. Such silence renders one's political judgments incomplete. It is a mockery of human wisdom and produces a sterile education.

It is the very purpose of values education to expose students to the great variety of possible interpretations and applications. Values education seeks neither to be a pedantic ideology nor to be some academic legerdemain for prejudicial brainwashing. It assumes that the more concrete elements or data that are present in a field of study, the more difficulty there is in arriving at any exclusive resolution. This lack of definition does not suggest total relativity among values, nor does it preclude the existence of absolute values. It merely points to the need for critical analysis. Such informed reflection demands an examination and understanding of these various perspectives. Every system, every ideology, every political, economic, and social perception and method presupposes one or more value judgments, which are inferred from a certain value-laden concept of human nature.

The final section of the course, "Influence," is designed to expose the students to possible avenues for the exercise of their political influence. The most interesting experience for the students in this course has been a day of personal lobbying. Because of Villanova University's proximity to Washington, D.C., the class visits the United States Congress. Students have prepared themselves throughout the semester for this event. Each chooses a topic of personal concern. Each reads the available literature on any bill pending in the legislature that deals with the issue they have chosen. A representative of Network, the Catholic lobbying group, or Common Cause can provide needed assurance to the students. Most of the students fail to realize that, since they are well read on their specific topic, and since the politicians often have many bills with which to concern themselves, they (the students) are usually more knowledgeable than their representatives on their issue. Moreover, politicians know that they must listen to their constituents in order to survive in public office.

Apathy, in the final analysis, is the greatest enemy of wisdom and the body politic. True wisdom cannot survive without application. The greatest barrier to implementation is acceptance of the claim that "what you do really does not matter." Aristotle and Thomas Aquinas both define the prudent person as one who not only knows what is good and what ought to be done but also knows how to achieve this good. Though we may question with Plato whether or not virtue can be taught, we can, nevertheless, include in our courses on political science an exposure to some of the existing instruments for exerting political influence. Besides those organizations mentioned in the syllabus, one could add SANE and Amnesty International, among others.

In spite of the claims of politicians every election year that they wish only to serve their constituency, an alarming number of citizens do not treat their elected representatives as their servants. Though parents may not notice such reticence at home, today's youth are often reluctant to disturb their senators and representatives. A course requirement of political lobbying, whether done at the local, state, or national level, can change that perception in a fundamentally sound way. Most Americans today are unaccustomed to the role of command of servants. Yet the very essence of participatory democracy demands that its citizens realize that they are in command—and insist that the government serve the people. The people do not exist to serve the government. For this reason an introductory course on political science should include a section on citizen influence.

NOTE

1. Paul M. Dietterich, "Some Discussions of International Affairs Education," in *Education for Justice: A Resource Manual,* ed. Thomas Fenton (Maryknoll, N.Y.: Orbis Books, 1975).

SELECTED READINGS FOR FACULTY

Barnet, Richard, and Ronald Muller. *Global Reach.* New York: Simon and Schuster, 1974.

Brown, Lester R. *By Bread Alone.* New York: Praeger Publishers, 1974.

Freire, Paulo. *Pedagogy of the Oppressed.* New York: Herder and Herder, 1970.

Goulet, Denis. *The Cruel Choice: A New Concept in the Theory of Development.* New York: Atheneum Publishers, 1971.

Gutiérrez, Gustavo. *A Theology of Liberation.* Maryknoll, N.Y.: Orbis Books, 1974.

Hollenbach, David. *Claims in Conflict.* New York: Paulist Press, 1979.

King, Martin Luther, Jr. *Stride toward Freedom.* New York: Ballantine Books, 1961.

Klineberg, Otto. *The Human Dimension in International Relations.* New York: Holt, Rinehart and Winston, 1966.

Lefever, Ernest. *Ethics and United States Foreign Policy.* New York: Meridian Books, 1957.

Locke, John. *Two Treatises on Civil Government.* New York: E. P. Dutton, 1924.

Malloy, James M. *Authoritarianism and Corporatism in Latin America.* Pittsburgh, Pa.: University of Pittsburgh Press, 1977.

McGinnis, James B. *Bread and Justice.* New York: Paulist Press, 1979.

Melden, A. I., ed. *Human Rights.* Belmont, Calif.: Wadsworth Publishing Company, 1970.

Melman, Seymour. *The Permanent War Economy: American Capitalism in Decline.* New York: Simon and Schuster, 1974.

Mische, Gerald and Patricia. *Toward a Human World Order.* New York: Paulist Press, 1978.

Nelson, Jack A. *Hunger for Justice.* Maryknoll, N.Y.: Orbis Books, 1980.

———, and Vera Green, eds. *International Human Rights: Contemporary Issues.* White Plains, N.Y.: Earl M. Coleman, 1980.

O'Brien, David, and Thomas Shannon, eds. *Renewing the Earth.* Garden City, N.Y.: Doubleday Image Books, 1977.

Sharp, Gene. *The Politics of Non-Violent Action.* Boston, Mass.: Porter Sargent, 1973.

Sivard, Ruth Leger. *World Military and Social Expenditures 1980.* Leesburg, Va.: World Priorities, 1980.

Spangler, David. *Toward a Planetary Vision.* Edinburgh: Findhorn Publications, 1976.

Tucker, Robert W. *Nation or Empire? The Debate over American Foreign Policy.* Baltimore, Md.: Johns Hopkins University Press, 1960.

Universal Human Rights (quarterly published at Johns Hopkins University Press, Baltimore, Md.).

Welch, William. *The Act of Political Thinking.* Totowa, N.J.: Helix Books, 1981.

8

Psychology

MARGARET GORMAN, R.S.C.J.
BOSTON COLLEGE

Most teachers of undergraduates are faced with somewhat conflicting goals. Is the goal of their teaching to be the imparting of the knowledge and methodology of their discipline or is it to be the further intellectual and personal development of their students? Do they primarily teach the subject matter or do they primarily educate their students by teaching that subject matter? The teacher of psychology is not exempt from this seeming conflict. When, therefore, a proposal is made that the teaching of psychology should be concerned with justice and peace, this may, on the surface, look like further confusion over the goals of teaching psychology.

Moreover, there is growing concern among psychologists that psychology is developing too rapidly and is too diffuse for the teaching of it to have any value, especially for undergraduates. The need for one or some synthesizing themes is gradually being recognized. The American Psychological Association (APA) has stated as its goals the advance of psychology as a science and a profession as well as the advancement of society. In a discussion of this problem, Richard D. Mann adds another aspect to the understanding of the discipline: psychology is "one of the liberal arts, a contemporary form of the ancient search for wisdom, meaning and beauty."[1] Mann believes that, especially in the teaching of undergraduates, the identity of psychology will rest less upon its status as a science and more upon its status as a helping profession and carrier of human wisdom. Finally, he points out what most psychology professors are beginning to recognize: many students are not as interested in the study of psychology as a science as they are in the ability to foster their self-development. He gives a strong warning about the growing influence of psychology as a part of this culture's storehouse of wisdom and the need to alert the students to the danger of making it an ideology. Others have claimed that psychology has replaced religion.[2]

There are perhaps three levels on which teachers of psychology, interested in justice and peace yet confronted with the increasing mass of psychological research, could infuse their courses with those themes and still be faithful to their discipline. The levels, briefly presented now, will be developed more fully later in this essay.

If the concern and chief goal of psychology teachers is to present the research and methodology of psychology, the first level of presentation should include a discussion of the growing body of research on moral development, justice, conflict resolution, peace, altruism, and prosocial behavior. To omit a discussion of such research would deprive the students of an adequate presentation of the discipline. Unfortunately, most of the introductory texts do not incorporate these developments. Therefore, this paper will present some of the early and current developments in these topics.

The second level of presentation should include the considerable discussion today as to whether or not altruism and justice are essential components of psychological health. For the psychologists interested also in the personal development of their students, a presentation of both the research and the controversy would be necessary.

The third level is perhaps the deepest and most challenging one—that of the justice of the teachers themselves in their classrooms, in the way they conduct their classes, respect their students, give assignments and examinations, and evaluate the work of their students.

CONTENT OF CURRENT RESEARCH IN PSYCHOLOGY

The emphasis of most introductory texts is on such topics as methods of research, conditioning and learning, perception, and memory. Usually only one-sixth or one-fifth of the material is on the whole person. Rarely is there consideration of the implications of the growing research on moral development, empathy, altruism, and justice. Nor, in any presentation of the history of psychology, is there anything on the growing number of psychologists interested in these topics. Yet more and more developmental psychologists and social psychologists have turned their interests to themes of justice and peacebuilding.

Only in 1936 was an official organization formed, the Society for the Psychological Study of Social Issues (SPSSI), and only in 1975 did the *Journal of Social Issues* publish a whole issue on the justice motive. Morton Deutsch admits that the term "justice" received very little mention in successive editions of the *Handbook of Social Psychology*.[3] By 1975, however, this had changed so greatly that several substantive volumes were published on the subject of justice, and more are being published (see Selected Readings for Faculty at the end of this essay).

In the preface to *Equity and Justice in Social Behavior*, the authors, Jerald

Greenberg and Ronald Cohen, summarize their view of the importance of this topic in social psychology:

> We have tried to compile contributions that show how the broad concept of justice pervades the core literature of social psychology and how concepts, theories, and research findings from this literature bear on several theoretical formulations of justice. . . . By showing how the justice theme is involved in a vast array of social behaviors, we intend not only to demonstrate the breadth of justice concepts per se but also to highlight a wealth of critical issues that may otherwise have escaped attention. . . . The ubiquity of the justice concept makes it one that pervades all aspects of social psychological inquiry.[4]

The research on justice encompasses individual relationships (such as fairness in interpersonal relations, in intimate relations, and in parent-child relations) as well as legal and procedural justice, retributive or punitive justice, and justice in the marketplace, as the Greenberg and Cohen volume cited above demonstrates. From this research, it is possible for psychology teachers to have their students look at justice from an international point of view. The research has recognized that justice can be based on equity (not the Aristotelian equity but one based on Aristotle's distributive justice), on equality, and on need. In periods of abundance, where economic productivity is the primary goal, justice based on equity is the prevailing form. In situations where the fostering of enjoyable social relations is the primary goal, justice is based on equality. In situations of scarcity or situations where personal development is the goal, justice based on need is the common goal.[5] Students need then to examine the plight of minorities and of the third world in the light of these three forms of justice. The relationship between scarcity of resources and the prevailing power, justice, and peace situations can then be explored. For example, the criteria for distribution of resources in a country devastated by famine would be different from the criteria for the distribution of wage increases in a well-established industry in the United States. In order to avoid violence and establish peace in both cases, some form of justice is needed but the form differs for each situation.

Two groups of psychologists have recently concentrated on issues of justice and peace. The April 1983 *Newsletter* of the Society for the Psychological Study of Social Issues had as its theme "Psychologists and Peace." Therein, SPSSI's Task Force on Peace described its two main concerns: "the imminent danger of nuclear disaster, whether by intention or by accident, and the practical steps psychologists can take as professionals and concerned citizens to lessen the danger of such a disaster." SPSSI also appointed its first Public Policy Fellow, Paul Kimmel, to enable him to develop a resource catalogue containing source material on social issues. He earlier developed testimony for United States Senate hearings on the National Peace Academy proposal.

Another group, Psychologists for Social Responsibility, is working closely with SPSSI. At the 1983 convention of the American Psychologists Association, Psychologists for Social Responsibility sponsored sessions on such topics as "Toward the Cause of Peace: What Can Psychology Contribute?," "Avoiding World War III: Military, Psychological and Political Perspectives," and "Psychologists in Response to the Nuclear Threat."

Substantive volumes on the psychological aspects of peace and conflict resolution refer to the role of beliefs and religion. Leonard Doob's *The Pursuit of Peace*, for example, has as its theme the need not only to avoid conflict but also (and even more urgent) to change human beings from *homines malefici* to *homines pacifici*. He indicates the importance of vision, commitment, and religion in order that this can be accomplished.[6]

Social psychologists are not alone in developing solid research on justice and peace. Developmental psychologists, from the time of Jean Piaget[7] onward, have been increasingly interested in the moral development of children and adults. Lawrence Kohlberg's seminal work[8] has produced critiques and replications. Carol Gilligan, Augusto Blasi, and others have tried to understand the affective aspects of moral development.[9]

Since 1958 Kohlberg has been doing research on the moral development of children and adults. His paradigm is based on his belief that "the first virtue of a person, school or society is justice interpreted in a democratic way as equity or equal respect for all people." His research has indicated that persons develop their reasoning about justice in three levels, each of which contains two stages. *Level 1*, the preconventional, is the level of most children under nine years of age, for whom wrongdoing is avoided or the just thing is done because of external consequences. Those on stage 1 decide to act or not act to avoid punishment. Those on stage 2 base decisions on rewards and one's own immediate interests. Persons judging according to *level 2*, the conventional level, make moral decisions based on group expectations (stage 3) or on authority's demands (stage 4). Persons on the postconventional level, *level 3*, (rarely reached and only after age twenty), make moral decisions according to principles that are understood and accepted. These principles are the equality of human rights and respect for the dignity of human beings as individuals. Whereas stage 5 is concerned about the possibility of the conflict between what is legal and what is moral, stage 6 is committed unequivocally to universal principles of justice.[10]

Meanwhile other developmental psychologists such as Martin Hoffman and Nancy Eisenberg have moved toward a more positive and affective type of moral development. As Gilligan has pointed out, Kohlberg's model stresses a kind of negative morality—do not violate the rights of others. Hoffman and Eisenberg are interested in the development of helping behavior, which seems to be facilitated by empathy—a concern for helping others in distress. Eisenberg even developed a schema of "prosocial reasoning" similar to the stages formulated by Kohlberg.[11] Teachers of child development should certainly include such studies and theories in their presentation.

Little or none of the developments reviewed above is incorporated into introductory-psychology textbooks. Thus teachers of introductory or general psychology could be exonerated if they did not consider the topics of justice, altruism, equity, and conflict resolution. Yet if the concern is to present the "state of the art" of psychology, it is incumbent on the teachers to acquaint themselves with the research and to present it to the students.

Introductory texts in *social* psychology usually do contain a larger proportion of chapters on moral judgment, prosocial behavior, and prejudice. But the more recent research, including the growing research on justice, is rarely presented. The psychologists concerned with justice and with being faithful to their discipline need to include these studies.

The same is true for introductory texts in child development. Rarely do they include sections on the development of the concepts of justice and fairness in children. The fourth edition of the *Handbook of Child Psychology*, published in 1982, does include a chapter, not on moral development, but on "Children's Prosocial Dispositions and Behavior." Whereas earlier psychologists viewed children and even adults as being motivated solely by self-interest, many psychologists today view altruism as equally fundamentally human and as capable of being developed.[12]

Thus for psychologists teaching undergraduate courses in social psychology, general psychology, introduction to psychology, and child development, it is becoming evident that materials on conflict resolution, peace, justice and equity theory, and altruism should be included in their courses. This is merely to be faithful to the content and methodology of psychology as it is today.

THE DEVELOPMENT OF HEALTHY PERSONS

Psychology as a science is concerned not only with social structures that create or prevent peace and justice. Its original concern, especially as a profession, was the development of healthy persons. The question to be raised is: Does the notion of psychological health include the qualities of justice and concern for others? The same conflict that social psychologists recognized between self-interest and concern for others is present in theories of psychological health and sickness.

Sigmund Freud was perhaps the first to describe this conflict in psychological terms and to attribute psychological illness to the frustration of the pleasure principle. His definition of social justice again emphasizes his view that all motivation is self-oriented: "Social justice means that we deny ourselves many things so that others may have to do without them as well, or, what is the same thing, may not be able to ask for them. This demand for equality is the root of social conscience and the sense of duty."[13] According to some rather severe criticisms of psychology, this cult of selfishness has pervaded the psychological field. Daniel Yankelovich blames Maslowism as the prime force in this cult of self-fulfillment, although he says that he feels some remorse about "making Abe Maslow, who was a generous and sympathetic person, the symbol of the most flawed aspect of the search for self-fulfillment."[14]

Others are particularly critical of the human-potential movement, claiming that the goal of humanistic psychology is the development of selfish persons.[15] Certainly there is evidence that abuses of the humanistic theories have occurred. But there is also growing evidence that emphasis on "doing my thing" (Fritz Perls) is not necessarily part of the humanistic credo. In fact, Abraham Maslow, Rollo May, and David Bakan emphasize quite the opposite.[16] An examination of Maslow's description of the self-actualizing person reveals an emphasis on justice and concern for others. Maslow lists the motivations of self-actualizing persons, evident in their work as well as in other areas of living: ". . . delight in bringing about justice; delight in stopping cruelty and exploitation. They hate (and fight) corruption, cruelty, malice, dishonesty, pompousness, phoniness and faking. They enjoy taking on responsibilities (that they can handle well), and certainly don't fear or evade their responsibilities. They respond to responsibility."[17]

Salvatore Maddi also presents a model of psychological health in contrast to persons with an existential neurosis. Persons prone to existential neuroses see themselves as mere carriers of social roles and embodiments of bodily needs. The healthy person, in contrast, is one who has developed the psychological side of his or her nature—primarily symbolization, imagination, and judgment: "The individualist would not feel powerless in the face of social and biological pressures because he puts heavy reliance on the processes of symbolization, imagination and judgment. He would perceive many alternatives to simple role playing and isolated biological satisfaction. Because he sees himself to be a fountain of power, his social and biological living transcend the concrete instance."[18] Thus Maddi's individualism is focused on transcending extreme conformism, not on extreme selfishness. Rollo May, too, presents the goal of existential therapy as self-transcendence. This includes self-awareness, and "care for and concern for the welfare of [others]."[19]

Psychology teachers, then, while warning against the view of the person advocated by such books as *Looking Out for Number 1*, also have an obligation to present objectively, in the words of the psychologists themselves (such as Maslow, Maddi, and May), their view of the healthy person. For while these psychologists describe self-fulfillment or self-actualization as the goal, their ideas include the notion of self-transcendence and going out to others. As Maslow says: "All such people are devoted to some task, call, vocation, beloved work ('outside themselves')."[20] Again, such a presentation of what it means to be psychologically mature and healthy is rarely found in psychology textbooks.

A PROPOSED MODEL

An "Introductory" or "General Psychology" course is a good setting for the inclusion of those themes of justice, altruism, responsibility, and peace that have just been discussed. The following proposal for a course including these themes is based on several assumptions: (1) that the majority of the students taking the course are probably not going to make psychology their specialty; (2) that the topics of most interest to these students concern their own psychological, intellectual, and moral development rather than subdisciplines such as sensory processes, advanced statistics, and the like; (3) that because of prevalent national and international tensions, students are also interested in understanding the dynamics of living in groups such as family, nation, and world community (and such causes of tension and conflict as misperceptions and structural injustice, as well as factors facilitating living and working in harmony, are all open to psychological investigation); (4) that psychology, as a science, is relatively new and has many unsettled issues (and thus the goal of the teacher is not merely to impart facts but to spark inquiry); (5) that any "Introductory Psychology" course must be related to the concerns of everyday life.

With these assumptions in mind, the course is not organized around topics found in most standard "Introductory Psychology" textbooks. The textbook suggested for use with the syllabus below is *Psychology* by Roediger, Rushton, Capaldi, and Paris. Although the organization of the topics is according to the traditional scheme (in which the early topics concern sensation, learning, and language), it is possible to reorganize the topics around the central concept of the person and relationships. This text is chosen because one of the authors has done considerable research on altruism and the need to develop prosocial behavior in society today. Even more than Kohlberg's concept of justice as the foundation of moral behavior, this notion of altruism and prosocial behavior is related to concepts of social justice.

GENERAL PSYCHOLOGY (three credits)

This course presents an overall view of the methodology, theories, and research in the field of psychology. Since the material is so vast and complex, a deliberate focus will be on those topics dealing more directly with the understanding of the person, living with other human beings. The topics will include moral development, the development of prosocial behavior, and the development and channeling of aggression. The emphasis, then, will be on those aspects of psychology that may help to work toward improving society, creating justice, and working for peace.

REQUIRED READING

Text: Roediger, Henry; J. Philippe Rushton; Elizabeth Capaldi; and Scott Paris. *Psychology*. Boston, Mass.: Little, Brown and Co., 1984. Study Guide also required.

American Psychological Association. "Ethical Principles in the Conduct of Research with Human Participants." Washington, D.C.: APA, 1982.

————. "Ethical Principles of Psychologists." Rev. ed. Washington, D.C.: APA, 1981.

Axline, Virgisco M. *Dibs: In Search of Self*. New York: Ballantine Books, 1964.

Freud, Sigmund. *Civilization and Its Discontents*. New York: W. W. Norton, 1961.

Golding, William. *Lord of the Flies: Text, Notes and Criticism*. Ed. J. Baker. New York: G.P. Putnam, 1964.

Jung, Carl. *The Undiscovered Self*. New York: Mentor Books, 1974.

Lifton, Robert, and Richard Falk. *Indefensible Weapons*. New York: Basic Books, 1982.

COURSE OUTLINE

Week One: "Introduction to the Field of Psychology." Text, chap. 1, and the two pamphlets of the American Psychological Association on professional ethics.

Week Two: "Development and Socialization." Text, chap. 8, pp. 277–301, and *Dibs*. Discussion of the forces that shape the child to be just and moral as well as the justice issue of child abuse, from the Study Guide. Also, describe Final Projects, which are to be selected by Week Four.

Week Three: "Moral Development and Adolescent Development." Text, pp. 302–17, supplemented with notes on Gilligan's theory of moral development.

Week Four: "Personality Theory." Text, chap. 13. Emphasis here is on the understanding of oneself and others, as seen by different theorists. Select Final Projects.

Week Five: "Motivation." Text, chap. 11. This text touches many topics, among them sexual motivation and achievement motivation, as well as extreme motivation and injustice to oneself, such as anorexia nervosa.

Week Six: "Emotion and Stress." Text, chap. 12. An understanding of healthy ways to cope with stress. Discussion of the use of alcohol to cope with stress, from the Study Guide.

Week Seven: "Abnormality" (with emphasis on character disorders). Text, chap. 14. Discussion of the justice issue and criminal responsibility. The Study Guide discusses the ethics of therapy with homosexuals.

Week Eight: "Therapies." Text, chap. 15. Emphasis here is on the variety of therapies and on the controversy as to their effectiveness.

Week Nine: "Social Psychology." Text, chap. 16. Emphasis is on the formation of stereotypes and on person-misperception as a possible cause of unjust behavior. The discussion of mindlessness, conformity, and compliance is supplemented by a discussion of Jung's *The Undis-*

covered Self and his proposal of religion as the counterbalance to mass-mindedness.

Week Ten: "Aggression." Text, chap. 17, pp. 611–24, and Freud's *Civilization and Its Discontents*. Is aggression instinctual, learned,or a natural reaction to frustration? Discussion of the effect, on children, of violence on television.

Week Eleven: "Altruism." Text, chap. 17, pp. 624–43. Discussion of the stages of prosocial reasoning and the possibility of television offering the role model for prosocial behavior.

Week Twelve: "International Conflict and Peace." Lifton and Falk, *Indefensible Weapons*. The application of theories of misperception, aggression and prosocial behavior to the international scene (supplemented by relevant journal and newspaper articles).

ASSIGNMENTS

1. Due at end of first month: annotated bibliography of six items on one topic chosen by the student (e.g., aggression, equity, justice, prejudice, war, peace, moral development, empathy, guilt). This assignment acquaints the student with Psychological Abstracts and the vast research going on.
2. Due at end of second month: workbook sheets, with all projects from the Study Guide done so far, to be turned in.
3. Final (twofold project):
   a. Research project on some topic. For example, sex differences in empathy; justice issues, and the like. (The Workbook gives projects at the end of each chapter, from which the student chooses.)
   b. Take-home examination, enabling the student to synthesize material, with such questions as: (1) From your study, describe the qualities of a healthy person living in this decade, and indicate from which psychological theories you drew your description. (2) From your study of aggression, summarize those theories that maintain that aggression is or is not innate. Propose ways by which aggression, personal and international, may be channeled constructively. (3) Present the theories of moral development and the development of empathy. Show how family, school, and instruments of mass communications can help in this development.

The first week of this course concentrates on the history and methodology of psychology. The assigned text refers to the ethical issues special to psychology, but it would be good for the students to have in their hands the two brochures of the American Psychological Association setting forth ethical principles for both research and therapy.

A large part of the course focuses on personal development in response to the question: How do people develop into caring, moral, responsible, choosing (rather than free) persons? The emphasis is on choice rather than freedom, for in studying how persons make morally mature choices, consideration must be made of the limits on human freedom—limits of the real, of other persons, and of the situation.

Since the students are very interested in their own growth and development, the second and third weeks of the course explore development and socialization. In addition to chapter 8 in the text, the students read Axline's *Dibs: In Search of Self*. This book can be used throughout the period devoted to development and personality topics, for it reveals the injustice of parents as well as the development of healthy and unhealthy coping mechanisms. The third week of the course considers moral development and should include not only Kohlberg's theory but also Gilligan's.[21] While the text takes no stand on the final norm of morality, students often ask the questions: "What is right or just?" and "How can we know what is right or just, since there is so much disagreement?" It is important at this time to clarify the role of psychology with regard to what it can and cannot discover about morality. Psychology can describe only *what is*—what human beings do, how they decide, and what the consequences are on others. When psychology moves beyond description to prescription, it has moved into the normative, into the field of moral philosophy or moral theology. The professor has a choice—either to present simply the results of psychological research and theoretical formulations or (and this is preferable) to present the norm of justice, charity, and natural law as presented by moral theologians. It is important to indicate clearly that these norms are not derived from psychological research but from philosophical and theological reflection (selections from Pope Paul VI's *Populorum Progressio*, "On the Development of Peoples," and Vatican II's *Gaudium et Spes*, "Pastoral Constitution on the Church in the Modern World," would be helpful here). The experience of this writer has been that students want to know the classical statements on moral norms and what disciplines to turn to for norms; and they respect the clarification as to what psychology can or cannot give us on this matter.

After two weeks on the development of the person, the fourth week of the course explores different personality theories. Many of these theorists present views on how society shapes the person. An important goal of the course is to help students understand how easily and strongly they can be shaped by society and yet how possible it is for them in turn to shape that society themselves. They should discuss at this time and throughout the course Abraham Maslow's two questions: "How good a society does human nature permit?" and "How good a human nature does society permit?"[22]

By this time the students will have begun the experiential component of their course—their projects, which are linked especially with the sections on aggression, justice, moral reasoning, altruism, and conflict resolution. They will be done in groups to encourage cooperation as opposed to the competition model so prevalent in college courses. A list of suggested projects follows.

SUGGESTED EXPERIENTIAL PROJECTS

1. Volunteer for Meals on Wheels for a specified length of time. In a reflection paper, examine misperceptions of the elderly; poor distribution of resources; powerlessness.

2. Examine letters to the editor in a newspaper for examples of bias and misperception as well as "belief in a just world."

3. Develop a file of news clippings on aggression and helping behavior.

4. Interview representatives of peace groups and analyze their literature to understand their perceptions of peace and justice.

5. Volunteer to tutor disadvantaged students.

6. Study the positions of one union and those of the management with whom they are in conflict.

7. Interview inhabitants of different neighborhoods in your town or city to see their perceptions of other ethnic groups.

8. Work with a Human Services Agency (in a town or small city) as it strives to help the homeless and those without fuel.

9. Join a Friendship Group that visits prisoners, and reflect on powerlessness and justice.

10. Analyze prime-time programs on television for incidents both of aggression and of helping and cooperation. Or, do the same for the evening news programs.

For an understanding of themselves, students must certainly explore the concept of motivation. The fifth week is devoted to this. Since one aspect of injustice can be in the area of sexual relations, the text's chapter on motivation gives some insight into sexual motivation. The issue of gender identity, of concern to many students, is also considered here.

The topic for the sixth week is emotions. The text assignment, together with discussion, should help the student in understanding healthy ways of coping with stress. Since alcoholism is a growing phenomenon on campuses, this subject is discussed in the Study Guide. The professor can use the chapters on motivation and emotions to discuss justice to oneself as being prior to justice to others.

In the topics of abnormality and therapies (seventh and eighth weeks), the justice issue naturally arises. Chapter 14 of the text considers the responsibility of criminals for their actions and to what extent they can be legally prosecuted. The authors' discussion of therapy with homosexuals enables the student to see that justice issues arise in a variety of contexts.

The last third of the course emphasizes social psychology (chaps. 16–17 of the text). There can be a fruitful discussion of stereotypes and misperceptions as a cause of unjust behavior. The Study Guide gives excellent, short tests of perceptions of other nationalities and of the authoritarian personality. A discussion of Jung's *The Undiscovered Self* should supplement the text's treatment of mindlessness, conformity, and compliance. The students are still struggling with the question of how to relate to society without being suppressed by it. Jung's proposal that a genuine relation with the transcendent enables one to resist mass-mindedness brings another dimension to the problem.

Perhaps the most important topic for justice and peace will be that on aggression, discussed in the first half of chapter 17 of the text. Students should compare Freud's view of aggression as described in *Civilization and its Discontents* [23] with the other theories outlined in the text. An understanding of the differences between nonhuman aggression (largely instinctive) and human aggression (more open to social learning) may help the student to understand some of the causes of violence and war. The discussion of aggression will be more concrete if it is made in conjunction with the reading of *The Lord of the Flies*. At this point the professor can present some of the recent research on justice. The fact that we are possibly approaching an era of scarcity of natural resources (especially food and replenishable energy), coupled with an expanding population, is a challenge to notions of distributive justice. Material from Melvin and Sally Lerner about justice in a period of scarcity could be presented at this time. [24] The students should examine some of the research on the effect of television on children's aggressive behavior.

The movement now is toward developing positive modes of behavior and thinking. Thus the last section of chapter 17 of the text, on altruism, is most important. The students should be encouraged to see that television could also be a powerful educational tool for developing helpful and cooperative behavior. Indeed, throughout the course the students should be encouraged to see that although psychology gives insights into abnormal and aggressive behavior, its greatest value lies in the insights it can give into how to improve society, and how to develop caring, responsible persons. Martin Hoffman's work on the best methods of developing empathy and altruism should be presented here. [25] The emphasis can then move from the control or channeling of aggression (tenth-week materials) to the development of altruism. Since social-learning theory holds that the development of both aggression and altruism (although they may be innate) is largely due to socialization, the students ought to reflect on this in the light of their own development and the development of the next generation.

Reflection on the research on altruism and empathy leads, in the final week of the course, to a consideration of what psychology can offer toward the understanding of peace-making and peace-building. In this last part of the course, students consider how what they have learned earlier about theories of misperception, aggression, and prosocial behavior can be applied to the international scene. Robert Lifton and Richard Falk's *Indefensible Weapons* attempts to apply psychological insights to the threat of nuclear war. The professor can supplement the Lifton material with other readings and films. Playing the game "Prisoner's Dilemma"[26] would be an experiential component of value, helping students to understand why extreme and consistent cooperation is not necessarily productive of just and peaceful results. Juergens Dedring has summarized some of the best of this psychological research on peace and conflict.[27]

At this time, students could analyze John F. Kennedy's June 10, 1963, speech at American University on the pursuit of peace in the nuclear age, as well as the 1983 pastoral letter of the United States Catholic Bishops, "The Challenge of Peace." Both works draw on the insights of psychology into conflict resolution, and help to show how spokespersons for peace can make use of psychology.

The course, then, is an introduction to those psychological concepts and theories of concern to present-day college students—how human beings develop intellectually and morally so as to become responsible persons in their families, their nation, and the international family. Through a course like this, students may come to see how much persons are shaped by society, and how, when, and why they could shape society and events that might lead to injustice and conflict and turn them into occasions for cooperation. Above all, the students may emerge from the course with hope that they can make a difference.

INTERDISCIPLINARY POSSIBILITIES

It would be valuable to have an interdisciplinary course on "Personality Theory" team-taught with philosophers or theologians, or both. Each of the disciplines would present its views of what it means to be human. Some of the earlier psychological theories of personality from Europe (those of Freud and Jung especially) were deeply influenced by philosophers. The existential psychologists also acknowledge their indebtedness to Martin Heidegger and Jean-Paul Sartre.[28] The underlying theme of the course could be an exploration of the question: What does it mean to be human? Since human beings need to live in society, the norms of justice and how to live in society in harmony are of concern to psychologists, philosophers, and theologians.

After presenting the philosophical statement of Aristotle on happiness as acting and being on the most human level (seeking the truth and living the good), there could be an examination of Freud's discussion of happiness in *Civilization and Its Discontents* as well as a discussion of Maslow's self-actualizing person. Aristotle's three grades of being (vegetative, animal, and human) could be compared with Maslow's hierarchy of needs and Maddi's description of the existential neurosis.[29]

As the course moves to a consideration of the person in society, some other comparisons and contrasts can be made between philosophy and psychology.

B. F. Skinner's *Beyond Freedom and Dignity* [30] can be studied in connection with Jung's view of the persona as a fruitful source of neurosis[31] and Heidegger's criticism of *Das Man*.[32]

The final section would be a comparison and contrast of the themes of morality. Themes of justice (Aristotle; Plato's *Republic*), duty (Kant[33]), and enlightened self-interest (Hobbes[34] and Adam Smith[35]) can be compared with the work of the psychologists on equity theory and the justice motive. After examining the description of moral choice and deliberation in Aristotle, the students could examine the insights of Kohlberg into the process of moral decision-making. Kohlberg could be seen as a Neo-Kantian or as a natural law theorist. The work of Bernard Haring on the goal of morality as the humanizing of persons[36] and the work of Josef Fuchs on natural law[37] would be a fruitful source of comparison with the work of the psychologists. Fuchs also has engaged in a dialogue with the humanists and maintains that humanists and Christians alike accept love as the highest moral value. His discussion of love and Heidegger's discussion of care and responsibility should be studied with Erik Erikson's[38] and Carol Gilligan's[39] descriptions of care and responsibility.

The experiential component could well consist of tutoring or of working with the elderly, with delinquent adolescents, or with prisoners, and reflecting on how the social structures with which these persons are connected do or do not enable them to develop in a genuinely human way. Or, students might examine television shows or advertisements to see how they do or do not portray images of what it means to be genuinely human.

The goal of the course, then, is to show, from the perspective of two or three separate disciplines, a more complete picture of what it means to be human—intelligent, deliberating according to the norms of justice and love, and working responsibly for peace.

JUSTICE IN THE CLASSROOM

It is not enough simply to change the course content to include justice and peace considerations. We need also to change the way we teach in order to include justice considerations. All teachers can attempt to be models of justice in the way that they conduct their classes and interact with their students.

Teachers' fairness in presenting clearly the goals of the course and their expectations of the students is assumed. However, some teachers arbitrarily add extra assignments or readings toward the end of a course, possibly because new material has just been found. But there is an implicit contract between student and teacher that should be respected. Students should perform their duties: regular presence at class, fulfillment of reading and other assignments. Teachers should organize and present the material clearly, be available for consultation in regular office hours, and not add to the initial requirements presented in the first days of the course.

Moreover, students' perceptions of their teachers as models of justice would be enhanced if the professors, not only verbally but in actuality, indicated that their primary concern was the development of the students' knowledge and skills and not their own research. The moral environment of the school is a more powerful teacher than words.

Examinations, too, should be presented not for the purpose of tricking the students or "catching" them unaware of minute facts, but for the purpose of enabling them to synthesize what they have learned, present it clearly, and evaluate it critically. It is important to realize that the material facts of psychology are accumulating so rapidly that students must be helped to sift out the meaningful from the meaningless, the substantive from the ephemeral.

Since some of the students may choose the profession of psychology, and all of them will read about psychological research, every introductory course should contain a section on "Ethical Principles of Psychologists" and "Ethical Principles in the Conduct of Research with Human Participants."[40] Discussion of particular cases that the American Psychological Association has compiled would be very helpful for these students. The teachers must in their own research reveal to the students their careful adherence to the principles laid down by their official organization.

Moreover, the insight into human behavior that the teachers have should enable them to help guide any student who may have emotional problems toward professional help. Teachers cannot ignore signals that their very profession helps them to recognize. Finally, rather then turning out students with a view of psychology as a mere accumulation of isolated facts about sensation, perception, neuroses, psychoses, development, and so forth, psychology teachers should enable their students to see, by the end of the course, how they can incorporate what they have learned into their own lives.

As models of justice in the classroom, psychology professors should present the goals of the discipline as more than a science and a profession. The American Psychological Association specifically lists "the advancement of society" as one of its goals. It is therefore only just to the students and to the discipline of psychology to present its goals as including help for the mentally ill as well as a capability of designing programs that may prevent or alleviate injustice and war, and advance justice and peace.

NOTES

1. R. D. Mann, "Psychology," in *The Modern American College: Responding to the New Realities of Diverse Students and Changing Society*, ed. A. W. Chickering et al. (San Francisco, Calif.: Jossey-Bass, 1980), p. 398.

2. P. C. Vitz, *Psychology as Religion: The Cult of Self-Worship* (Grand Rapids, Mich.: Wm. B. Eerdmans Publishing Co., 1977).

3. M. Deutsch, "A Critical Review of 'Equity Theory': An Alternative Perspective on the Social Psychology of Justice," *International Journal of Group Tensions* 1, no. 4 (1979): 20–49.

4. J. Greenberg and R. Cohen, eds., *Equity and Justice in Social Behavior* (New York: Academic Press, 1982), p. xix.

5. M. Deutsch, "Equity, Equality and Need: What Determines Which Value Will Be Used as the Basis of Distributive Justice?" *Journal of Social Issues* 31, no. 3 (1975): 143.

6. L. W. Doob, *The Pursuit of Peace* (Westport, Conn.: Greenwood Press, 1981).

7. Jean Piaget, *The Moral Judgment of the Child* (Glencoe, Ill.: Free Press, 1932).

8. L. Kohlberg, "The Development of Modes of Moral Thinking in the Years Ten to Sixteen" (unpublished Ph.D. dissertation, University of Chicago, 1958).

9. C. Gilligan, *In a Different Voice* (Cambridge, Mass.: Harvard University Press, 1982). A. Blasi, "Moral Cognition and Moral Action: A Theoretical Perspective," *Developmental Review* 31 (1983): 178-210.

10. See L. Kohlberg, *The Psychology of Moral Development: The Nature and Validity of Moral Stages* (New York: Harper & Row, 1984), pp. 172-79; quotation from p. xv.

11. N. Eisenberg, ed., *The Development of Prosocial Behavior* (New York: Academic Press, 1982).

12. See, e.g., M. L. Hoffman, "Is Altruism Part of Human Nature?" *Journal of Personality and Social Psychology* 41 (1981): 121-37; M. Toi and C. D. Batson, "More Evidence That Empathy Is a Source of Altruistic Motivation," *Journal of Personality and Social Psychology* 43 (1982): 281-92.

13. See Sigmund Freud, *Group Psychology and the Analysis of the Ego* (New York: W. W. Norton, 1959). First published, in German, in 1920.

14. Daniel Yankelovich, *New Rules: Searching for Self-Fulfillment in a World Turned Upside Down* (New York: Random House, 1981), p. 236.

15. See, e.g., M. and L. Wallach, *Psychology's Sanction for Selfishness* (San Francisco, Calif.: Freeman, Cooper and Co., 1983); P. C. Vitz, *Psychology as Religion*; Daniel Yankelovich, *New Rules*; W. Kilpatrick, *Psychological Seduction* (Nashville, Tenn.: Thomas Nelson, 1983).

16. Abraham Maslow, *The Farther Reaches of Human Nature* (New York: Viking Press, 1971); Rollo May, *The Discovery of Being: Writings in Existential Psychology* (New York: W.W. Norton, 1983); D. Bakan, *The Quality of Human Existence* (Chicago, Ill.: Rand McNally, 1966).

17. Maslow, *The Farther Reaches of Human Nature*, p. 298.

18. S. Maddi, "The Existential Neurosis," *Journal of Abnormal Psychology* 72 (1967): 320.

19. May, *The Discovery of Being*, p. 149.

20. Maslow, *The Farther Reaches of Human Nature*, p. 291.

21. For an excellent discussion of both Kohlberg's and Gilligan's points of view, see M. Brabeck, "Moral Judgment: Theory and Research on Differences between Males and Females," *Developmental Review* 3 (1983): 274-91.

22. Maslow, *The Farther Reaches of Human Nature*, p. 335.

23. Sigmund Freud, *Civilization and Its Discontents* (New York: W. W. Norton, 1961). First published, in German, in 1930.

24. M. J. and S. C. Lerner, eds., *The Justice Motive in Social Behavior* (New York: Plenum Press, 1981).

25. M. L. Hoffman, "Is Altruism Part of Human Nature?"

26. The Prisoner's Dilemma is a classical interaction game illustrating the value and hazards of cooperation and competition. If two persons cooperate, both will get some reward. If one cooperates and the other competes, the competitor will gain and the cooperator will lose. If both compete, both lose. This paradigm is useful in illustrating the value of selective cooperation, for if one cooperates all the time, the competitor will take advantage and perhaps destroy the cooperator.

27. J. Dedring, *Recent Advances in Peace and Conflict Research* (Beverly Hills, Calif.: Sage Publications, 1976).

28. See e.g., Rollo May, *The Discovery of Being*.

29. Aristotle, *The Nichomachean Ethics*, trans. W. D. Ross (New York: Oxford University Press, 1980), book 5 S. Maddi, "The Existential Neurosis."

30. B. F. Skinner, *Beyond Freedom and Dignity* (New York: Bantam Books, 1972).

31. Carl Jung, *The Undiscovered Self* (New York: Mentor Books, 1957).

32. Martin Heidegger, *Being and Time*, trans. John Macquarrie and Edward Robinson (New York: Harper & Row, 1962).

33. Immanuel Kant, *Groundwork of the Metaphysics of Morals* (New York: Harper & Row, 1964).

34. Thomas Hobbes, *Leviathan* (New York: Penguin Books, 1982).

35. Adam Smith, *Wealth of Nations*, ed. A. Skinner (New York: Penguin Books, 1970).

36. Bernard Haring, *Free and Faithful in Christ: A General Moral Theology for Clergy and Laity* (New York: Seabury Press, 1978).

37. J. Fuchs, *Human Values and Christian Morality* (Dublin: Gill and Macmillan, 1970), and *Personal Responsibility and Christian Morality* (Washington, D.C.: Georgetown University Press, 1983).

38. Erik Erikson, *Insight and Responsibility* (New York: W. W. Norton, 1964).

39. C. Gilligan, *In a Different Voice*.

40. See the two pamphlets by the APA: "Ethical Principles in the Conduct of Research with Human Participants" (Washington, D.C.: APA, 1982), and "Ethical Principles of Psychologists," rev. ed. (Washington, D.C.: APA, 1981).

SELECTED READINGS FOR FACULTY

JUSTICE

Note: The titles below that are published by Plenum Press are volumes in a series entitled "Critical Issues in Social Justice." As of this writing, new titles are being added.

Folger, R., ed. *The Sense of Injustice: Social Psychological Perspectives*. New York: Plenum Press, 1982.

Greenberg, J., and R. Cohen. *Equity and Justice in Social Behavior*. New York: Academic Press, 1982.

Lerner, M. J. "The Justice Motive in Social Behaviour." *Journal of Social Issues* 31 (1975): 1-19.

———. and S. C. Lerner, eds. *The Justice Motive in Social Behavior*. New York: Plenum Press, 1981.

Meese, L. A.; N. L. Kerr; and B. L. Watts. *The Sense of Justice in Men and Women: A Socio-Psychological Analysis of Sex Differences in Procedural and Distributive Justice*. New York: Plenum Press, 1983.

Mikula, G., ed. *Justice and Social Interaction: Experimental and Theoretical Contributions from Psychological Research*. New York: Springer-Verlag, 1980.

Sampson, E. E. *Justice and the Critique of Pure Psychology*. New York: Plenum Press, 1983.

ALTRUISM AND SELF-INTEREST

Eisenberg, N., ed. *The Development of Prosocial Behavior*. New York: Academic Press, 1982.

Mussen, P., and N. Eisenberg-Berg. *Roots of Caring, Sharing and Helping.* San Francisco, Calif.: Freeman, Cooper and Co., 1977.

Rushton, J. P. *Altruism, Socialization and Society.* Englewood Cliffs, N.J.: Prentice-Hall, 1980.

Staub, E. *Positive Social Behavior and Morality.* 2 vols. New York: Academic Press, 1978. Vol. 1.

Vitz, P. C. *Psychology as Religion: The Cult of Self-Worship.* Grand Rapids, Mich.: Wm. B. Eerdmans Publishing Co., 1977.

Wallach, M. A., and L. Wallach. *Psychology's Sanction for Selfishness: The Error of Egoism in Theory and Therapy.* San Francisco, Calif.: Freeman, Cooper and Co., 1983.

Yankelovich, Daniel. *New Rules: Searching for Self-Fulfillment in a World Turned Upside Down.* New York: Random House, 1981.

PEACE AND CONFLICT RESOLUTION

American Journal of Orthopsychiatry. 1982; entire volume.

Dedring, J. *Recent Advances in Peace and Conflict Research.* Beverly Hills, Calif.: Sage Publications, 1976.

Deutsch, M. "Recurrent Themes in the Study of Conflict." *Journal of Social Issues* 3, no. 1 (1977): 222–25.

Doob, L. W. *The Pursuit of Peace.* Westport, Conn.: Greenwood Press, 1981.

Kelman, H. ed. *International Behavior: A Social-Psychological Approach.* New York: Irvington Publishers, 1980.

Lifton, R. *The Broken Connection.* New York: Simon and Schuster, 1979.

———, and R. Falk. *Indefensible Weapons.* New York: Basic Books, 1982.

Teachers College Record 84, no. 1 (1982); entire issue.

9

Sociology

MARIE AUGUSTA NEAL, SND de Namur
EMMANUEL COLLEGE

In the decades prior to 1960 sociologists aspiring to be more scientific (in the style of the physical sciences) argued for a value-free sociology, one rooted primarily in hard data without pointing a direction toward preferred social, political, or economic structures. With the introduction of the anthropological perspective into sociology—that is, the systematic study of values, symbols, and the rest of culture, including religion—in the 1950s, it appeared as if this physical-science model might be effective. All this was challenged in the 1960s when effective movements toward third-world liberation demonstrated the non-neutrality of functionalism used unwittingly as a value rather than as a tool of analysis. Trying to keep things as they are to provide more objective study, sociologists acted effectively to prevent directional change in social situations needing change. (Whether this consequence was intended or unintended is not an issue here; that it was a consequence is the point proposed.)

Once sociologists became aware that critical social analysis is itself a tool, not an ideology, we were faced in the early 1970s with the pressure to make explicit our own preferred form of social order as well as our own preferred style of analysis. At this time the social justice perspective of many Christian churches was becoming explicit, thanks to the fine assemblies of the late 1960s that brought to fruition the justice journey of the churches. These assemblies include Vatican Council II; the Medellín, Colombia, Second General Conference of Latin American Bishops, held in 1968; and the Uppsala Conference of the World Council of Churches in the same year. All of these assemblies took seriously the challenge of nineteenth-century critics, including Karl Marx, that religion is opium for the people when and if it lulls the masses into a waiting posture for eternal reward, when they should be reaching out to claim their just

121

share of the world's resources, whether through organized labor or through just revolution against oppressive political and/or economic systems.

Somewhat like churches, established sociological associations were challenged by the movements of peoples to take sides for or against their liberation because their learned skills helped them to see more clearly than the untrained person how social systems work and affect those playing roles within them. Many chose not to challenge structures already in place. As a result professional journals, textbooks, and sociology departments in leading universities became centers of learned resistance to social change wherever such change threatened the established order of races, classes, sexes, and other structured relationships. This choice was faced similarly by the other social sciences: economics, political science, and anthropology. Related to this, a psychology characterized by assumptions of systems as constants within which the self adapts became the corresponding personal-behavior-analysis focus of those taking the nonchange option. Values clarification became the modish form for adaptive adjustment, and "managed change" the limit of study of social change.

This made sense until the churches moved into the examination of social systems. Their move was a function of reports from missions in third-world areas struggling for change. On the basis of these reports, formal church bodies adopted in assembly a policy of judging the goodness of action and the need for change according to whether or not systems prevent the development of peoples and exploit human beings as workers without power in the interests of those with power. Sociologists have the analytic tools to address these issues, but as human beings are as free as others to choose to use or not to use them toward the end of helping those human beings who lack access to resources and power to participate in the decisions that affect their lives. Such decisions require a commitment to human rights. Such a commitment requires a self-conscious acceptance of these rights as values to be achieved. Action to achieve human rights for peoples constitutes a social-justice perspective in the teaching of the social sciences.

Although academic sociologists and others have a history of introducing methods to teach from a social justice perspective, those who choose to do so do not as of this writing represent the majority in the field. One fine example of such an effort, which forms the background experience for this present proposal, occurred in 1965. At that time a group of social scientists met at a series of institutes at Tufts University, Massachusetts Institute of Technology (MIT), and Rutgers University in order to review critically current ways of presenting the social sciences in undergraduate university courses, in the light of manifestly conservative influences in the then current theories of their several disciplines. The timing of the institutes was determined by a desire to respond to the grave social problems of the mid-1960s, which had been instrumental in stirring college students into action. These included, specifically, the liberation struggles in third-world countries, especially in Africa, and the civil rights movement of blacks in the United States. The group calling the institute series into existence included physical scientists and mathematicians who had already reviewed their own approaches and initiated reforms for more inspirational teaching from elementary through high school to university education. The funding came from the United States Department of Education.

Beginning with the assumption that science is intended to be in the service of the human community, this group—including such well-known persons as Jerrold Zacharias of MIT; mathematician Andrew Gleason of Harvard University; historian Paul Ward, then executive secretary of the American Historical Association; Jaqueline Grennan, later president of Hunter College; Jaqueline Mattfeld, academic dean at Sarah Lawrence, among others—was really addressing in practice the legitimacy of physical and social scientists participating in value-oriented education. These academicians agreed that a direction gives life to a discipline and that the challenge of good teaching is to provide effective skills in using the analytic tools to some good end. But to what end?

Four of the social scientists attending—economist Douglas Dowd of Cornell University; political scientist John Rensenbrink of Bowdoin College; social psychologist Michael Maccoby, then working with Erich Fromm in Mexico; and this writer, a sociologist from Emmanuel College, Boston—developed a cross-disciplinary social science introductory course focused on the problem of why there are poor people in a rich society like that of the United States. Clearly we had decided that commitment to the elimination of poverty was a legitimate perspective for teaching social science. We also decided that the method of teaching had to bring the issues to life and action and that the disciplines had to be effectively introduced.

With these three principles agreed to, we then determined what was the minimum set of concepts each of our disciplines required that we include to provide an effective analysis of that question. Then each prepared a corresponding set of five lectures that we would give to a group of students in a large course, 150 students or more, using our respective disciplines to respond to that question. We hypothesized that if we lectured in each others' presence, we could create an authentic critical atmosphere for learning. We further theorized that by locating ourselves among the students and agreeing to speak out, to question for clarification, to challenge interpretation toward clearer explication and provision of more substantial evidence for positions taken and claims made during the lecture, we would engage the students in an experience of concerned disagreement, shared ignorance, and joint learning.

Obviously we had already assumed that straight lecture was not effective for new learning. We wanted to introduce the teacher as learner as well as knower. We wanted people to discover the persuasiveness of evidence over the authority of status, but to do this without losing the quality of respect for the thinking of the other. Our experience with social analysis of existing world realities convinced us that those conditions needing change are so serious that they require the informed skill of newly committed students and workers as well as the experience of older scholars to generate effective action. Our earlier critique of education objected to indoctrination and to a too great docility in learners. We wanted a style, however, that would discourage idle conversation in the classroom stemming from uninformed interveners who were not caught up seriously into the learning process and who, through failure to be seriously engaged with the evidence under consideration, were not only uninformed on the subject matter under discussion, but uninspired to want to learn the skills of scientific analysis and criticism necessary to act responsibly and effectively. We also wanted to develop a course that would teach caring about the distress of those living in poverty, sufficiently infused to generate a desire to change conditions that cause human misery. We agreed that we can learn effectively by correcting each other and replanning when interpretation from another perspective seems to contradict, diminish, deny, or exploit those with less access to power than is possessed by those who provide analysis and point direction for proposed action. For this correction and planning, we agreed that those whose power is inadequate for the development of their life situation need to be present and involved in the learning and teaching or none would learn. We did not feel we knew how best to create this environment for new learning, but we wanted to try to do so.

We took the opportunities available to us at that time and brought together, in a summer experiment at Cornell University, sixty students who were signed up as incoming freshmen at Cornell University and Emmanuel College the following September. Fifteen of the invited students were blacks coming to Cornell from New York City's Harlem and the rural south of the United States. Together with the one black faculty member, Gloria Joseph, a graduate student and dean of admissions, the black students reported a different definition of the situation, the discovery of which changed all of us. We all learned to learn as we teach.

Why do I recount this experiment here? Because it provides both a precedent and a framework for social-justice education today, gives evidence that innovation can be effective, and sets aside the reservation that secular institutions cannot participate in value-based curriculum building or that "real" scientists do not engage in such practice. Just as that group organized itself to do what needed to be done for the 1960s, so we must organize to do what needs to be done today. Then the issue was: Who shall decide? Today it is this and more: Who shall survive? Our task now is to set up a course that has all those qualities yet fits today's learning environment stimulated by a new church involvement in the transformation of the world through justice and peace and education.

The church's new mandate to provide education for social justice stems from Pope John XXIII's *Pacem in Terris* ("Peace on Earth," 1963), Vatican Council II, and Pope Paul VI's 1967 encyclical *Populorum Progressio* ("On the Development of Peoples"). These were followed by Paul VI's *Octogesima Adveniens* ("A Call to Action") commemorating in 1971 the eightieth anniversary of the original social encyclical, *Rerum Novarum*. "Justice in the World," the document prepared by the Second General Assembly of the Synod of Bishops (Rome, 1971), was designed to implement Paul VI's "Call to Action." The Catholic bishops in the United States began their implementation of this recommendation in regional hearings. The first of these was held in Appalachia, and the publication of its proceedings, "This Land Is Home to Me," was a breakthrough document for people-participation.[1] The first national initiative in America in response to "Justice in the World" was the Call to Action conference in 1976. Held in Detroit, Michigan, it examined the justice needs of the United States in its bicentennial year.[2] In the United States, the Catholic Bishops' pastoral letter on war and peace ("The Challenge of Peace") put the object of social analysis into world perspective and invited the social sciences to apply an effective, critical social analysis to the arms race and its effect on the poor of the world.[3] At the same time, the United Nations urged the consideration of a new international economic order in which the voices of the poor would be heard in the planning for the use of their resources.[4] More recently, the pastoral on the United States economy is a further church effort toward a just social order. These church documents, plus the plight of third-world peoples expressed in United Nations literature, suggested the agenda for a new introductory sociology course.

This course focuses on three interrelated transitions that have occurred since the mid-1960s: the legalization of universal human rights by the United Nations;[5] the prediction of leveling-off of world population growth for the year 2110 at about 10.5 billion;[6] and the uncontrolled proliferation of arms production in the face of manifest possible solutions of problems of human need. A significant element in all three is the successful struggles of a number of third-world countries in achieving their independence from earlier colonial control. These nations now take new responsibility for their own governance. They were aided by the initial United Nations Universal Declaration of Human Rights, adopted by the U.N. General Assembly in 1948 and now formalized and explicated as the International Bill of Human Rights with the binding quality of law for those nations that have signed the covenants.[7] Included in these covenants is the affirmation that all peoples have economic rights to such basic necessities as health care, food, shelter, and income, and the right to organize as workers, as well as rights to free speech, freedom to migrate, fair trial, various political freedoms including freedom from arbitrary arrest, and finally, the right "to self-determination and to enjoy and utilize fully and freely their natural wealth and resources."[8] The recognition of these human rights and their existence in the operating life of an international body provide the groundwork for social justice education.

Social justice, as distinct from narrower concepts of justice limited to justice under existing legal systems, extends human rights to all peoples irrespective of whether or not the sovereign states within which they now live recognize those human rights in currently codified law. The covenants make action for social justice encompass the entire human family. They open our basic communal concern to all peoples and extend our consciousness to the peoples of the world. A corresponding church document, *Laborem Exercens* ("On Human Work"), urges a new degree of human solidarity and provides for a new sense of hope inviting us to respond to the just demands of the poor as they organize themselves to claim their rights as human beings. Understanding the interrelationship of all these social-system elements and the value choices embedded in them now becomes the challenging content for effective sociological analysis.

This course begins by listening to third-world peoples recounting their efforts at organizing for action and then proceeds to the raising of questions that lead to social analysis of the conditions of these struggles.

THE INTRODUCTORY SOCIOLOGY COURSE

This course guarantees a complete introduction to the discipline of sociology with the added feature of sensitizing the class to the issues of social justice that can be investigated and acted upon in sociological perspective. The focus differs from many sociology courses now taught in that the system under analysis is the world system rather than the structure of a single nation-state, the customary focus of many but not all standard introductory textbooks.

A classic example of the standard text from which this course will deviate is the long-time high-selling text by Leonard Broom and Philip Selznick. Revised and summarized to present the bare essentials in 1984, with Dorothy H. Broom as an additional author, they produced a book entitled *The Essentials of Sociology.*[9] It provides chapters with the following content: first, an overall perspective on "doing" sociology, followed by the "essential elements," namely: culture, socialization, interaction and social participation, bureaucracy and its alternatives. Next comes a section entitled "The Great Divides: Inequality and Discrimination." This includes age and sex, minorities, and strata and classes. The last section is entitled "Population Perspectives" and includes a section on demographic analysis and population change.

If you reflect on these categories and divisions of topic, what the sociologist sees is a finely tuned description of society in its current forms with the suggestion of points of tension in prejudice and discrimination, while change occurs through population shifts (both declines and increases). In contrast, note the divisions of topic in C. Michael Otten's *Power, Values, and Society.*[10] It is divided into three main sections. The first treats of science, technology, and the human condition. Within this, science is examined as a tool for analysis of social concerns. The possibility of science being used to achieve different interests is emphasized and then the theme becomes "moral foundations and theoretical perspectives." Theories are presented with their presuppositions regarding human nature. Students are thus introduced to the discipline with a challenge to their own critical perspective on knowledge and the process of learning. In the second section, entitled "Power, Production and Control," the entire sweep of history from preindustrial, through industrial, to current postindustrial times is surveyed. Deviance is examined with domination rather than with institutions, and national states controlling and being controlled are presented. The American capitalist state is presented as just one form of political economy among others. The uses of power are considered as a problem, and social change as something that can be planned and rooted in values. The student is invited to evaluate possible values with the analytic tools being learned. In the last section, power is examined as an analytic concept and is juxtaposed with culture and socialization as one of the structures of consciousness. American culture, religion, education, and family life are presented as the sources of values and interests and as the milieu of socialization, which in turn is presented as the development of consciousness within which situations are defined as real. Personal good and social need are studied together.

Not many textbooks take this kind of critical approach. Choosing to use such a text places on the teacher the task of selecting the emphases for lecture and projects that fit values and interests having some directional concern. The following presentation of two specific courses is an attempt to provide that emphasis, as developed earlier in the discussion of social justice.

The assumptions undergirding the courses are these: (1) For learning about human need, the voices of those with the need must be heard. People speak their own truth best once they organize sufficiently to have support against opposing powers. (2) Understanding processes of social change, of dominance and control, and of choice are as essential for an effective social analysis as concepts of structure and socialization, yet these are weakly taught in standard courses in sociology. For learning, they probably require involvement in action for change. (3) Although population shifts are the basic factor in social change, control of them is the determinant of social change. (4) Without the teaching of how social change occurs, standard social science is itself an implement of indoctrination to effect support of the status quo.

INTRODUCTION TO SOCIOLOGY *(three credits)*

A Problem Approach to Sociological Analysis

PROBLEM NO. 1 (WEEKS ONE AND TWO): "POVERTY AND THE USES OF EVIDENCE"
Listening to the Poor
  Through slides, film, newsprint, or in person, the organizing poor tell their stories.
Discussion and Project on Poverty
  Questions
    1. Why is it that two-thirds of the world's peoples are poor when humankind has a technology that could provide adequately for human needs?
    2. Why are there poor people in a rich society like that of the United States?
  Project
    Prior to any discussion, each student will write for ten minutes her or his response to questions 1 and 2 above. These responses will be saved for future reference.
  Materials for Examination of the Topic
    "World Population Data Sheet" plus graphs and charts from the Population Reference Bureau.

Discussion: Uses of Evidence
  Questions

> What makes evidence compelling? Who provides it? How do we judge its accuracy? Relevancy? What shapes our Point of View on problems of human concern?

Assignment:

1. Text: C. Michael Otten, *Power, Values and Society* (New York: Random House, 1982), chap. 1, "Society and Social Concerns."
2. Elaine Murphy, "Food and Population" (Washington, D. C.: Population Reference Bureau, 1984).

PROBLEM NO. 2 (WEEKS THREE AND FOUR): "THEORY IDEOLOGY, BELIEF"

Questions

> How do sociologists develop theories of society? What is the relationship among theory, ideology, research, belief, and opinion?

Discussion

> Are communism and capitalism methods, beliefs, ideologies or theories?

Story

> South Africa–A Case Study

Assignment:

1. Text: chap. 2, "Moral Foundations and Theoretical Perspectives."
2. C. Wright Mills, *Sociological Imagination* (London: Oxford University Press, 1959) chap. 1.
3. Pablo Richard, et al., *Idols of Death and the God of Life* (Maryknoll, N. Y.: Orbis Books, 1983), introductory essay.
4. Richard J. Cassidy, "Catholic Teaching Regarding Capitalism and Socialism" (Archdiocese of Detroit: Office for Justice and Peace, 1979).

PROBLEM NO. 3 (WEEKS FIVE AND SIX): "POWER, PRODUCTION, AND CONTROL"

Questions

> What relationships exist between the political and economic structures of society? Why is there unemployment when there is so much work that needs to be done? How does work get done in a society?

Discussion

> Work and human need: the case of Nicaragua.
> World map of grain consumption (Population Reference Bureau).

Assignment
1. Text: chap. 5, "Domination, Direction, and Deviance: The Modern State and Societal Control," pp. 109–40.
2. Amata Miller, "U.S. Economics: Alternative Approaches," *Network* 9, no. 6 (November–December 1981).
3. Slides and oral accounts from people who have recently returned from Nicaragua.

PROBLEM NO. 4 (WEEKS SEVEN AND EIGHT): "CULTURE AND SOCIETY"

Questions

What are the elements of the culture? What is the relationship among culture, society, and social class?

Discussion:

Why is the situation in Nicaragua defined so differently by northern and southern hemisphere peoples, by state and church at the present time? Where does religion fit in? What determines style, custom, rightness, and wrongness? Are there subtle forms of social control operating in society? If so, what are they and why do they work? What happens when they are not effective? What are anomie, apathy, alienation?

Assignment:
1. Text: chap. 7, "Culture, Making Up Reality."
2. Garrett Hardin, "Living on a Lifeboat, "*Bioscience* 24, no. 10 (October 1974): 561–68; and John Vandermeer, "Hardin's Lifeboat Adrift," *Science for the People,* January 1976, p. 16–19.
3. Lieberson, "Theory of Race and Ethnic Relations," *American Sociological Review* 26, no. 6 (December 1961).

PROBLEM NO. 5: (WEEKS NINE AND TEN): "INSTITUTIONS AND SOCIAL CLASS"

Questions

What are social institutions? What is the process of socialization? Whom do the rules serve? Are human rights institutions, values, or norms? Whom do they bind and under what conditions? What makes a right a right?

Discussion:

Why was the "lifeboat ethic" introduced? Whose interests does it serve? How is it related to the population question? How does one become a member of a society? of a social class? of an ethnic group? of a community? How do you know who belongs and who is an outsider? How does one learn the rules? What happens if you do not live according to the rules? Are there

really any rules? Who makes them? How do you leave the group if
you do not want to belong? Can you leave?

Assignment:

1. Text: chap. 8, "Institutions, Ideals and Self-interest: The American Faith."

PROBLEM NO. 6 (WEEKS ELEVEN AND TWELVE): "COMMUNI-CATION AND SOCIAL CHANGE"

Questions

What is the basis of the thesis that this is an age of communication
rather than of industry? What is different about communication
today from any earlier period? In social change, what changes?
What is the relationship between prophecy and social change?

Assignment:

1. Text: chap. 9, "Socialization, the Process of Becoming Human."
2. United Nations, "International Bill of Human Rights" (New
   York: United Nations, 1978).

PROBLEM NO. 7 (WEEK THIRTEEN): "ASSESSMENT OF METHOD OF LEARNING"

Questions

What constitutes a good textbook? What other materials are
needed to learn a social science?

Project and Discussion:

1. Critical evaluation of a textbook. Each group will have a different book to assess. The task is to assess this standard text as
   more, or less, useful than the Otten textbook for an introduction
   to sociology, with reasons for the choice based on learnings from
   the course.
2. Apply the standards of human rights to the problems of society.

Term Paper

An outline for solving a problem scientifically will be distributed
early in the course. Each student will investigate the current
situation of a third-world country that he or she has become
interested in from what has been seen or heard in the media. She
or he will investigate reports presented in the regular and alternate media and write a report of the situation, as judged most
accurate from the sources examined. The paper will conclude
with an assessment of sources of information.

Final Examination

The original questions of the course, under Problem No. 1, will be
asked again. The response will be compared with the earlier one
and assessed in terms of the use of evidence and sociological
analysis.

THE ORGANIZATION OF THE COURSE

The first experience is the hearing of the stories of poor people as they strive to organize themselves to claim their rights as human beings. Using stories of the organizing poor is a new idea. It derives from reports of the effectiveness of the method of conscientization used in Latin America. This is a method of teaching literacy by means of which local groups name the reality experienced, raise to consciousness the political, social, and economic oppressions of their lives, and take action to change those conditions. This method cannot be taught in the university. It is done in the village or the ghetto, wherever the dispossessed live. (For those unfamiliar with this method, a demonstration of its use should be introduced at this point. See Paulo Freire's *Pedagogy of the Oppressed.*[11]) University education that is social-justice-oriented is a response to the organizing efforts of the poor.[12]

After hearing the stories of the poor through film, slides, a discussion and response, or other method, the analysis begins with a thorough examination of the distribution of population across first-, second-, and third-world nations. "First world" is defined as the capitalist countries with structures of high technology; "second world" refers to communist countries with state-controlled economies; "third world" means the countries of the world whose economies are dependent on but unaligned with either of these systems. With this focus and the use of the "Population Data Sheet," which shows population distribution, infant-mortality and life-expectancy rates, gross national product (GNP) per capita, rate of natural increase, and urban/rural distribution, each student using his or her own individual copy can study these distributions for each of the 161 nations of the world and discover their interrelatedness. The data sheet is updated each year. Each student can examine the census evidence of poverty. "Poverty" is here defined as a characteristic of a people with high infant mortality and low life expectancy. Students can see by the data that a short lifespan is directly associated with a low GNP per capita. With one added graph showing the income distribution for each fifth of United States population for each year from 1947 to the present,[13] students are equipped from the very beginning of their introduction to sociology to associate social structure and change with the size, and change in size, of population and its geographical location. Another essential graphic is a world map that has Europe and Africa in the center so that students can readily see the relationships among the world land masses, rather than a distorted focus on the Americas centrally placed at the expense of dividing the land masses of Asia. From the examination of such a map, which will necessarily put Africa in the middle, race differences can be reexamined in the light of migrations, colonization, and prehistoric land movements into current continental and island segments.

Once population, access to resources, and rates of natural increase are compared, students discover that development is associated with reduction of the rate of natural increase, because, when children have a low mortality rate and hence will be growing up and needing family care, and the elderly are thus assured of progeny to provide the care that they will need, choice of family size follows. Discussion of population control and economic development are then linked experientially. Moving next to the discussion of political economies allows a central focus on the question of high technology and its positive potential for providing food, clothing, and shelter, with fewer people doing handwork and more people available for human services. The link between work, income, social security, health care, education, and the uses of taxes— that is, common wealth for human needs—becomes focused. This raises the question of ideology and organization: capitalism, communism, and other forms of socialism as modes of social organization can now be considered without threat of indoctrination or subversion. Culture and socialization come next, as we consider where and how we learn what is defined as the right and the good. Family and religion are included here. Finally, existing programs for addressing apparently insoluble problems of overpopulation, hungry peoples (organized and unorganized), uses of violence against the poor, and production and deployment of nuclear defenses are examined. The course ends with students and teacher stating theses that need further investigation. These provide potential sociology majors with problems for research in advanced research methods courses and with a challenge to learn research skills to initiate or extend current inadequate knowledge that informs manifestly inhumane solutions of problems of human need.

For a course with this focus, the sociology text must have a world perspective, as Otten's does. The population data can be provided by the Population Reference Bureau in Washington, D.C. Stories of the struggles of poor peoples must be authentic and presented in a "local voice." Films are good for this feature. There should be a specific action component. The United Nations covenants are currently published as the "International Bill of Human Rights." The fact that the United States has not yet adopted the covenants is a good place to begin a course initiative toward immediate social action to move the adoption of the covenants by the Senate. Although signed by President Jimmy Carter in the fall of 1977 they have not yet been incorporated into law to make them a binding factor in United States foreign and domestic policy. As of this writing, such action has not yet been achieved and very few Americans are aware of the fact.

The approach to sociological analysis just considered for an introductory course can be used or elaborated upon in any standard course, including sociology of family, race and ethnic relations, deviance and social control, and urban sociology. It could be applied, for instance, in an advanced research methods course by focusing that course on serious urban problems.

THE ADVANCED RESEARCH METHODS COURSE

An advanced research methods course can take up any number of issues suggested by the introductory course. One of these is the problem of where the poor will live when high technology makes the city an attractive place for the professionally trained elite to live and work. Few skilled or semiskilled assistants are needed in these highly productive professions in the telecommunications industry, insurance, banking, publishing, transportation, medicine, law, and other computer-assisted professions.

RESEARCH METHODS IN SOCIOLOGY (three credits)

The Problem: Who will be living in Boston [or whatever city is selected for the course study] in 1990? (For five years, the advanced research methods course will compile data on this question, each class building on the findings of the previous research teams.)

Course Goal: The course seeks to develop a further understanding of the relationship between theory and research; to develop the uses of research in policy-making; to understand the role of ideology in the design and use of research findings; to make a critical examination of ideological perspectives; to develop a body of data that can be used to improve the quality of life for poor people in the city; to teach students how to do science for the people by addressing a live question and orienting career preparation to its solution.

MATERIAL NEEDED

Boston People's Yellow Pages, 5th ed. Boston, Mass.: Vocations for Social Change; publication now discontinued. A reference book for the location of organizations in the people's interests, for interview possibilities, for data gathering.

Boston Public Library. *Boston: An Urban Community.* Boston, Mass.: Boston Public Library, 1977. Annotated reading lists.

U.S. Bureau of the Census. *Censpac* (Census Software Package), *User Reference Manual.* Washington, D.C.: U.S. Government Printing Office, 1981.

Dutka, Solomon; Lester R. Frankel; and Irving Roshwalb. *A Marketer's Guide to Effective Use of 1980 Census Data.* New York: Audits and Surveys, 1981. (Available from Audits and Surveys, One Park Ave., New York, NY 10016.)

Lin, Nan. *Foundations of Social Research.* New York: McGraw-Hill, 1976.

———; Ronald S. Bart; and John C. Vaughn. *Conducting Social Research.* New York: McGraw-Hill, 1976.

Statistical Abstracts of the United States, 1980 (section on principal cities). Washington, D.C.: U.S. Government Printing Office, 1981.

Survey Research Center. *Interviewer's Manual.* Rev. ed. Ann Arbor, Mich.: Survey Research Center, University of Michigan 1976.

Newspaper and magazine articles on city issues that the research will address will also be used.

COURSE OUTLINE

Weeks One and Two:

The problem: Who will be living in Boston in 1990? Background of the question: read articles about the ethnic struggles; access to resources; political and economic interests.

Assignment: In no more than five double spaced, typewritten pages answer the following question: Who has been living in Boston in the past three hundred years? Use the census data and Boston Public Library, *Boston: An Urban Community,* annotated reading list, 1977, as sources.

Weeks Three and Four:

The problem: Who knows the city, understands its problems? Who are its people? Prepare and use an interview schedule. First, decide whom to interview: local experts, community workers, agency personnel, elected officials, residents. Then, provide in-class practice in interviewing. Develop one schedule for "experts," and one for a sample of residents. Discuss advantages and disadvantages of interviews in comparison with mailed questionnaires.

Field trip: In a school van, visit the waterfront (or similar) area of the city. Stop in each area to talk with local organizing-group personnel. Discuss observations on return.

Weeks Five and Six:

Refine hypotheses. Mail prepared questionnaires. Participate in the writing of an SPSSX program that incorporates measures for everyone's hypotheses. (SPSSX is a software package for statistical analysis designed especially for social science research. See *SPSSX: User's Guide* [New York: McGraw-Hill, 1983] distributed by SPSSX Inc., Chicago, Illinois.)

Weeks Seven and Eight:

Introduction to the 1980 census data and its storage on tapes. Discuss who has access to tapes, costs, and use. Examine data as collected in previous years. Decide what is needed for this year. Get it.

Weeks Nine and Ten:

Students (in pairs) will visit sections of the city assigned to them, and compare what they see with census data. As a group, discuss the living conditions, the migrations, and implications of condominium conversion in the light of national migration trends.

Weeks Eleven and Twelve:

Analyze questionnaire returns and computer program findings in the light of hypotheses developed from interviews, library research, interpretations of professionals. Discuss the meaning of the findings.

Weeks Thirteen and Fourteen:

Make projections from the evidence. Discuss the place of commitment to justice in policy formation and implementation. Prepare final research report and be prepared to defend it.

The members of the class make their presentations to each other. After the close of the course, people who work in the city on social justice for housing, schools, neighborhood, or medical services and community organization are invited to a presentation of the findings presented by the students. They discuss the findings and examine the evidence. Sometimes students are invited to neighborhood organizations to present their findings.

This course begins with a question that is the statement of a problem: Who will be living in Boston [the city] in 1990? Hypotheses are then invited from the experience of the researchers in training. A field trip, visiting the several ethnic areas of the city where condominium development is proceeding, is scheduled. It builds on the findings of students of the previous three years whose recorded observations, having been filed, are reexamined. Using the 1980 national census data tapes, the sections of the city are sorted out with their specific social characteristics, including age, sex, education, occupation, home ownership, ethnicity, generation in America, income, condition of plumbing, crowdedness of residence, and condominium potential. After examining these data the class is divided into interviewing teams. Each team visits a different section of the city. By pooling their resources, they learn the local history from the district library's local archives; from interviews with current city personnel, the student researchers learn about police and fire service, health, education, and welfare programs. With this general background, the students each year single out some group for special study. It may be teachers, tenants, professionals, students, other workers, or a new ethnic minority. By preparing an interview schedule and drawing a random sample, the students learn these skills, and, in using them with their selected interviewees, they are then able to record from the perspective of that group what is happening in the city, and to focus on specific needs, concerns, and interests. After studying the census data, the students can record the ethnic-group characteristics and on graphs plot and compare them with national trends. Movements in and out of urban areas can be charted, and hypotheses about migration tested. While students are learning to use sources for the history of the city as well as its current census characteristics, its problems and their interpretation from organizational files, they also learn standard methods of sampling techniques, questionnaire construction, interviewing skills, theory construction and testing, hypothesis formulation, and measurement. They become acquainted with the uses of statistics, computer programming, and report writing. More than simply acquiring these necessary skills, they learn to use them in the interests of the people whose stories they are learning. By discovering how people live, struggle, survive, and use the resources of their cities, they can begin to make more informed choices if, in the larger context of their education, the social justice agenda is seriously interwoven. They also learn what resources are made available to populations, whether or not people are neglected, how people are moved about, understood, treated; how to identify and assess from interest groups claims and counter-claims of social justice; and how to proceed from information to action. They learn how to ground action in information and how to listen to people in order to understand human need.

Most of us are aware at this point that all education has a point of view. To choose the doing of a social justice agenda in the academic setting is as fine a commitment to academic excellence as to choose to produce humanistic scholars with trained competency to anguish in the face of manifest injustice. The difference seems to be that the training for social justice helps to develop that human passion for action to eliminate oppression. Conditioned by trained competency and directed by knowledge, we are addressing problems with technical solutions currently prevented from solution by false assumptions of scarcity and enlightened self-interest.

NOTES

1. For copies of these documents, see David O'Brien and Thomas A. Shannon, eds., *Renewing the Earth: Catholic Documents on Peace, Justice, and Liberation* (Garden City, N. Y.: Doubleday Image Books, 1977).

2. Joseph Varacalli, *Toward the Establishment of Liberal Catholicism in America* (Washington, D. C.: University Press of America, 1983).

3. United States Catholic Bishops, "The Challenge of Peace" (Washington, D. C.: United States Catholic Conference, 1983); "Catholic Social Teaching and the U.S. Economy," *Origins* 15 (November 1984).

4. "Declaration on the Establishment of a New International Economic Order" (New York: United Nations, 1974).

5. "International Bill of Human Rights" (New York: United Nations, 1978).

6. See "Population Data Sheet" (Washington, D. C.: Population Reference Bureau, 1980).

7. The "International Bill of Human Rights" states:

"When the 'Universal Declaration of Human Rights' was proclaimed by the General Assembly in 1948, it was viewed as the first step in the formulation of an 'international bill of human rights' that would have legal as well as moral force. In 1976—three decades after this comprehensive undertaking was launched by the United Nations—the 'international bill of human rights' became a reality, with the entry into force of three significant instruments:

"The International Covenant on Economic, Social and Cultural Rights;

"The International Covenant on Civil and Political Rights; and

"The Optional Protocol."

8. "International Bill of Human Rights," p. 2.

9. Leonard Broom; Philip Selznick; and Dorothy H. Broom, *The Essentials of Sociology* (Ithaca, Ill.: F. E. Peacock Publishers, 1984).

10. C. Michael Otten, *Power, Values and Society* (New York: Random House, 1982).

11. Paulo Freire, *Pedagogy of the Oppressed* (New York: Seabury Press, 1970).

12. Marie Augusta Neal, *The Gospel Agenda in Global Perspective,* Research Paper no. 1, Sisters of Notre Dame de Namur, Pedagogy Project, Emanuel College, Boston, 1981.

13. See Douglas F. Dowd, *The Twisted Dream: Capitalist Development in the United States from 1776* (Cambridge, Mass.: Winthrop Press, 1977).

SELECTED READINGS FOR FACULTY

Avila, Charles. *Ownership.* Maryknoll, N. Y.: Orbis Books, 1983.

Baum, Gregory. *The Priority of Labor.* New York: Paulist Press, 1982.

Cabestrero, Teófilo. *Ministers of God, Ministers of the People,* Maryknoll, N.Y.: Orbis Books, 1983.

Cardenal, Ernesto. *The Gospel in Solentiname.* Maryknoll, N.Y.: Orbis Books, 1976.

Charover, Stephan L. *From Genesis to Genocide: The Meaning of Human Nature and the Power of Behavior Control.* Cambridge, Mass.: MIT Press, 1979.

Cussianovich, Alejandro. *Religious Life and the Poor: Liberation Theology Perspectives.* Maryknoll, N.Y.: Orbis Books, 1979.

De Santa Ana, Julio. *Towards a Church of the Poor.* Maryknoll, N.Y.: Orbis Books, 1981.

Dorr, Donal. *Option for the Poor: A Hundred Years of Vatican Social Teaching.* Maryknoll, N.Y.: Orbis Books, 1983.

Dowd, Douglas F. *The Twisted Dream: Capitalist Development in the United States from 1776.* Cambridge, Mass.: Winthrop Press, 1977.

Eagleson, John, and Philip Scharper, eds. *Puebla and Beyond: Documentation and Commentary.* Maryknoll, N.Y.: Orbis Books, 1979.

Freire, Paulo. *Pedagogy of the Oppressed.* New York: Seabury Press, 1970.

George, Susan. *Ill Fares the Land: Essays on Food, Hunger and Power.* Washington, D.C.: Institute for Policy Studies, 1984.

Gutiérrez, Gustavo. *The Power of the Poor in History.* Maryknoll, N.Y.: Orbis Books, 1983.

Hanks, Thomas D. *God So Loved the Third World: The Bible, Reformation, and Liberation Theology.* Maryknoll, N.Y.: Orbis Books, 1983.

Hardin, Garrett. "Living on a Lifeboat." *Bioscience* 24, no. 10 (October 1974).

Herzog, Frederick. *Justice Church: New Function of the Church in North American Christianity.* Maryknoll, N.Y.: Orbis Books, 1980.

Holdgate, Martin W. et al. *The Global Possible: Resources, Development and the New Century.* Washington, D.C.: World Resources Institute, 1984.

Holland, Joseph, and Peter Henriot. *Social Analysis: Linking Faith and Justice.* Rev. ed. Maryknoll, N.Y.: Orbis Books, 1983.

Lappé, Frances Moore, and Joseph Collins. *Food First: Beyond the Myth of Scarcity.* Boston, Mass.: Houghton Mifflin, 1977.

Lieberson, Stanley. "A Societal Theory of Race and Ethnic Relations." *American Sociological Review* 26, no. 6 (December 1961).

Maduro, Otto. *Religion and Social Conflicts.* Maryknoll, N.Y.: Orbis Books 1982.

Martin, James. *The Telematic Society: A Challenge for Tomorrow.* Englewood Cliffs, N.J.: Prentice-Hall, 1981.

Neal, Marie Augusta. "Accepting Our Progeny: The Gospel Agenda in Global Perspective." In *The Gospel Agenda in Global Perspective.* Research Paper no. 1, Sisters of Notre Dame de Namur Pedagogy Project, 1981.

———. *A Sociotheology of Letting Go: A First World Church Facing Third World People.* New York: Paulist Press, 1977.

O'Brien, David, and Thomas A. Shannon. *Renewing the Earth: Catholic Documents on Peace, Justice and Liberation.* Garden City, N.Y.: Doubleday Image Book, 1977.

Otten, C. Michael, *Power, Values and Society: An Introduction to Sociology.* New York: Random House, 1982. (Formerly published by Scott, Foresman.)

Piven, Frances Scott. *The New Class War: Reagan's Attack on the Welfare State and Its Consequences.* New York: Pantheon Books, 1982.

Richard, Pablo et al. *Idols of Death and the God of Life: A Theology.* Maryknoll, N.Y.: Orbis Books, 1983.

Sivard, Ruth Leger. *World Military and Social Expenditures.* Box 1003, Leesburg, Va.: World Priorities, 1983.

Sklar, Holly. *Trilateralism: Elite Planning for World Management.* Boston, Mass.: South End Press, 1980.

United States Catholic Bishops. "The Challenge of Peace: God's Promise and Our Response." *Origins* 13, no. 1 (May 19, 1983).

Vandermeer, John. "Hardin's Lifeboat Adrift." *Science for the People,* January 1976.

Varacalli, Joseph. *Toward the Establishment of Liberal Catholicism in America.* Washington, D.C.: University Press of America, 1983.

CHURCH DOCUMENTS

Bishops of Appalachia. "This Land Is Home to Me" (1975). Prestonsburg, Ky.: Catholic Committee of Appalachia, 1975.

John XXIII. *Mater et Magistra* ("Christianity and Social Progress," 1961). New York: America Press, 1961.

———. *Pacem in Terris* ("Peace on Earth," 1963). Boston, Mass.: St. Paul Editions, 1963.

John Paul II. *Laborem Exercens* ("On Human Work," 1981). Boston, Mass.: St. Paul Editions, 1981.

Leo XIII. *Rerum Novarum* ("Of New Things," 1891). Washington, D.C.: National Catholic Welfare Conference, 1942.

Paul VI. *Octogesima Adveniens* ("A Call to Action," 1971; eightieth anniversary of *Rerum Novarum*). Washington, D.C.: United States Catholic Conference, 1971.

———. *Populorum Progressio* ("The Development of Peoples," 1967). Boston, Mass.: St. Paul Editions, 1967.

Pius XI. *Quadragesimo Anno* ("Fortieth Year [after *Rerum Novarum*]," 1931). Washington, D.C.: National Catholic Welfare Conference, 1942.

Synod of Bishops. "Justice in the World," 1971. Boston, Mass.: St. Paul Editions, 1971.

Vatican II. *Gaudium et Spes* ("Pastoral Constitution on the Church in the Modern World," 1965). Boston, Mass.: St. Paul Editions, 1965.

OTHER RESOURCES

Murphy, Elaine M. "The Environment to Come: A Global Summary." Washington, D.C.: Population Reference Bureau, 1983.

"Population Data Sheet." Available from Population Reference Bureau, 1337 Connecticut Ave., N.W., Washington, DC 20036.

United Nations. "International Bill of Human Rights." New York: United Nations, 1978.

United Nations. "Toward a World Economy that Works." New York: United Nations, 1980.

United Nations. "A Declaration on the Establishment of a New International Economic Order." New York: United Nations, 1974.

PART III

THE PROFESSIONAL DISCIPLINES

10

Business and Management

OLIVER F. WILLIAMS, C.S.C.
UNIVERSITY OF NOTRE DAME

People who are successful in the business world are often caricatured as "knowing the cost of everything and the value of nothing." Those of us teaching students in colleges or universities with a religious affiliation like to think that our students who go into business will be different from the caricature, that they will be exemplars of Christian virtue, even in the face of great difficulties.

Yet what does it mean to be a Christian in today's business world? Among other things, it means to be one who stands for justice. But justice has many dimensions. In discussing the marketplace, justice must be considered on at least two levels: the level of economic systems and the level of specific performance within a system. For example, in the world today there is a great debate on whether the structures of capitalism or those of socialism offer more possibility for justice. The majority of the courses treating justice questions in business schools, however, assume that the American economy is fundamentally legitimate, and then go on to focus on ways the system might be made more just. It may be helpful to outline how justice questions might be considered on this second level.

A shorter version of this essay was published as "Being a Christian in the Business World: The Challenge and the Promise," *Horizons* 11, no. 2 (1984): 383–92.

JUSTICE IN ACCOUNTANCY

The second level is essentially a reformist posture and it allows for the infusion of justice issues into the whole range of business courses. For example, in one course, "Cost Accounting," ethical issues are routinely interjected. The syllabus poses a question for each section, which is designed to engage the student about the fairness of the way in which benefits and burdens are distributed in an accounting procedure. For example, in studying overhead costs, the following question is offered: "Should an organization be allowed to include in its overhead costs for pricing purposes the expenses involved in product liability suits where the organization has clearly been at fault?" Along with learning a new accounting procedure, the class also learns how one ascertains the rightness or wrongness of such procedures.[1]

The American Accounting Association has a Public Interest Section that encourages a number of activities that would integrate justice issues into accountancy. The Public Interest Section Charter highlights social-responsibility accounting, public-issues work, and direct-assistance programs. Perhaps the most effective way to sensitize accountants to justice is through direct-assistance programs. For example, in the College of Business Administration of the University of Notre Dame, a number of students in accountancy volunteer time to provide assistance in tax-return preparation for disadvantaged and minority persons in the South Bend, Indiana, area. Sharing their time and talent with the poor, students may come to see that this world needs not only their competence but also their compassion.

JUSTICE IN MANAGEMENT

The touchstone of all ethical analysis is whether or not the policy or activity in question promotes and protects human dignity, so it is not surprising that a course in basic management would be replete with justice issues. For example, a typical course, "Principles of Management," addresses the following topics: Motivation, Evolution of Management Theory, Leadership, Authority and Power, Organizational Design, and Conflict within Organizations.[2] Each of these areas has a justice dimension revolving around whether persons are afforded the opportunity of developing and exercising their capacities as free persons, or not. Managers have vast power to shape their organizations and to design systems for common ends. Understanding power not as a manipulative tool but as an opportunity to serve the common good is the challenge.

Research and experience in industry are confirming the fact that when people are treated in accord with their dignity, absenteeism declines and the quality of work rises. Much management theory echoes the justice literature in exhorting managers to move beyond the concept of the "hired hand," of labor as a commodity. Strategies of "team building," "organizational development," and "job enrichment" are in the forefront of management theory today because they are tools to increase productivity and job satisfaction. These same strategies are advocated in the name of justice, for they enable the person to grow in creativity with freedom and dignity.

A COURSE ON JUSTICE IN BUSINESS

It is important that students encounter justice issues in lower-level courses from professors in their major business disciplines. However, in order to grasp the ever expanding role of business in society and to see the justice issues in the context of global problems and the economic system itself, a single course devoted to this theme is helpful. What follows is the rationale and outline of "Modern Decision-Making in the Christian Tradition," a course designed for upper-level students.

Our Students: What Sort of Persons Are They?

It has been my experience that students in the course are serious about their Christian faith, that is, they attend church services and they strive to live the sort of life that they understand to be Christian. They are largely from good homes and have learned the value of friendship and love from dedicated parents. Most of them, however, have not been challenged to think through the implications of their Christian faith for their life in the business world or in the wider social order.

While they may be models of compassion and generosity to those in their immediate circles, many of our students today have a blind spot for responsibilities in the socio-political order. In the traditional vocabulary, they are strong on charity but weak in justice. Justice in our time is often equated with "law and order," the quid pro quo that ensures that each gets what he or she deserves. One of the objectives of the course is to widen the horizons of the students so that they come to see more adequately what is entailed in calling oneself "Christian." To begin, I ask them to reflect on sections of "Justice in the World," the document issued by the Roman Synod of Bishops, Second General Assembly (1971). For example: "Action on behalf of justice and participation in the transformation of the world fully appear to us as a constitutive dimension of the preaching of the Gospel, or, in other words, of the Church's mission for the redemption of the human race and its liberation from every oppressive situation."[3]

After a brief introduction to the overarching concerns of the course, the class begins to read the books assigned. The semester is divided into three parts, each one representing a key goal of the course: *1*. The Challenge: Understanding the Problem (sessions 1–10); *2*. The Promise: Mining the Christian Tradition (sessions 11–21); *3*. The Promise Applied: Living the Tradition in the Business World Today (sessions 22–28).

MODERN DECISION-MAKING AND THE CHRISTIAN TRADITION *(three credits)*

"Economic activity is to be carried out according to its own methods and laws but within the limits of morality, so that God's plan for humankind can be realized" [*Gaudium et Spes*, no. 64].

PURPOSE

The course will focus on one central question: "How might Christian faith influence life in the business world?" After reviewing some of the basics of what it means to be a Christian, the course explores cases of actual situations likely to be encountered in business life today.

REQUIRED TEXTS

All should have the following books for the course (all paperbacks):

Berger, Peter. *Pyramids of Sacrifice*. Garden City, N.Y.: Doubleday, 1976.

Birch, Bruce and Larry Rasmussen. *The Predicament of the Prosperous*. Philadelphia, Pa.: Westminster Press, 1978.

Bolt, Robert. *A Man for All Seasons*. New York: Random House, 1962.

Sinclair, Upton. *The Jungle*. New York: New American Library, 1960.

United States Catholic Bishops. "Catholic Social Teaching and the U.S. Economy." *Origins* 14 (1984): 337–83.

Williams, O., and J. Houck. *Full Value*. New York: Harper & Row, 1978.

———. *The Judeo-Christian Vision and the Modern Corporation*. Notre Dame, Ind.: University of Notre Dame Press, 1982.

John Paul II. *Laborem Exercens*. Washington, D.C.: USCC, 1981.

ASSESSMENT FOR FINAL GRADES

Class Participation: Effective class participation includes listening skills; analysis abilities; insightful contributions; and last but not least, a willingness to risk, testing new ideas. It is assumed that students will not be absent from class more than three times during the semester.

Examinations: There are two examinations, a midsemester and a final.

Final Paper: For the subject of the final paper the student has several choices. The basic question of the course is "How might Christian faith influence life in the business world?" One option is to write the story of a person who is trying to take that question seriously. A second option is to write a projection of one's own story reflecting how one's Christian faith could influence one's life in the business world. A third option is for the student, in consultation with the instructor, to select another theme of special interest related to the central question of the course. Papers are to be ten to fifteen pages in length, typed double-spaced.

COURSE OUTLINE

The course meets two times a week for seventy-five minute periods. Note that *The Judeo-Christian Vision and the Modern Corporation* is referred to as *JCV.*

Session	Topic	Readings
1	Opening Discussion	"Justice in the World," 1971 Synod Document
2–3	Understanding the Problem	*The Jungle*
4	History of Religion and Business	O. Williams, "Introduction," *JCV,* pp. 1–21
5–8	The Bible Speaks to Our Times	*The Predicament of the Prosperous*
9	Some Conflicting Interpretations	M. Novak, "Can a Christian Work for a Corporation?" *JCV,* pp. 159–94
10	More Conflicting Interpretations	C. Wilber and K. Jameson, "Goals of a Christian Economy," *JCV,* pp. 203–17
11–12	The Catholic Teaching	*Laborem Exercens*
13–16	Living a Christian Story	*Full Value,* chap. 1–3
17–19	The Ethics of Development	*Pyramids of Sacrifice*
20–21	Having a "Sense of Self"	*A Man for All Seasons*
22	Case: "Walnut Ave. Church"	*Full Value,* pp. 95–106, and J. Schall "Catholicism, Business, and Human Priorities," *JCV,* pp. 73–81; 107–33
23	Case: "The Eli Black Story"	*Full Value,* pp. 141–53, and J. Gustafson and E. Johnson, "The Corporate Leader and the Ethical Resources of Religion: A Dialogue," *JCV,* pp. 306–29
24	Case: "Agenbite of Inwit"	*Full Value,* pp. 107–15, and C. Cleary, "Women in the Corporation: A Case Study about Justice," *JCV,* pp. 292–305
25	Case: "Give Us This Day"	*Full Value,* pp. 130–40, and D. Goulet, "Goals in Conflict: Corporate Success and Global Justice?" *JCV,* pp. 218–43

26	Case: "Caribbean Corporate Strategy"	*Full Value,* pp. 116–29, and K. Hanson, "Corporate Decision-Making and the Public Interest," *JCV,* pp. 330–42
27	Case: "The John Caron Story"	*Full Value,* pp. 206–17, and C. Stone, "Corporate Accountability in Law and Morals," *JCV,* pp. 264–87.
28	Conclusion	*JCV,* pp. 249–63

The Challenge: Understanding the Problem

In 1983 the United States Census Bureau reported that 15 percent of Americans, 34.4 million people, were below the poverty threshold. While one could quibble over just what qualifies as being "below the poverty threshold," at the very least the statistics are a reminder that, for many Americans, the United States is not the land of plenty. A cursory study of third-world statistics is much more disconcerting. Poverty and hunger are a way of life for many millions of people. The problem is that the majority of our students have been raised in relative affluence and have little experience of poverty.

While one could show students reams of statistics highlighting the gap between the haves and the have-nots, this approach has not proved effective. Most of them have never really had the opportunity to know what it is like to be poor and powerless in our society, for they have been gifted with what it takes to get ahead. One way—and perhaps the best way—to help students empathize with the plight of the powerless is to arrange for them to live and work with the poor for a short time. At the University of Notre Dame, a one-credit course called the "Urban Plunge" is offered. Here the student is assigned to spend several days in a poor, urban setting, usually over a vacation period, and then write a reflection paper on the experience. Some of the students have had this course before taking the "Modern Decision-Making" course, and they clearly have a more profound understanding of poverty. Most, however, have not participated in the "Urban Plunge."

As a way of trying to lead the students into some empathy with the poor, the class reads and discusses Upton Sinclair's novel *The Jungle.* Sinclair tells the story of a young immigrant who comes to the New World to find a new life for himself and his family. The setting is the factory life of Chicago in the early twentieth century, and the reader is confronted with a tale of crushing poverty and despair that seems to know no bounds. No matter how hard they try, this lovable little family meets one setback after another. They are vividly portrayed as pawns in the game of powerful politicians and leaders of industry. Many of the students candidly admit that they were moved to tears as they experienced the shattering of one dream after another of the novel's hero. After this book, the students have a feeling for what it means to be on the bottom rungs of the socioeconomic ladder. They begin to understand the problem of the American economy: some people are poor and powerless in the face of the market system.

Sinclair's purpose in writing *The Jungle* was to convince people that capitalism was a brutal system that must be abandoned. As a convinced socialist, Sinclair intended to depict the depravity of American industry (in particular, of the Chicago slaughterhouses) in such a way that no one would come to its defense. It is somewhat ironical that because of Sinclair and other like-minded radicals, capitalism has continued to survive—and even thrive. For the sections of the book describing the horrible details of meat production caused such a national furor that within six months the U.S. Congress passed the Pure Food and Drug Act and the Beef Inspection Act. One lesson many learn from this whole episode is that the system is reformable, and that persons skilled in the ways of changing structures can make it more humane and responsive.

Sinclair's argument against capitalism, flowing through *The Jungle,* is incisive and provides a way into some critical issues for the course. His argument against capitalism is based on two points: (1) Sinclair focuses on what capitalism does to people, not only what it does to the poor and powerless but, perhaps more importantly, what it does to the rich. It makes them greedy and insensitive, he argues. The system accents the worst character traits of a person and mutes the more noble ones. (2) Sinclair repeatedly argues, through the novel, that socialism is mandated by the Bible. In Sinclair's words: ". . . the Socialist movement was a world movement, an organization of all mankind to establish liberty and fraternity. It was the new religion of humanity—or you might say it was the fulfilment of the old religion, since it implied but the literal application of all the teachings of Christ."[4]

In order to ascertain the truth of Sinclair's second assertion, that Scripture mandates that we strive toward a socialist economy, it is necessary to explore the religious heritage in some depth. This is the task of the second part of the course. Sinclair's first assertion must be addressed before the course can proceed. If capitalism inevitably shapes people into greedy and insensitive human beings, how could humane and religious people have supported it over the centuries?

Sinclair's criticism takes us back to the first, and probably the most compelling, apologist for capitalism, Adam Smith. It is important that the students be exposed to Smith's *The Wealth of Nations,* for—although published over 200 years ago (1776)—it is still considered to be the bible of capitalism. Smith assumed the truth of the Judeo-Christian vision of a land where all might enjoy the fruits of creation. Smith's insight was that only certain places were generating sufficient wealth so that all might enjoy the good things of creation. What characterized these places was what we now call a market economy. When each person pursues his or her own self-interest the common good is enhanced. The baker bakes the very best bread he can and sells it so that he can use the proceeds of his sale to buy what he wants. Although motivated by self-interest, the net result is that the community has quality products at a reasonable cost.

What Smith did was to show how economic action based on self-interest could be beneficial for the community. This was indeed a remarkable turn of events, for economic self-interest was heretofore not thought to be respectable. Smith assumed that economic self-interest would be kept in check by the moral forces in the community. His argument for the morality of a market economy was utilitarian: The end (a community where all could obtain the fruits of creation) justified the means (economic action based on self-interest).

What seems to have happened in Sinclair's *The Jungle* is that the means has become the end, that is, making a profit has become an end itself with no reference to the humane community that Smith envisioned as the net result. Instead of an acquisitive economy enabling a humane community, we see an acquisitive economy *overwhelming* the community and shaping it into an acquisitive society. Respect for human dignity, the touchstone of the whole process, is reduced to near zero. Is this our situation today? The students have cause for serious reflection.

Since Sinclair wrote *The Jungle* there have been numerous government regulations and programs designed to harness a market economy—child-labor laws, minimum-wage laws, provisions for unions, social security, medical plans, and so on. Even with this, the student must still ask the hard question posed by Sinclair: Is it possible for *me* to participate in the market economy, the business world, and not be overcome by greed and insensitivity? To demonstrate that all Christians do not have to answer Sinclair's question the same way, four distinguished speakers are brought into the class, some business leaders, some social critics, all of whom are known for their fidelity to religious values. The notion of vocation that leads some to follow Dorothy Day and others Thomas Aquinas Murphy (former president of General Motors), some to follow Father Daniel Berrigan, S.J., and others Father Theodore Hesburgh, C.S.C., is crucial, but this is to anticipate the second part of the course.

The Promise: Mining the Christian Tradition

The issue that opens this section has been lingering since it was raised by Upton Sinclair: Is socialism mandated by the Bible? First, it is necessary to clarify some terms. In short, "socialism" and "capitalism" are two different theories of distributive justice. Distributive justice concerns the principles for allocating scarce benefits and undesirable burdens, and capitalism and socialism are two distinct ways for accomplishing this allocation. Socialism makes the allocation on the basis of needs and abilities: work burdens are distributed according to a person's abilities and benefits according to a person's needs. Capitalistic theory allocates benefits on the basis of the contribution one makes as this is determined by the market forces of supply and demand.

To be sure, the early Christian communities seem to have been models of socialistic justice (e.g., read Acts 2:43–45). Students are asked to consider Sinclair's question and then to take a position and defend it. It is generally a heated debate with the class divided about equally. Those arguing that socialism is mandated by the teachings of Jesus cite text after text from the Bible. Those arguing against this position point out that it is naïve to think that you can organize whole societies on the model of familial relationships, and that socialism saps freedom with its strong paternalism. Who determines what *my* needs are? Can you motivate a society without self-interest?

At this point the position of the 1981 papal encyclical *Laborem Exercens* ("On Human Work") is discussed. (Only paragraphs 11 and 13 are read at this time.) Here there is no endorsement of either system but a prophetic call for reform of all economic systems so that human dignity and creativity can flourish. The American economy is a mixed economy with elements of socialistic theory in a dominant capitalistic model. Yet *Laborem Exercens* argues that it is not beyond reform. The promise is that intelligent and compassionate citizens can participate in the system and make it better. (The pastoral letter of the United States bishops, "Catholic Social Teaching and the U.S. Economy," could be used here as well.)

Before moving to case studies that rehearse what it might mean to improve the American economic system, it is necessary to have good grounding in the religious perspective. We use five books for this purpose: Birch and Rasmussen, *The Predicament of the Prosperous*; Williams and Houck, *Full Value*; John Paul II, *Laborem Exercens*; Peter Berger, *Pyramids of Sacrifice*; and Robert Bolt, *A Man for All Seasons*.

As an introduction to the study of what theology has to say to our times, we spend several classes on the history of the interaction between religion and commerce. A brief look at the church fathers, Thomas Aquinas, Martin Luther, John Calvin, and the struggles of workers in the early twentieth century sets the stage for the 1980s, with which this class is concerned. The class syllabus opens with a quotation from the Vatican II document *Gaudium et Spes* ("The Church in the Modern World"): "Economic activity is to be carried out according to its own methods and laws but within the limits of morality, so that God's plan for humankind can be realized."[5]

The students are asked to read some sections of the work of Thomas Aquinas and try to discern how he understood "God's plan for humankind." What is God's plan for creation? I leave this question open and suggest that the forthcoming theology books should provide some answers.

The first book, *The Predicament of the Prosperous,* is co-authored by two theologians at Wesley Theological Seminary, Bruce Birch and Larry Rasmussen, and presents an incisive analysis of our times in light of the biblical perspectives. It is a provocative book and, while I point out areas where I am in disagreement, its key thesis speaks to the issues of the course. The authors argue that America has come to understand itself as "God's special delivered people" who now have a mission to bring such deliverance to others. We are the "heroic deliverers" and consequently are pictured entirely as part of the solution and not at all as part of the problems of the world economy.

Birch and Rasmussen predict a terrible crisis in the world as a result of the scarcity of global resources, and they argue that America is partially responsible, for it has failed to use the world's goods wisely. They suggest that rather than "heroic rescuer," a more appropriate image is "Exile in Babylon." We are about to experience God's judgment and we must repent, reshaping our priorities on how we use God's resources and how we share them with our fellow human beings, both in the United States and worldwide.

The authors argue that just as Sinai followed exodus (embodiment in social systems followed proclamation), so too systemic and perspectival change must follow conversion. It is not enough to focus on aid and relief efforts but, rather, we must get to the root causes of oppression, hunger, and poverty. This will entail seeing ourselves, United States citizens, as part of the problem.

Although the authors are not specific in suggesting reforms, they at least point toward trade and tariff concessions and financial assistance for developing countries. The students are challenged to examine their own perspectives on these questions and are pressed to take a stand for or against Birch and Rasmussen's position.

At this juncture two essays are assigned from *The Judeo-Christian Vision and the Modern Corporation*. These articles have quite diverse perspectives on the need to reform the American economy. One, by Michael Novak, "Can a Christian Work for a Corporation? The Theology of the Corporation," is relatively content with the present arrangements in the American economy. The other, by Charles Wilber and Kenneth Jameson, "Goals of a Christian Economy and the Future of the Corporation," is strident in its opposition. It argues that Adam Smith's apology for capitalism no longer applies, since we are in an era of *corporate* capitalism where largeness and high concentration impede the workings of the market. They suggest some significant reforms. Students are asked to formulate their own positions.

The next topic for discussion is John Paul's encyclical *Laborem Exercens* ("On Human Work"). While it is difficult for students, it does offer an attractive vision pointing us toward God's intentions for the quality of life in our world. Our work in making the world more humane actually furthers the kingdom of God. We are called to be co-creators with God, fashioning his creation. In particular, co-creators are charged to work for sociopolitical changes that are aimed at improving the quality of life of the least advantaged. The encyclical offers a number of suggestions for improving the economies of the world, including co-determination, economic planning, and worker participation in management. Many of these suggestions are discussed at length in a companion volume to the encyclical, *Co-Creation and Capitalism: John Paul II's* Laborem Exercens, edited by John Houck and Oliver Williams.

At this point in the course the students are offered one way of appropriating the biblical and theological themes of the class. Using *Full Value: Cases in Christian Business Ethics,* the students are introduced to narrative theology— seeing life as a story. It is as if life is one giant play that has already been written in outline by the Author of Life.

We find the plot revealed to us in Scripture through the church. This

"Christian story" informs our moral vision, sustains our loyalties, and nurtures our character. The Christian story tells us what life is about; it provides images from the Bible stories and stories of the saints that can serve as models in shaping our own story. "I am an Exile in Babylon but I want to change and become more of a co-creator as David was." "I want to cooperate rather than control."

The notion of role model is similar to the notion of "master image guiding one's story." It is pointing to the idea that a fulfilled life entails settling the question of the sort of person one would like to become. It is possible to avoid the question, but at one's own peril, I argue. A famous quotation from John Ehrlichman, one of Richard Nixon's chief staff officers, shocks most of the students. Reflecting after he had been fired by Nixon in the aftermath of the Watergate affair, Ehrlichman said:

> I'm more and more realizing that I lived 50 years of my life without ever really coming to grips with the very basic question of what is and is not important to me, what is and is not right and wrong, what is and is not valuable and worthwhile. . . . I've begun a process that my own kids began almost from the beginning . . . developing my sense of values. I'm a beginner. . . . [6]

Each of us has an image of the sort of person we would like to become, even if only unconsciously. Students are encouraged to see that Jesus offers images through his many stories of the sort of person God intends them to be. Whether it be "Servant of the Lord," "Pilgrim of the People of God," or "Co-Creator"—different images fit the uniqueness of individuals—one or another biblical image can help people to find their way through life.

With a master image from the Bible, one slowly shapes oneself by many little decisions into the sort of person one is called to be. Adam Smith said that if each person pursued his or her own self-interest, then the common good would be enhanced. Smith never assumed that "self-interest" would always be "selfishness." *What sort of self is it that is self-interested?* A self shaped by the church and other moral communities would be interested in the community, the poor, developing nations, and so on. Religious images and sacramental life are presented as ways that shape the community, giving its members an expanded horizon for action and a wider agenda for life. *Full Value* is replete with biblical stories and applications aimed at aiding the reader in coming to understand narrative theology. Most students find this approach helpful.

Because many students will work for corporations with third-world subsidiaries, it is important that they have some familiarity with the anguish of developing countries. I have found Peter Berger's *Pyramids of Sacrifice* a good introduction to the issues. Berger's thesis is that social change, whether it be by developmental growth or by revolution, cannot be ethically pursued at *any* price. The human costs in terms of suffering and loss of meaning must be considered. He examines two case studies of rapid social change, Brazil (developmental growth-capitalism) and China (revolution-socialism) and is critical of both. Leaders of both these nations have been too willing to sacrifice generations for the sake of some elusive future paradise. More attention to the needs of the poor and suffering in the present is his constant refrain.

Berger has chosen a powerful metaphor to make his point that development and revolution are often the twentieth-century version of the ever present false gods. The title *Pyramids of Sacrifice* refers to the Great Pyramid at Cholula, Mexico, where the Aztecs regularly sacrificed humans because of their conviction that the gods required it. The executioners blindly followed the theorists and sacrificed untold numbers of victims. So too, Berger argues, do some politicians, planners, revolutionaries, and so on, blindly follow one or another social theorist (Milton Friedman? Karl Marx?) and continue the slaughter. He is *not* arguing that because change entails suffering, nothing should be done. His point is, rather, that the social, political, and human consequences of economic decisions must be factored in when considering a program or a plan. A tolerable human cost is the goal.

The final book of the course is a play by Robert Bolt, *A Man for All Seasons*. This book prepares the students for the last section of the class, applying their knowledge to actual cases. The play tells the story of Sir Thomas More, the brilliant young lawyer who rose to be an ambassador and finally the Lord Chancellor under King Henry VIII. Here is a man with whom many students in the course can identify—talented, witty, upwardly mobile, and yet a serious Catholic.

In the preface to the play, Robert Bolt asks *the* penetrating question: "Why do I take as my hero a man who brings about his own death because he can't put his hand on an old black book and tell an ordinary lie?"[7] None of our students will be in quite the predicament of Thomas More, but all of them will need to have a fairly good "sense of self" to withstand the temptation to do "whatever it takes to get along and get ahead." That is where More's life is a helpful model. He got ahead and there were certain kinds of compromises he was willing to make, but there was a point beyond which he would not go, no matter what. Many of my former students come back and speak of colleagues that they meet in the business world about whom one could truly say: "There is nothing they would not do to get ahead." How does one become like More with that "adamantine sense of self"? More tells us that it is his relationship with Christ and the community of believers in the church that make him what he is.

To explain how More might be gathering the strength to stand firm, the notion of master image is developed. More has a master image from the Bible guiding his story, and from that master image he has a place to stand and to limit what he will do in his professional role as Lord Chancellor. In many ways More was a "company man" as Lord Chancellor, but there was a loyalty to God stemming from his master image that far surpassed his loyalty to the king stemming from his professional image. The professional (Lord Chancellor) was only part of the man, not the whole man. He could step outside his professional role and assess what the limits of that role might be. He had a story, the Christian story, with a dominant image sufficient to keep him humane through it all. His Christian story could encompass his professional story and put it in perspective. He knew where to draw the line. This skill is the subject of the third part of this course.

The Promise Applied: Living the Tradition in the Business World Today

The final section of the course consists of six case studies (six chapters of *Full Value*), which call for decisions about how one is to understand some data or act in a certain situation. The thrust of the course is to say that most people never fully explore what their faith ought to mean in the sociopolitical order. These cases are designed as one way to awaken this awareness. The subject matter varies from world hunger, multinationals in the third world, and the humanization of work, to the challenge of one executive trying to live his values at work and still survive.

In discussing cases, the four-step decision-making model in *Full Value* is used: (1) ascertain the data; (2) interpret and clarify the data; (3) discern the values in conflict in the case; (4) consider the alternatives and make a decision.

One learns in doing the cases that often it is in interpreting the data that Christian faith has its primary import. Deciding what facts are to be taken as significant is a key step. For example, an economist might argue that the poor must go hungry so that the infrastructure can be constructed and allow for an advanced economy. The Christian would weigh the fact that people are going hungry as critical and would strive to find some way to provide for them, even at the expense of the economic-growth process. Similarly, the value trade-offs in unemployment, inflation, reindustrialization, and so on, are considered.

When one is forced to study concrete cases, it becomes clear that being a visionary is not enough. Developing the skills to bring good intentions to fruitful outcomes is the crucial task. I argue that it is indeed true that the American economy is unjust to some, but compared to what? How can things be better? The American economy is "a moving target"; it can be reformed. No doubt, it is our hope as teachers in schools espousing Christian values that our students will be on the leading edge.

CONCLUSION: BUSINESS AS A "NOBLE" OCCUPATION

It is commonplace to assume that there is an inherent antagonism between the intellectual class and the business world. Intellectuals celebrate the heroic, the saintly, the noble, and the virtuous. The great intellectuals of the world—Aristotle, Thomas Aquinas, the fathers of the church, for example—had a certain disdain for commerce. Business was never considered to be a noble profession. Consider Aristotle's definition of "noble."

> . . . those actions are noble for which the reward is simply honor, or honor more than money. So are those in which a man aims at something

desirable for someone else's sake; actions good absolutely, such as those a man does for his country without thinking of himself; actions good in their own nature; actions that are not good simply for the individual, since individual interests are selfish.[8]

Adam Smith in *The Wealth of Nations* supposedly captured the dominant motivation of business people. For Smith, business is motivated by economic self-interest, the acquisitive impulse, and hence it is not a virtuous or *noble* endeavor. It is, however, a *respectable* occupation, he argues, because the aggregate of "self-interests" results in great benefits for the whole society. If each person pursues his or her own self-interest, then the common good will be enhanced, according to Smith. He saw that the sum total of individual self-interests resulted in a market economy that allowed all to better their own condition. A market economy is moral because it raises the level of living for all—even though it is based on acquisitiveness. In Smith's words:

> In civilized society he stands at all times in need of the cooperation and assistance of great multitudes, while his whole life is scarce sufficient to gain the friendship of a few persons. Man has almost constant occasion for the help of his brethren, and it is vain for him to expect it from his benevolence only. He will be more likely to prevail if he can interest their self-love in his favour, and show them that it is for their own advantage to do for him what he requires of them. Whoever offers to another a bargain of any kind proposes to do this. It is not from the benevolence of the butcher, the brewer, or the baker, that we expect our dinner, but from their regard to their own interest.[9]

The thrust of my course, however, is to say that Christians can and do participate in the market (business world) without being solely motivated by economic self-interest. The profit motive, that is, economic action based on self-interest, is not their single-minded concern. I suggest that business *is* a noble occupation when it is consciously concerned to enhance the common good, and not simply to make money. One can live a Christian vocation in the world of commerce. The course argues that it is not easy but that it is possible.

The role of business is changing in American society, expanding to encompass a wider role of service to the common good. For example, some corporations have resisted moving plants from the inner city to the suburbs because of a commitment to the community. Adam Smith assumed that God would work to transform self-interested behavior to a good end. His view of God's providence was naïve. He seemed to think that God would override human freedom and by a "hidden hand" make things come out for the common good in spite of bad judgment. Christians, as an imperative of their faith, must consciously and deliberately work for the common good.[10] The poor in the third world, pollution control, and the quality of life all need conscious care. We must make God's work our own. Christians who are managers are called to embody the faith, the hope, and the love of Christ, and by their free decisions to make the world a more humane place. The hope is that some of our students may be called to be leaders in this challenging work.

NOTES

1. For further information, write Professor Ken Milani, Department of Accountancy, University of Notre Dame, Notre Dame, IN 46556.

2. For further information, write Rev. David Tyson, C.S.C., Department of Management, University of Notre Dame, Notre Dame, IN 46556.

3. Synod of Bishops, "Justice in the World," *The Gospel of Peace and Justice: Catholic Social Teaching since Pope John,* ed. Joseph Gremillion (Maryknoll, N.Y.: Orbis Books, 1976), p. 514.

4. Upton Sinclair, *The Jungle* (New York: New American Library, 1960), p. 310.

5. "Pastoral Constitution on the Church in the Modern World," *The Documents of Vatican II,* ed. Walter M. Abbott, S.J. (New York: Guild Press, 1966), par. 64, p. 273.

6. Quoted in Richard Reeves, "What Ehrlichman Really Thought of Nixon," *New York* 9, no. 19 (May 10, 1976): 42.

7. Robert Bolt, *A Man for All Seasons* (New York: Random House, 1962), p. xii.

8. Aristotle, *Rhetoric,* 1, chap. 9.

9. Adam Smith, *The Wealth of Nations,* ed. Edwin Cannan (Chicago, Ill.: University of Chicago Press, 1976), p. 18.

10. Some interpreters of Adam Smith, citing his earlier work in ethics, argue that Smith assumed that the good citizen would promote the common good. Cf. Adam Smith, *The Theory of Moral Sentiments* (Indianapolis, Ind.: Liberty Classics, 1976; originally published in 1753, twenty years earlier than *The Wealth of Nations*).

SELECTED READINGS FOR FACULTY

Bradshaw, Thornton, and David Vogel. *Corporations and Their Critics.* New York: McGraw-Hill, 1981.

Calian, Carnegie Samuel. *The Gospel according to the Wall Street Journal.* Atlanta, Ga.: John Knox Press, 1975.

Cavanagh, Gerald F., S.J. *American Business Values in Transition.* Englewood Cliffs, N.J.: Prentice-Hall, 1976.

Clark, John W. *Religion and the Moral Standards of American Businessmen.* Chicago, Ill.: South-Western Publishing, 1966.

Dawson, Christopher. *Progress and Religion.* Garden City, N.Y.: Doubleday, 1960.

Ellis, John Tracy. *American Catholicism.* Chicago, Ill.: University of Chicago Press, 1969.

Forell, George, and William H. Lazareth, eds. *Corporate Ethics: The Quest for Moral Authority.* Philadelphia, Pa.: Fortress Press, 1980.

Fuller, Reginald H., and Brian K. Rice. *Christianity and the Affluent Society.* Grand Rapids, Mich.: Wm. B. Eerdmans, 1966.

Gustafson, James M. *Protestant and Roman Catholic Ethics.* Chicago, Ill.: University of Chicago Press, 1978.

Holland, Joe, and Peter Henriot, S.J. *Social Analysis: Linking Faith and Justice.* Washington, D.C.: Center of Concern, 1980.

Houck, John W., and Oliver F. Williams, C.S.C., eds. *Catholic Social Teaching and the U.S. Economy: Working Papers for a Bishops' Pastoral.* Washington, D.C.: University Press of America, 1984.

———, eds. *Co-Creation and Capitalism: John Paul II's* Laborem Exercens. Washington, D.C.: University Press of America, 1983.

Jones, Donald G., ed. *Business, Religion, and Ethics.* Cambridge, Mass.: Oelgeschlager, Gunn & Hain, 1982.

Kelly, George A. *The Catholic Church and the American Poor.* New York: Alba House, 1976.

Kerans, Patrick. *Sinful Social Structures.* New York: Paulist Press, 1974.

Maguire, Daniel C. *A New American Justice.* Garden City, N.Y.: Doubleday, 1980.

Maida, Adam J. *Issues in the Labor-Management Dialogue: Church Perspectives.* St. Louis, Mo.: Catholic Health Association of the United States, 1982.

Novak, Michael. *The Spirit of Democratic Capitalism.* New York: Simon and Schuster, 1982.

O'Connell, Timothy E. *Principles for a Catholic Morality.* New York: Seabury Press, 1976.

Sampson, Anthony. *North-South: A Program for Survival.* Cambridge, Mass.: MIT Press, 1980. Brandt Commission report.

Schumpeter, Joseph A. *Can Capitalism Survive?* New York: Harper & Row, 1950.

Silk, Leonard, and David Vogel. *Ethics and Profits: The Crisis of Confidence in American Business.* New York: Simon and Schuster, 1976.

Stevens, Edward. *Business Ethics.* New York: Paulist Press, 1979.

Tawney, R. H. *Religion and the Rise of Capitalism.* New York: New American Library, 1926.

Thomas Aquinas. *Treatise on Law.* Chicago, Ill.: Regnery Company, 1970.

Velasquez, Manuel G. *Business Ethics.* Englewood Cliffs, N.J.: Prentice-Hall, 1982.

Weber, Max. *The Protestant Ethic and the Spirit of Capitalism.* New York: Charles Scribner's Sons, 1958.

11

Education

MILDRED HAIPT, O.S.U.
COLLEGE OF NEW ROCHELLE

In preparation for this essay on educating for justice and peace in teacher education, I conducted a survey of ninety colleges and universities having membership in both the Association of Catholic Colleges and Universities (ACCU) and the American Association of Colleges for Teacher Education (AACTE). The latter organization represents a group of colleges and universities with a special commitment to teacher education. My intent in surveying preservice teacher-education programs was, first, to determine the extent to which teacher educators incorporate concepts, issues, and courses related to justice and peace education into their professional-studies curriculum. A second purpose was to identify the interest and needs of teacher educators for developing such practices.

The questionnaires were distributed (Spring 1983) to the institutions' liaison persons listed in the *AACTE 1982 Directory.* Forty percent of those who received the two-page survey responded. Among the thirty-six persons who completed the questionnaires, twenty-three (64%) checked "yes" to the question were they interested in including justice and peace education in the professional-studies curriculum of their teacher-education programs. Eleven persons (30%) indicated they were not interested in doing so, and two (6%) checked neither response.

Reasons cited by the teacher-educator respondents for and against the inclusion of justice and peace education in the professional-studies curriculum of teacher-education programs provide a background for this essay. In the opinion of this author, peace and justice concepts, issues, attitudes, and skills do have a rightful place in the preparation of teachers. The position has been arrived at after several years of reading, reflection, discussion, and attempts to educate for justice and peace through the professional-studies curriculum. It is taken with due respect for those teacher educators who maintain that peace and justice are more appropriately addressed through various liberal-arts courses and campus organizations and activities.

"YES" TO JUSTICE AND PEACE IN TEACHER EDUCATION

The basis for justice and peace education in teacher education at Catholic colleges and universities rests upon three sets of factors: those that pertain to the Roman Catholic Church; to present-day society; and to the teaching profession itself.

The 1983 United States Catholic Bishops' pastoral letter on war and peace states that the content of the letter will become a "living message" only through the work of educators. Moreover, it expresses the confidence that "all models of Catholic education, which have served the church in our country so well in so many ways, will creatively rise to the challenge of peace."[1] If graduates of today's colleges and universities, representing the Christian tradition, are to become the teachers of tomorrow, they have a responsibility to raise moral and religious questions about contemporary issues in education. For example:

- Is it right that more than half the school-aged children in the world are not receiving any formal education?[2]
- Is it right that in America two million children are barred from school because they are considered "different"?[3]
- Should more than half of every federal income-tax dollar be spent on defense and the military while millions of children do not have adequate food, health care, and educational opportunities?[4]
- How are women, minorities, and the handicapped discriminated against in the educational system?

Surely, those of us who bear the gospel message and carry on the religious values and traditions of the church cannot avoid questions such as these. Nor can we say that true peace is possible without justice in these matters as well as in other areas of our life. As Betty Reardon wrote:

> In its simplest terms, peace is a state of order in which justice can be pursued without violence. . . . If we are working toward justice, then we are working toward a state of affairs in which as many members of society as possible have a fair share of power and wealth. People will have a fair share of wealth and power if they have enough of both to fulfill themselves and to determine within the limits of the good of the community how they want to live.[5]

A second set of factors that urges us to train teachers to educate for justice and peace is found in society, which today provides a radically unique situation. For the first time since the creation of the world, humankind has the power to destroy the planet by the use of nuclear weapons. Planet earth is threatened by survival in a world that produces nuclear arms daily. Stockpiles of weapons and militarization are on the increase in many of the developing as well as the industrialized nations. At the same time, there is a continuing tendency among individuals, groups, and nations to settle conflicts and disputes by means of violence. Evidence of this type of behavior in the classroom prompted one teacher, Patricia S. Ward, to write:

> Pupils just didn't seem to possess the important skills needed to work and play successfully in groups, to cooperate with each other on a daily basis, or to resolve differences without resorting to shouting matches—or worse—fistfights. And equally troubling, during our Friday morning current-events hour, students were reporting on riots, assassinations, and armed conflicts as if they were inevitable everyday matters—like the weather. Violence in its many forms had become an accepted part of my students' consciousness and daily lives. As naïve and old-fashioned as it sounded even to me, I knew I had to introduce a new subject into my curriculum: peace.[6]

Experiences such as this emphasize the need for educators to help build a more equitable society, one in which humankind struggles for peace at any cost. The classroom is one place where teacher and student alike can learn how to achieve peace at a personal, interpersonal, and structural level.

The third set of factors that forms a rationale for justice and peace education in teacher education pertains to the teaching profession itself. Physicians, lawyers, and scientists are not the only professionals speaking out on war and peace. Individually and corporately, teachers have become part of the nuclear-education movement. Educators for Social Responsibility (ESR) was founded in May 1981 by teachers and parents concerned about the threat of nuclear war. Within three years ESR had some seventy chapters in twenty-seven states across the country. Members strive to understand issues related to the arms race. They also aim to teach "the skills of analysis, cooperation, and negotiation; the knowledge of our social, economic and biological interdependence; and the ethics that will help ensure the survival of humanity."[7]

On June 25, 1982, Willard H. McGuire, then president of the National Education Association (NEA), gave an address before the second special session on disarmament of the United Nations General Assembly. He concluded his remarks with these words: "We must educate the world's children to believe that real peace is possible. A peace free of nuclear threats and counter threats. A peace where human life is something more than a list of numbers on some benighted general's chart. Such a peace can only be possible through world disarmament. The world's teachers must work toward this goal."[8]

Several curricula have already been developed to assist classroom teachers to teach about war and peace, the arms race, and disarmament. The most noteworthy include the following: (1) "Choices: A Unit on Conflict and Nuclear War," prepared by the National Education Association and the Union of Concerned Scientists. This is a two-week unit for junior high school students, and grew out of a July 1982 resolution of the NEA National Assembly. (2) "Crossroads: Quality of Life in a Nuclear World," prepared by the Educational Task Force for Peace in Cambridge, Massachusetts. The booklets incorporate week-long curricula for secondary school English, social studies, and science classes. (3) "A Day of Dialogue," prepared by Educators for Social Responsibility as a planning and curriculum resource guide dealing with nuclear issues in the classroom. The materials are appropriate to grades K–12.

Other resources, such as Edward Van Merrienboer's *Seeking a Just Society,*[9] contain explicit religious and moral treatment of peace and justice. They also give practical suggestions for implementing education for justice and peace in the classroom. While these materials attempt to engage the religious motivations of elementary and secondary school students, they are primarily meant to provide a framework for students to think about problems raised by social injustices in a nuclear age and to help them make life-giving decisions.

It is important to note that the impetus for justice and peace education at the elementary and secondary levels is coming not only from teachers and other professional groups, but also from local citizens. The action of the School Committee of the Cambridge, Massachusetts, City Council illustrates the kind of mandate on education for the nuclear age that is possible for schools at the district level. Members of this committee voted to support "children's and young people's understanding of the history, scientific background, economics, and politics of waging peace in the nuclear age."[10] Milwaukee's school board also voted to incorporate "peace studies and the dilemma of the nuclear arms race" into the curriculum.[11]

While it may be true that these actions represent pockets of interest, and that they are encountering some opposition, it is also fair to say that the nuclear dialogue is growing rapidly among school people. Whether the introduction of the dialogue into the classroom is formal or informal, the issues are being raised. One example of the growing awareness of the nuclear threat, among teachers and students, struck this writer while observing a humanities lesson at a large local high school. Tacked to the board in front of the room were the following sayings:

- Stop the arms race, not the human race.
- Split wood, not atoms.
- Better active today than radioactive tomorrow.

These statements, crowded among the bulletin-board announcements, the fire-drill regulations, and the class reading lists contain a serious and sobering message.

This experience relates to a cartoon that appeared around the same time in the *Phi Delta Kappan*. The cartoon showed a young child and an adult in the room of a modern-art gallery. They were standing in front of an abstract line drawing and the child was saying, "I see it as humanity's struggle for identity in a threatening world and the hope of a new day shining through—either that or a duck." A conclusion that can be drawn in both instances is that the interpretation and impact depend upon the viewer's point of view. The understanding proceeds through the eye of the beholder.

WAYS OF INTEGRATING JUSTICE AND PEACE EDUCATION INTO TEACHER EDUCATION

Several of the teacher educators who responded negatively to the question on including justice and peace education in the professional-studies curriculum of teacher-education programs mentioned the matter of time. Some indicated that there are already too many needs and other topics to be covered; other respondents made reference to the fact that they were obliged to fulfill standards imposed by the state, which left no room in the curriculum for justice and peace education.

Once again, the position taken by this author is that, given a justice and peace perspective, teacher educators *can* find various ways of incorporating concepts, attitudes, and skills related to education for justice and peace into the content and process of the teacher-education program. Moreover, by changing their methods of presentation and the emphases given to certain concepts and issues, teachers can educate for justice and peace within a set program and a limited time frame.

When presented with the question, "How do you think peace and justice can *best* be included in the professional-studies curriculum of your teacher-education programs?" thirteen of the respondents checked the infusion of concepts, such as community and cooperation, and an additional eleven checked the incorporation of issues, such as conflict management and children's rights. Only three of those who answered this question checked "a separate course." Thus the preferred method among this group of teacher educators is the integration of justice and peace into the existing professional-studies curriculum.

We shall now describe three models or possible ways of accomplishing this integration of concepts and issues and thereby preparing teachers to educate for justice and peace. The first is an adaptation of the social-analysis model developed by Joe Holland and Peter Henriot, S.J. The second is a problem-posing strategy for teaching critical thinking based on the work of Paulo Freire and developed by the Nuclear Disarmament Project of the Archdiocese of San Francisco, California. The third is an infusion model designed and disseminated by the Justice and Peace Education Council of New York.

The Social-Analysis Model

The social-analysis model suggests that there are injustices present in all social institutions, including education. According to Holland and Henriot, the formal analysis that is at the heart of the social-analysis methodology aims "to obtain a more complete picture of a social situation by exploring its historical and structural relationships."[12] Because justice in the practical order relates to wealth and power, it is possible (as a first step) to identify injustices by reflecting upon personal experiences in the educational structure, especially as they relate to power and to the distribution of personnel and material resources.

A second step in the social-analysis process is to analyze the experience by posing questions such as: Who is paying for education in our society or in a particular system? Who is making the decisions with regard to what is being taught? Who is benefiting the most from the education? Does the educational system promote justice and equity, and protect human rights? If not, why not?

A third step in the social-analysis process requires teacher and students to explore the culture of ordinary people and to find the symbols and myths that are used to express their values, hopes, and dreams. In this particular analysis, one would further need to ask how these connect with educational opportunities. What things or conditions thwart people's educational values and ideals? Or, on the other hand, how does the educational system in its present or in a reconstructed form contribute to their attainment?

Out of these reflections, teacher and students can begin to generate a course of action to rectify the injustices present in education. They can, for example, advocate plans that provide for a more equitable distribution of tax dollars to poorer school districts, and that continue to remove barriers of discrimination against the poor, the handicapped, and racial and ethnic minorities. To make the social-analysis process productive, they need to take direct action at the local level that can and will impact on the system.

The social-analysis model described here can readily be applied to the "Foundations of Education" course. In this case, the educational system provides the content for analysis. However, the content differs, depending upon the nature of the course taught. The social-analysis approach teaches a process; the content that the teacher selects varies and transcends the limits of the professional-studies curriculum.

A Model for Positive Problem-Posing Strategy

The model for positive problem-posing strategy was first developed by Paulo Freire for adult literacy programs in Brazil. Freire's approach has been applied to various subjects by many groups and individuals throughout the world. It begins with the personal experiences of the students and the social context in which they occur. It seeks to empower the students either to accept their life situation or to challenge and change it. The role of the teacher is not to transmit knowledge but, rather, to learn jointly with the students. Analysis and critical thinking are two skills central to the use of this model.

The problem-posing process has three parts: listening, dialogue, and action.

Together they constitute what Freire calls "conscientization," which, in the words of Bruce Boston, "means an awakening of the consciousness, a shift in mentality involving an accurate, realistic assessment of one's locus in nature and society; a capacity to analyze the causes and consequences of that locus; the ability to compare it with other possibilities; and finally a disposition to act in order to change the received situation."[13]

Freire's approach is appropriate for use with student teachers or with students who have engaged in field work. It begins with students and teachers describing to one another the concerns that they have experienced through their field work, and by their examining together the social situations that contain the problems.

Violence in some form or other is a concern that frequently arises in this type of sharing. The violence may be expressed by an outburst of words, by destruction of property, or by physical fighting. Forms of violence observed and experienced by the group are listed in simple declarative statements such as the following:

- Two students were hitting one another in the school corridor after lunch.
- A student let out a stream of swear words when he received a failure on his test paper.
- A rash of initials, words, and sayings have appeared on the walls of the school.

Dialogue follows the identification of the groups' concerns. At this stage, the teacher encodes the problem of violence in the schools and presents a "discussion-object." The teacher engages the students in a role-playing situation, for example, that illustrates the use of abusive language. Following the role play (in other instances this encoding may be in the form of stories, photographs, drawings, songs, collages, cartoons, etc.) the teacher asks a series of inductive questions to decode the discussion-object and to identify the problem. The questions might run as follows:

- What did you observe about the teacher, offender, and onlookers in this situation?
- What emotions did they express? How would you feel as a teacher or onlooker in this situation?
- How does this role play match your own experience with student outbursts in the classroom or school?
- What is the problem portrayed in this scene? What causes the problem for the student and for the teacher?
- How could this scenario be changed so that the violence does not occur?
- What actions can you as teacher or student take to prevent verbal abuse of this kind?

In the third and final phase of the conscientization process the group articulates various action steps. Since role play was used to code the problem initially, it would be helpful at this point to role play the alternatives for action identified by the group. This would ensure that teachers learn new ways of relating to students that prevent abusive behavior and respond to the problem in a positive, constructive manner.

Teacher educators have a valuable resource for teaching creative approaches to living and problem-solving in Prutzman's *The Friendly Classroom for a Small Planet*.[14] The program of exercises presented in this handbook is built around four themes, namely: communication, cooperation, affirmation, and conflict resolution. This program is an excellent supplement to the problem-posing strategy insofar as it attempts to get at the roots of conflict and violence by building positive self-concepts and a sense of mutual trust within a supportive atmosphere.

A Model of Concept Infusion

Although the infusion method is often talked about, little has been written to describe the method in detail. The Justice and Peace Education Council of New York has developed a series of curriculum training workshops and a manual called "Infusion."[15] In the opening pages of the manual, the infusion technique is described as "incorporating justice and peace concepts, knowledge, skills, attitudes, and activities into appropriate segments of the basic content of the curriculum. It consists of matching concepts and matching activities." Included in the concepts related to justice and peace are communication, cooperation, interdependence, multicultural understanding, human rights, liberation, power, nonviolence, citizenship, and empowerment. The workshop manual contains descriptive elements of these and similar concepts. However, teacher educators can adapt the council's list in terms of their own audience and subject matter. It is important to note that the concepts are to be seen and studied in relation to the socioeconomic and cultural context of society.

After the concepts have been identified and discussed, teacher and students explore ways in which the concepts are integrated or could be integrated into the existing professional-studies curriculum or into the subjects taught at the elementary and secondary levels. The group then selects those concepts that match the topics taught in particular courses. For example, in treating the topic of education and schooling, the concept of human rights can be incorporated into the lesson without compromising its original goal.

As noted in the United Nations Declaration of the Rights of the Child (1959), every child is entitled to an education as a human right. What barriers are there in the United States and around the world that prevent millions of children from exercising that right? What can be done to make schooling and educational opportunities available to all children? Why do some countries make a conscious choice to perpetuate illiteracy among the people?

According to the infusion model, it is always through the learning activities that the concepts are communicated. Thus, introducing preservice or in-service teachers to the United Nations Declaration of the Rights of the Child provides a matching activity for the matching concept of human rights that accompanies the basic lesson. UNICEF (United Nations Children's Fund) has slides that show children from different countries of the world. A set of these slides or comparable photographs can serve as "codes" for a discussion of children's rights. The plight of children in other countries can be compared to those in the United States. As one of the Justice and Peace Education Council members has written, "[The infusion method] does not make justice/peace education an 'add on,' but demonstrates that justice/peace concepts belong appropriately wherever human learning takes place."[16]

ORIENTATION TO TEACHING (two credits)

GOALS

The purpose of this course is to examine the ways in which school, community, and society respond to the educational needs of youth, and the role of teachers in the educational system and in society. The course is also designed to help students make a realistic appraisal of their own strengths and weaknesses, and aspirations in relation to the teaching profession.

Since a major part of the course is devoted to a study of the educational system, with its historical structure and function, the student is introduced to the process of social analysis. Both positive and negative aspects or injustices of the system are explored. Education for justice and peace is also emphasized by the incorporation of "matching concepts" (such as cooperation, interdependence, nonviolence, and human rights), and "matching activities."

RESOURCE MATERIALS

Text: Ellis, Arthur, et al. *Introduction to the Foundations of Education.* Englewood Cliffs, N.J.: Prentice-Hall, 1981.

Beckman, David M., et al. *The Overseas List: Opportunities for Living and Working in Developing Countries.* Minneapolis, Minn.: Augsburg Publishing House, 1979.

Prutzman, Priscilla, et al. *The Friendly Classroom for a Small Planet.* Wayne, N.J.: Avery Publishing Group, 1978.

Volan, Sissel. *An Approach to Peace Education* (UNICEF Development Kit no. 6 [1980], available from Development Education Office, UNICEF, United Nations, NY 10017).

Topic	Matching Concepts	Matching Activities
I. *Teaching: The Personal Choice.* Who are the teachers who have made a difference in your life? Why do you want to be a teacher? What are your concerns about education?	Communication, Cooperation	Informal survey of overseas experiences (e.g., schooling or travel). Did you talk with other students abroad? What were your conversations about? What did you learn about their educational system and experiences?
II. *Teaching: The Profession.* What opportunities are available for teachers? What are the rights and responsibilities of today's teachers? How have organizations helped or hindered the profession?	Interdependence, Multicultural Understanding	Brainstorming in small groups for five minutes. What are some opportunities for teaching at home and abroad (i.e., school and nonschool settings)? See Beckman, et al., *The Overseas List: Opportunities for Living and Working in Developing Countries.*
III. *Education and Schooling.* What is the difference between education and schooling? What is the context (socioeconomic, physical, psychological) in which education and schooling take place? (Begin the "social analysis" cycle at this point; develop it over the next four topics.)	Human Rights	Presentation and Discussion. Introduce students to the UN Declaration of Rights of the Child. In view of the health, education, and labor statistics, how are these rights observed? violated? What is being done to promote observance of human rights?
IV. *Historical Perspective.* How did the educational system develop in the United States? Have we developed schools that meet our needs? What other kinds of educational systems are there in the world?	Liberation	Presentation and discussion. How do countries fare when they do not have a well-developed school system? What kinds of educational opportunities do the people have? What is being done to expand these opportunities (e.g., literacy campaigns and nonformal education)?
V. *Political Dimensions.* What are the respective roles of the federal, state,	Power, Structural Transformation	Comparisons. Draw comparisons between a country such as the United States,

and local governments in education? Who has the critical decision-making power at these various levels of the structure? Who benefits from the decisions? Who gets excluded from the decision-making process?

which has locally controlled school systems, and one in which the federal government controls the school system.

VI. *Financial Dimensions.* Who pays for public and private schooling? What is the per-pupil expenditure from state to state and district to district? Who makes the decisions about how the monies are used? Who gains and loses from the way resources are used?

Distribution, Interdependence

Simulation. Planning a school budget. Examine federal, state, and local budget allocations. What would you do with money if tax dollars were diverted from war and military budgets?

VII. *Contemporary Issues in Schooling.* What issues (global and local) impact on the school? What steps can be taken to resolve the issues, to bring about more equitable and just educational opportunities?

Peace, Nonviolence, Conflict (analysis and management)

CCRC slide show. Role playing and conflict-management activities: examine forms of violence prevalent in the schools. How do we contribute to that violence? How do computer games contribute to that violence? What can be done to resolve conflict? See Prutzman, et al., *The Friendly Classroom.*

VIII. *Curriculum: Purpose, Patterns, Techniques.* What are our educational values and goals? How does the curriculum promote these values and contribute to the attainment of these goals?

Citizenship, Global Community

Panel with foreign students from the college community.

IX. *Multicultural Education.* What makes ours a multicultural society? What values are important in a multicultural society? What militates against these values? How effectively does our educational system serve a multicultural society?

Multicultural Understanding

Learning stations in the media center. View materials related to global issues that bear on education (e.g., sexism).

| X. *Future Directions.* What will the schools be like in the next twenty to fifty years? Will the changes help people to adjust to society or to reconstruct it? | Empowerment, Stewardship | Draw up a scenario. What will the world be like in twenty years, fifty years? What will you be doing? How can you as teacher and educator shape the future? |

NOTE: The remaining five weeks of the semester are spent visiting field sites (multicultural and multiracial) and videotaping in an effort to "try on" some teaching styles.

Application of the Models

This course outline incorporates both the social-analysis and concept-infusion models. I chose the social-analysis model because the content of the "Orientation to Teaching" course, as a whole, addresses itself to various aspects of the educational system. That is to say, the social, political, and economic dimensions of education constitute major topics of the foundations course.

A consideration of the politics of American education, for example, illustrates the appropriateness of the social-analysis model. Under this topic are discussed the respective roles of the federal, state, and local governments, the process of decision-making that directly affects schooling at the district level, formal and informal power groups influencing education, and who in the society benefits and who loses from the educational decisions that are made. Using this model, one can also draw comparisons between a centralized or federally controlled educational system of a foreign government, and the American educational system that is more decentralized or locally controlled.

The social-analysis model introduces a cyclical diagram that provides a framework for similar discussions pertaining to the social and economic factors of the educational system. Such a diagram also serves as a focal point for the higher-level thought processes of analysis, synthesis, and evaluation. Students of education can begin either with a description of the educational system as they know and experience it, or by expressing the educational values, hopes, and dreams that they share with their contemporaries. In each case, they eventually move through two other steps, which involve a formal analysis of the educational structure in terms of injustices, and identifying courses of action to rectify them.

Several key concepts emerge from the use of this methodology. As indicated in the syllabus, they include the ideas of power, structural transformation, distribution, interdependence, human rights, conflict, multicultural understanding, and nonviolence. Thus the infusion model becomes a natural corollary to the social-analysis model. When school finances are being considered, teachers can stress an equitable distribution of resources and personnel. A matching activity of the distribution concept would be to debate the relative merits of different funding formulae or to design a budget at the federal, state, and local levels that would reflect education as a top priority.

According to the infusion model outlined by the Justice and Peace Education Council of New York, key concepts are integrated into the course by means of their matching activities. Choice of the latter depends upon the subject matter and the particular needs and interests, knowledge and skills of the students. The purpose of the activities is to take learners beyond a basic comprehension of the concepts to a realization of their fundamental importance in contributing to a peaceful and just system of education.

In addition to the methods already described, the "Orientation to Teaching" course lends itself to an issues approach. Contemporary issues in schooling offer teacher educators an opportunity to consider problems—such as violence in the schools—that have a direct bearing on justice and peace. In instances where students are also in the field on a regular basis, the model for positive problem-posing strategy might likewise be employed.

All three models discussed in this essay are intended to show how justice and peace can be integrated into the professional-studies curriculum of teacher-education programs without introducing a separate course or set of courses. Implicit in the effective use of the three approaches suggested in this essay are two factors: (1) teacher educators have and continue to develop a justice and peace perspective; (2) a commitment on the part of teacher educators to train teachers to educate for justice and peace. This commitment requires that teacher educators themselves begin to possess the knowledge, skills, and attitudes that promote justice and peace at the personal, interpersonal, and structural levels. Only then will they be able to heed the admonition of Pope John Paul II, "To reach peace, teach peace."

NOTES

1. United States Catholic Bishops, "The Challenge of Peace: God's Promise and Our Response," *Origins* 13, no. 1 (May 19, 1983): 28.

2. According to figures on education released by the World Bank (1974) and cited in "Literacy and World Population," *Population Bulletin* 30, no. 2 (1976; Population Reference Bureau, Washington, D.C.).

3. See Thomas J. Cottle, *Barred from School* (Washington, D.C.: New Republic Book Co., 1976).

4. United States Budget, 1983, Office of Management and Budget, Washington, D.C.

5. Betty Reardon, "Education for Peace and Social Justice," *Geographical Perspectives,* no. 34 (Fall 1974). Reprint published by Department of Geography, University of Northern Iowa, and the Iowa Council for Geographic Education, Cedar Falls, IA 50613.

6. In Patricia S. Ward and Jeane J. Kirkpatrick, "How Your Students Can Give Peace a Chance," *Instructor* 91, no. 3 (October 1981): 76.

7. See "Educating for a World Free from the Threat of Nuclear Destruction," a

brochure available from Educators for Social Responsibility, 23 Garden St., Cambridge, MA 02138.

8. Willard H. McGuire, "An Address before the Second Special Session on Disarmament of the United Nations General Assembly," June 25, 1982. Mimeographed.

9. Edward Van Merrienboer, O.P., *Seeking a Just Society* (Washington, D.C.: National Catholic Educational Association, 1978).

10. Reported in *Salt* 2, no. 10 (November–December 1982): 9.

11. Reported in *Wall Street Journal,* May 24, 1983.

12. Joseph Holland and Peter Henriot, *Social Analysis: Linking Faith and Justice* (Maryknoll, N.Y.: Orbis Books, 1983), p. 98.

13. Bruce Boston, "The Politics of Knowing: The Pedagogy of Paulo Freire," *New Catholic World* 216 (January–February 1973): 28.

14. Priscilla Prutzman, et al., *The Friendly Classroom for a Small Planet* (Wayne, N.J.: Avery Publishing Group, 1978).

15. "Infusion" (New York: Justice and Peace Education Council, 1981). Mimeographed.

16. Loretta Carey, "Adapting the Infusion Method," *Momentum* 13, no. 3 (October 1982): 14.

SELECTED READINGS FOR FACULTY

Baines, James. "The Peace Paradigm." *The Whole Earth Papers* 1, no. 1; reprinted 1983.

Boston, Bruce. "The Politics of Knowing: The Pedagogy of Paulo Freire." *New Catholic World* 216 (January–February, 1973).

Boulding, Elise. *Children's Rights and the Wheel of Life.* New Brunswick, N.J.: Transaction Books, 1979.

Carey, Loretta. "Adapting the Infusion Method." *Momentum* 13, no. 3 (October 1982).

Cottle, Thomas J. *Barred from School: Two Million Children.* Washington, D.C.: New Republic Book Co., 1976.

Educators for Social Responsibility. *A Day of Dialogue: Planning and Curriculum Resource Guide/Dealing with Nuclear Issues in the Classroom.* Published in 1982, and available from Educators for Social Responsibility, 639 Massachusetts Ave., Cambridge, MA 02139.

Elam, Stanley M. "Educators and the Nuclear Threat." *Phi Delta Kappan* 64, no. 8 (April 1983).

Fenton, Thomas P., ed. *Education for Justice: A Resource Manual.* Maryknoll, N.Y.: Orbis Books, 1975.

Henderson, George, ed. *Education for Peace: Focus on Mankind.* Washington, D.C.: Association for Supervision and Curriculum Development, 1973.

Hofbauer, Rita, G.N.S.H., et al. *Making Social Analysis Useful.* Silver Spring, Md.: Leadership Conference of Women Religious, 1983.

Holland, Joseph, and Peter Henriot, S.J. *Social Analysis: Linking Faith and Justice.* Maryknoll, N.Y.: Orbis Books, 1983.

Jobs with Peace Education Taskforce. *Crossroads: Quality of Life in a Nuclear World.* Published in 1982, and available from Jobs with Peace Education Taskforce, 10 West St., Boston, MA 02111.

Justice and Peace Education Council. "Infusion—Curriculum Training Workshop." Mimeographed manual distributed to workshop participants. New York: Justice and Peace Education Council, 1981.

Kownacki, Mary Lou, O.S.B., ed. *A Race to Nowhere: An Arms Race Primer for Catholics.* Chicago, Ill.: Pax Christi-USA, 1980.

McGinnis, James and Kathleen, et al. *Educating for Peace and Justice: A Manual for Teachers.* St. Louis, Mo.: Institute for Peace and Justice 1981.

McGuire, Willard H. "An Address before the Second Special Session on Disarmament of the UN General Assembly," June 25, 1982. Mimeographed.

Meier, Paulette, and Beth McPherson. *Growing Up in a Nuclear World: A Resource Guide for Elementary School Teachers.* Published in 1983 by Nuclear Information and Resource Service, 1346 Connecticut Ave., N.W., Washington, DC 20036.

——. *Nuclear Dangers: A Resource Guide for Secondary School Teachers.* Published in 1983 by Nuclear Information and Resource Service, 1346 Connecticut Ave., N.W., Washington, D.C. 20036.

National Education Association. *Choices: A Unit on Conflict and Nuclear War.* Washington, DC: National Education Association, 1983.

Proceedings of the Symposium, "The Role of the Academy in Addressing the Issues of Nuclear War," Washington, D.C., 1982. Sponsored by Hobart and William Smith colleges, Geneva, N.Y., and American Council on Education, Washington, D.C.

Prutzman, Priscilla, et al. *The Friendly Classroom for A Small Planet.* Wayne, N.J.: Avery Publishing Group, 1978.

Reardon, Betty. "Education for Peace and Social Justice." *Geographical Perspectives,* no. 34 (Fall 1974). Reprint published by the Department of Geography, University of Northern Iowa, and the Iowa Council for Geographic Education, Cedar Falls, IA 50613.

——. *Militarization, Security, and Peace Education: A Guide for Concerned Citizens.* Valley Forge, Pa.: United Ministries in Education, 1982.

Sivard, Ruth L. *World Military and Social Expenditures.* Leesburg, Va.: World Priorities (Box 1003), 1982.

Teachers College Record 84, no. 1 (Fall 1982); entire issue.

Thompson, E. P., and Dan Smith. *Protest and Survive.* New York: Monthly Review Press, 1981.

Tonkin, Humphrey, and Jane Edwards. *The World in the Curriculum: Curricular Strategies for the 21st Century.* New Rochelle, N.Y.: Change Magazine Press, 1981.

United States Catholic Bishops. "The Challenge of Peace: God's Promise and Our Response." *Origins* 13, no. 1 (May 19, 1983).

Van Merrienboer, Edward, O.P. *Seeking a Just Society: An Educational Design.* Washington, D.C.: National Catholic Educational Association, 1978.

Volan, Sissel. *An Approach to Peace Education.* UNICEF Development Kit no. 6. United Nations, N.Y.: UNICEF, 1980.

Wallerstein, Nina, M.P.H., and Pia Moriarty. "Teaching about Nuclear War: A Positive Problem-Posing Strategy." Archdiocese of San Francisco, Calif.: Nuclear Disarmament Project, Commission on Social Justice, 117 Diamond St., n.d.

Wien, Barbara, ed. *Peace and World Order Studies: A Curriculum Guide.* 4th ed. New York: World Policy Institute, 1984.

12

Engineering

THOMAS A. SHANNON
WORCESTER POLYTECHNIC INSTITUTE

OVERVIEW OF ISSUES IN ENGINEERING EDUCATION

The perception of science as value-free has a long and honored tradition. It forms, consequently, the major value framework in which science is understood by scientists, as well as by a majority of other interested citizens. As a result, science and scientists have been able to stay free from many of the social or political controversies that have involved many other groups in society. The laboratory was perceived as a place in which pure knowledge was pursued for its own sake. Scientists were engaged in the exciting work of describing the basic elements of the universe. They were concerned with discovering how things work. They were fascinated by the interrelation of many little bits of knowledge and the consequent integration of theories to explain broader and broader areas of human knowledge and understanding. Because of this orientation, the perception that science and scientists have social obligations was deemphasized. Scientists were perceived to operate in a rarefied atmosphere to which few had access. It was almost as if society and science each went in its own direction, and the unspoken agreement was that there would be few relationships between them.

The first part of this paper was originally developed in collaboration with Professor Stephen Lammers of Lafayette College for presentation to the Ethics Section of the American Academy of Religion.

172

However, with the dawn of the atomic age, a new awareness came into the scientific community. This was the growing realization that the theoretical discoveries of scientists could have tremendous social impacts. The bombing of Hiroshima and Nagasaki demonstrated this as never before. Many persons began to be concerned about the so-called value-freedom of science and scientists. There was a growing perception that value judgments influenced what was studied and what was funded.

Another recent development that challenges the tradition of value-free science has come from studies in molecular genetics, especially the process of recombinant DNA. Here there has been a dramatic shift in the purpose of science. Traditionally, as stated above, science has been concerned with the *description* of nature. With the availability of the techniques of recombinant DNA, scientists now have the ability to *change* nature. Such a potential raises the question, On the basis of whose values will nature be changed? The 1980s have seen a tremendous debate concerning the developments in genetics, with special reference to the process of genetic engineering that has been made more easily available through the recombinant DNA process. Many value and ethical questions have been raised, many policy suggestions have been made and, as a result, a whole new discussion about values in science has arisen.

While there has been no complete resolution of the debate concerning whether or not science is "value-free," nonetheless many individuals have perceived that a variety of value questions surround the application of scientific discoveries and are at work in forming the kinds of research scientists engage in. Although science is done within a tremendously complicated mixture of public policy, fund allocation, and the desires of society, nonetheless scientists as members of a profession seem to be guided by values or ethical positions just as everyone else is.

These and other concerns provide a number of reasons why there is an interest in ethics courses in professional education. First, some students within the professional educational enterprise have found the process of professional education to be a dehumanizing one. It is hoped by some that the introduction of ethics courses may be part of a broader movement to make professional education more humane, and the professionals nicer persons. Second, many professionals and nonprofessionals argue that there should be training in ethics so that would-be professionals would become aware of the value dimensions implicit in what they do. For example, physicians should be aware that the concept of health is value-laden and engineers should know that their work often has profound social consequences. Third, other observers point to something that is potentially far more troubling. It has been argued that there has been a breakdown of whatever there was of a common social vision so that there is no longer a shared universe of discourse between the client and the professional. This new social situation is not necessarily an advance, but it is our new situation. Training in ethics would sensitize the professional to potential value differences in outlook between the client and the professional and would aid the professional by evaluating possible alternatives open in situations of this kind.

However, in the process of introducing ethics courses into the professional curriculum, it would appear that many proponents of these courses are not sensitive enough to the fact that not only value judgments but styles or forms of moral reasoning are already established in the professional context. One of the functions of an ethics course in a professional context is to open up the student to styles of moral reasoning other than his or her own and thus to broaden the student by showing him or her forms or styles of moral reasoning other than those that are already present in the particular professional context.

Styles of Moral Reasoning

What are these "styles of moral reasoning"? Thomas Ogletree distinguished three.[1] Ogletree identified these positions as "value-dominant," "obligation-dominant," and "virtue-dominant." He insisted that any perspective in ethics, to be adequate, should take account of the considerations raised by these styles of reasoning and that one could characterize different positions by discovering which of the orientations above was the dominant one.

In a value-dominant perspective, one focuses upon the significance of the consequences of action. Thus one speaks of what best enhances life or what minimizes pain where pain is unavoidable. Value-dominant thinking is a type of thinking that sees all values as equal. This type of thinking also points to the actors' personal stake in the values to be realized. The principal problem of this type of thinking is the relationship between means and ends. Thinkers in this tradition are taught to weigh the costs and the benefits of an action or, when they cannot know the results of an action with certainty, to weigh the risks against one another. Because of the interests and the results of action, there is a strong emphasis upon empirical investigation to determine exactly what will happen, when it is possible to make such a determination. The strength of this type of thinking is that it keeps us aware of the fact that many effects flow from action or inaction. Any ethical perspective must be interested in the results of actions at some point, even if a given perspective may not choose to put all the emphasis upon the expected or probable results of an action.

The second form of moral reasoning is called "obligation-dominant" by Ogletree. This type of moral reasoning insists that "a certain set of values— those linked to the minimal requisites of human life and dignity—have a privileged status in the valuation process." These values must be considered first in any valuation process, and only after they have been protected may one turn to other values. Second, this style of moral reasoning attends very carefully to the social circumstances within which the self is formed and continues to flourish. The others who form and shape the self make claims upon us and we have the feeling that we must serve them. Obligation thinking emphasizes the fact that others have needs, wants, and desires as *I* do and that at times they may require something of *me*. Ogletree argues that the strength of this type of thinking is that it prevents us from putting certain values on an equal level with others, that it forces us to give priority to certain values that enhance human dignity. Without this sort of procedure, certain fundamental rights would constantly be threatened in the name of some "greater good."

The third form of moral reasoning in Ogletree's schema is called "virtue-dominant." What is of concern in this style of moral reasoning is the formation of persons who are morally sensitive and morally mature so that they can make the best judgments possible for those situations in which they will find themselves. Virtue-dominant thinking usually involves an interest in developing persons who can "see" what is at stake morally. Virtue-dominant thinkers are concerned that persons be in contact with the reality of a situation so that they recognize the situation for what it is. This style of thinking proceeds out of the assumption that it is impossible to formulate in detail those moral principles that can guide us in all of the situations that we meet. Our lives are more confused and ambiguous than we care to admit and we often must confess that we have no firm guidelines for the situation in which we currently find ourselves. The only thing we can do in these situations of ambiguity is to try to understand what is happening, to act, and to be willing to defend our actions as the most appropriate ones, given our understanding of the situation.

WORCESTER POLYTECHNIC INSTITUTE: A CASE STUDY

Professional education can be characterized as swinging between the virtue and the value orientations described above. In some instances, there will be a heavier emphasis on the means and cost-benefit type of evaluation, which are common in the value orientation to ethics. In other instances, there will be a need for personal assessment and evaluation, which is characteristic of a virtue orientation toward ethics.

Worcester Polytechnic Institute (WPI) presents an interesting example of a response to several problems in engineering education, including the ethical ones. WPI, founded in 1865, began as a trade, or vocational, school for poor boys in the Worcester, Massachusetts, area. Its purpose was to teach these boys a craft so they would be able to be employed in various factories in the area. Eventually the school developed and became a college with accredited B.S., M.S., and Ph.D. programs in science, engineering, and management. With its emphasis on the development of professional knowledge and skills and its history as a vocational school, WPI quickly gained a reputation for producing engineers and scientists who were hardworking, dedicated, and competent. Thus, while research was not neglected, the emphasis was on producing engineers who were competent and qualified to do their job.

But after over a century of this orientation, other concerns, needs, and interests began to emerge. One major problem was tremendous unemployment in science and engineering in the early 1960s. This, in turn, affected enrollment. Another concern, raised especially at WPI, was that the educational system was too rigid. The curriculum contained extremely few electives and every major followed the same track, regardless of particular interests. Also, and more importantly, a feeling was beginning to develop among many of the faculty that the entire educational program was done within a professional vacuum. Students had little contact with engineers in the field and had little appreciation of the kinds of technical and social problems that they would be involved in resolving upon graduation. The process of education ironically, in some instances, served to narrow the students rather than to broaden them.

A faculty planning committee was established by the administration in 1969 to address these problems and to focus primarily on educational philosophy and curriculum reform. After two years, this committee submitted the WPI Plan, which consisted of a radical restructuring of graduation requirements, courses, teaching methodologies, and philosophy of education. The purpose of this educational program is "to impart to students an understanding of a section of science and technology and a mature understanding of themselves, and the needs of people around them."[2] Eventually, students should be able to demonstrate "that they can learn on their own, that they can translate the learning into worthwhile action, and that they are thoroughly aware of the inter-relations among basic knowledge, technological advances, and human need."[3] The graduates were encouraged to think of themselves as technological humanists, men and women who are professionally competent but also aware of what needs to be done and, more importantly, why it should be done and what the implications are of doing it.

One of the major purposes of this educational philosophy put into the curriculum was to help students to deal with the ambiguities arising out of the application of technological solutions to and within social and political problems and contexts. Thus, while the student is expected to be a knowledgeable and competent professional, he or she is primarily expected to be able to apply this knowledge within a social setting. This implies that a student must develop a sense of how to go beyond a mechanical application of formulae or methodologies in resolving a problem. Students must begin to see what is at stake not only technically, but also politically, economically, ethically, and socially. Though this implies an often difficult evaluation process, students will learn to make professional judgments that approach the most optimal decision possible, not only technically, but also socially. This approach to engineering education has elements of a virtue-dominant and a value-dominant approach. Insofar as students are being equipped with certain skills in order to solve problems in a complex environment, there are elements of a virtue-dominant approach. Insofar as they are expected to look for the optimal solution, there are elements of a value-dominant approach.

The means by which this educational philosophy has been institutionalized in the curriculum is through two degree requirements: the Interactive Qualifying Project and the Humanities Sufficiency. The Interactive Qualifying Project (IQP) helps the student to focus upon the relationship between the technical, social, and value dimensions of solutions to social problems. The purpose is to broaden the student's range of experience, understand the context in which engineering is being practiced, and give the student some approach to analyzing interdisciplinary problems, including the value dimension. While the means of the implementation of this degree requirement are varied, its purpose is to give the student exposure to, and experience in, solving problems that have no clear or single technical solution. The expectation of the faculty is that this orientation, emphasized through its being a degree requirement, will help the student to become aware of the broader context in which engineering is practiced as well as the value issues that are raised by choosing one solution among the many possible to particular problems.

The IQP is the equivalent of three courses and is typically spread over three terms. Students are encouraged to take relevant courses to prepare for their project. The work is done individually or in teams and is directed by a faculty member. Each IQP results in a report, which presents the findings of the study.

This degree requirement has made several important contributions with respect to justice education. First, the role model of the engineer has been changed. No longer can she or he be unaware of the context or implications of a specific solution. Second, the IQP has brought the world into the educational program. Engineers must be aware of, and concerned with, more than the technical because what they do affects society profoundly, and which problem they attempt to solve has important implications. Third, the IQP has forced students and faculty to reflect on their social responsibilities as engineers. While no clear consensus has emerged, the issue is recognized as important and is attended to through the student's Interactive Qualifying Project.

The Humanities Sufficiency requirement is also an important component of the educational philosophy at WPI. The intent here is not to try to expose the student to dribs and drabs of various ideas in the humanities but, rather, to allow the student to pursue a topic of interest to him or her by thematically relating five courses among the humanities offerings. Again, this allows a student to pursue a problem or a concern from many different points of view. While not directly impacting their perception of science or engineering—although it is possible to pursue one's humanities minor in the field of the history of science—the purpose is to make available to students another resource as they think through many of the problems that they must face. The concern is not to make humanities scholars out of the students, but to recognize that as well-educated and responsible citizens, other perspectives and means of analysis are important to them. Such different perspectives and means of analysis are extremely important when one realizes that many of the decisions that are made in engineering and science have to do with evaluating risks and benefits as well as many other social implications of particular engineering decisions.

The Humanities Sufficiency requirement concludes by having the student spend the equivalent of one course preparing a report on his or her research topic. Clearly topics differ, and although only some students focus on problems of ethics or justice, nonetheless the degree requirement as a whole shows the students a different side of life, provides different methodological resources, and helps them see and examine problems from a different perspective. The hope is that this will provide another resource for students in making professional decisions.

The entire curriculum and philosophy of education of WPI is a response to the problem of how to teach ethics within an engineering curriculum. Although WPI does offer, in the Humanities department, a course in professional ethics, what is most important is that the burden of providing some ethical analysis to problems in engineering does not rest upon that one course. Rather, the responsibility for such an evaluation is spread throughout the faculty.

A MODEL CURRICULUM

Another way to add justice and ethical issues to an engineering program is to put them into a specific course. The advantages of this—as opposed to the Interactive Qualifying Project—are: the issues can receive specific and thorough attention; guest speakers can be brought in to illustrate concretely the problems under discussion; students can be helped to prepare for problems they may face. The model curriculum is obviously not the only way to do this. It reflects my experience of introducing such a course and what I have found effective and important for the students.

I wish to make two preliminary comments. First, I have found guest speakers to be invaluable. Not only do they give both credibility and reality to the topics, they also provide vivid, complex problems for the students to discuss and examine. Cases from texts are most helpful, but I have found nothing as effective as an engineer coming into my class and saying, "Two weeks ago on a consulting job I had this problem. . . ." Additionally (something that I discovered only after having guest speakers a few times), such guest appearances by real engineers in the real world provide excellent role models for the students. Students can "excuse" ethics professors for being interested in the problem. They can't do that with practicing engineers—and that may be one of the most valuable features of the course.

Second, the majority of students have had some work experience somewhere—many in their own field of specialization. That presents another source of material for discussion in class. One has to make sure the students know and feel it is safe to discuss these situations. Once this is established, however, the most amazing statements will come out of students' mouths and splendid discussions will occur.

Three good textbooks are available for use in courses in engineering ethics, even though the titles of the texts do not specifically refer to engineering ethics. The first of these is *Business Ethics* by Richard T. DeGeorge (1982). This book is helpful because it has some basic discussion of ethical concepts at the beginning, but then goes into specific topics that relate to ethical issues in the professions. Many of the topics covered can easily relate to the engineering profession. A second text is Norman Bowie's *Business Ethics* (1982). This book is organized around the concept of role morality and how that applies to a variety of situations. This book is not as directly applicable to a specific course in engineering ethics, but several of the concepts that Bowie raises having to do with the organizational structure of corporations, whistle-blowing, and the moral assumptions in business are all relevant to issues raised in the practice of engineering. The major text specifically relating to ethical issues in engineering is the two-volume compilation of readings and cases edited by Robert Baum and Albert Flores, *Ethical Problems in Engineering* (1980), and is available through the Rensselaer Polytechnic Institute Studies in the Human Dimension of Science and Technology. These two volumes contain essays on specific topics in engineering as well as a variety of cases that can be used to help explain and illustrate several of the major problems that will arise. Each of these texts lists a large number of references and can be used to develop further resources in the area.

I assign three case studies, which enable students to apply the ethical concepts to a case and to discover what ethical concepts were or were not used in a case. I find these case studies more useful than traditional term papers because the students must wrestle with a concrete situation and cannot so easily take refuge in the abstract. Also the way in which students use and appeal to ethical concepts (or fail to do so) much more clearly reveals their comprehension of the issues. I have asked students to prepare these case studies, sometimes individually, sometimes in teams. When using the team approach I have volunteered myself as a resource person, but have taken no initiative to schedule meetings, appoint a leader, or give specific assignments. I have simply made sure that members of the team had each other's mailbox numbers and that they saw each other in class the day I assigned the teams. The process of working as a team is helpful because many things are (or should be) experienced: value conflicts, leadership, cooperation, responsibility, and delegation of authority. I grade the report of the team and assign that grade to each team member.

Course Content

As can be seen from the outline below, the first section of the course is a general introduction to ethics. It is important for any course on professional ethics to begin with identifying two or three ethical methodologies or concepts, particularly justice, confidentiality, and responsibility, as a way of helping to establish a general basis in ethics for the evaluation of concepts later on in the course as well as providing students who may not have a good background in philosophy or religion with an initial orientation to ethical means of analysis. This need not be done in depth or with the assumption that all of these individuals will be philosophers, because they will not be. What needs to be done, though, is to identify the contours of basic ethical theory, indicating at least the major differences between ethical relativism as well as other methods of objectivity in decision-making. The point here is to show the students how to begin analyzing various kinds of material that they are not in the habit of evaluating. This can be done within a few classes and can help the students to move into a different mode of analysis.

The section "Moral Issues in Business" opens up several thematic issues with respect to the values structure already present in business and engineering. Issues of rights and responsibilities of both the business itself and the employees, and issues of substantive and procedural justice can be raised, as well as the moral basis of the structure of business. This section is theoretical, but begins to focus on the realities of life for a professional practicing within a pre-established context.

ENGINEERING ETHICS (three credits)

REQUIRED TEXTS

Baum, Robert, and Albert Flores. *Ethical Problems in Engineering.* Troy, N.Y.: Rensselaer Polytechnic Institute, 1980.
Bowie, Norman. *Business Ethics.* Englewood Cliffs, N.J.: Prentice-Hall, 1982.
DeGeorge, Richard T. *Business Ethics.* New York: Macmillan, 1982.

COURSE OUTLINE

1. General Introduction to Ethics
    Readings: DeGeorge, chaps. 1–5;
                      Baum and Flores, chap. 1;
                      Bowie, chap. 1.
2. Moral Issues in Business
    Readings: Bowie, chaps. 2–3;
                      DeGeorge, chaps. 6–8, 13;
                      Baum and Flores, chap. 2.
3. Specific Problems
    a. Conflict of Interest. Readings: Baum and Flores, chap. 3; Bowie, chap. 5.
    b. Products Liability. Readings: Bowie, chap. 5; Baum and Flores, chap. 4.
    c. Trade Secrets. Readings: DeGeorge, chap. 12; Bowie, chap. 6.
    d. Whistle-Blowing. Readings: DeGeorge, chap. 9; Bowie, chap. 7; Baum and Flores, chap. 3.
    e. Work in Defense Industries.

Specific problems are addressed in the remainder of the course. One topic that inevitably comes up in the discussion of engineering ethics and professional ethics generally is the whole issue of conflict of interests. Minimally this conflict has potential for occurring among the engineer, the employer, the client, and society. It is necessary at this point in the course to identify the ways in which the interests of different individuals, while often complementary, can also at times be at odds with one another. Especially important here is the inclusion of the interests of society. While it is not always the case, frequently the interests of society are either ignored or not really taken into account. The engineer can have a very critical role here in helping to represent the interests of society by demonstrating what some of the short- or long-term consequences of particular decisions are. This topic also allows discussion of important virtues that are appropriate to the engineer as she or he begins the process of working with both an employer and a client. Often the engineer will be caught between these two poles and must be very clear about where one's interests lie. This is also a good time to talk about the whole concept of the formation of conscience and the role of individual conscience in both technical and ethical decision-making.

The "Products Liability" section focuses on the professional and ethical responsibilities of the engineer with respect to the design of products. While manufacturers have typically been perceived as being responsible for the products they produce, only recently has that obligation been taken much more seriously. One of the important functions that an engineer is frequently called upon to perform is to evaluate the design, construction, and quality of the components of a particular product. Because the consequences of mistakes are frequently costly, there is potential here for an enormous amount of conflict of interest and for compromising technical competence, and the need for an extremely high amount of personal integrity. The need for honesty and integrity on this level can also very easily be related to what students are currently doing in their own lab classes and other projects in which they might be involved. One can make the obvious point that if one is willing to compromise the integrity of reports and designs on the undergraduate level, such a mode of behavior might also transfer to professional settings, where the consequences might be much more severe.

The following section, on trade secrets, looks at the responsibility of an engineer to her or his own company with respect to knowledge gained or developed during the course of employment. Is one free to do with this information what one wants? Sharp justice issues are raised here as well.

"Whistle-blowing" deals with the issue of loyalty to one's company, profession, and colleagues, and with one's obligation to society and to one's moral standard. Blowing the whistle on one's colleagues or one's employer has become a serious problem in the practice of engineering. Tremendous personal, social, and professional problems follow from the fact that a person identifies publicly a problem in a particular organization or contract. The issue here is the conflict between loyalty to one's employer and loyalty to society. Questions of integrity and loyalty, as well as issues of public health and safety, become very critical in many engineering situations. Examining criteria under which whistle-blowing is appropriate and the means of doing it fairly and honestly will be extremely important for the student engineer. This is the place to bring in a variety of codes of ethics as well as to continue to focus on issues of personal integrity and technical competence.

Finally, the course addresses the ethics of work in defense industries. This particular issue is extremely delicate as well as timely. A large number of companies that are hiring engineering students are doing so because they have contracts from the United States Department of Defense or are subcontracting work that relates to the development of weapons systems. Two broad issues need to be addressed here. First is the examination of the moral implications of working for a particular industry. The engineer must have a clear sense of why she or he is or is not willing to work for a particular company. My view here is that whatever the engineer does should be done conscientiously. Helping a student to sort through the various issues involved in working for a company primarily engaged in defense work, for instance, will be a service to that student.

The second broad issue has to do with the implications of working in an industry with heavy security requirements. Many times the individuals working in such industries suffer grave lack of privacy because of the company's hiring procedures, and they may be subject to polygraph testing or psychological testing. While a company clearly has certain rights with respect to whom it hires and has responsibilities to maintain security standards, nonetheless employees may have questions about some procedures they must undergo. There is also the day-to-day pressure of working in an industry that one either knows very little about or may not discuss with anybody except one's immediate co-workers. While I would agree that shoptalk or talking primarily about one's means of employment is not the major element in one's conversation, nonetheless talking about where one spends a large part of one's day is an important part of conversation. This whole aspect of secrecy and confidentiality with respect to the material in which one is involved professionally can put strains on various relationships, and can have a depressing effect on the worker. A class in engineering ethics might help a person to think through some of the implications of actually working in such an industry and what that might mean for one's personal relationships as well as one's career.

BASIC RESOURCES

While I cannot cover all necessary bases, I would like to present some basic resources for use in designing a curriculum. These come from my experience with text materials and also reflect my interest and the concerns that I pursue in the classroom. Obviously, each professor has concerns of her or his own, but my hope is that these basic resources will be a help to all.

Books

A wide variety of books on professional and engineering ethics is now appearing. I mention three that I have found particularly helpful. The first is from the Hastings Center Series on the Teaching of Ethics: *Ethics and Engi-*

neering Curricula by Robert J. Baum. This book gives a good overview of some of the basic issues in designing a course in engineering ethics, and also lists resources. Another extremely good publication comes from the Center for the Study of Ethics in the Professions at the Illinois Institute of Technology in Chicago. This is *A Selected Annotated Bibliography of Professional Ethics and Social Responsibility in Engineering*, which lists many resources, including journals and newsletters. It is well indexed and covers a variety of topics. It is invaluable for anyone who is doing research in the field or is helping students to discover resources. Another major resource, published in 1980 by the American Association for the Advancement of Sciences, Committee on Scientific Freedom and Responsibility, is *Professional Ethics Activities in the Scientific and Engineering Societies*. This book presents the different initiatives that have been taken by professional societies and has some general discussion of ethical problems in the professions. One of its major advantages is the many up-to-date codes of ethics from a wide variety of professional societies reprinted in it.

Journals

Of the many journals available, I have selected five basic ones that can be used for the development of other resources in the area. *Business and Professional Ethics Journal* is available through the Office of Science and Technologies Studies Division at the Rensselaer Polytechnic Institute, Troy, New York. The journal reviews a broad number of issues in professional ethics and has many articles specifically on issues in engineering ethics. Another important general journal comes from the Program in Science, Technology and Society, published by the Massachusetts Institute of Technology Press, Cambridge, Massachusetts. This is *Science, Technology and Human Values*, which has many timely articles on general issues in science and society but, more valuably, has an excellent quarterly bibliography on the major books and articles of that quarter. The journal *Environmental Ethics*, available from the Department of Philosophy and Religion at the University of Georgia, in Athens, has a number of articles that are related to problems in engineering ethics. Another useful journal is the *Hastings Center Report*. While this journal began primarily to examine issues in life sciences, the mandate of the Hastings Center has broadened to include issues in professional ethics in general. An important resource of the *Hastings Center Report* is its bimonthly bibliographical listings. Finally, the journal *Ethics*, published by the University of Chicago Press, is beginning to include a wider variety of articles related to applied philosophy. Additionally, *Ethics* has a sizable book-review section, which is helpful for faculty members as well as students.

The journals mentioned here will provide a point of departure for someone beginning to work in the area of engineering ethics. Careful attention to the resources in these books and journals will provide a basis for the development of a comprehensive and adequate bibliography for courses.

CONCLUSION

One of the strongest points that a person in engineering ethics can make is to establish clearly and confidently that ethical issues are part and parcel of the role of the engineer. This can be accomplished readily by focusing on the consequences of engineering as a profession as well as by examining many of the issues that arise in connection with the design and production of various products. Important for the success of the course is the immediate establishment of the concept that part of the role of an engineer is to raise social and ethical issues. By linking the ethical and social aspects into the definition of the profession of engineering, one avoids the danger of finding these issues to be superfluous to the real world of engineering. Such linkage of the social and ethical issues of engineering to its daily practice also helps to integrate the individual who is an engineer by showing that this same individual has responsibilities not only as an engineer but also as a person and a citizen. Such linkage of the personal, professional, and social dimensions of the individual can help to provide or at least to set the framework for the development of more personal integration and integrity as one carries out one's professional duties. It also helps one to avoid the moral schizophrenia into which persons frequently fall, which suggests that from nine to five a person operates under one set of principles, and the rest of the time under a different set of principles.

The task of a course on engineering ethics should not be to convert a person to a particular way of thinking or form of reasoning. Rather, it should open up the individual to see her or his profession from a different point of view and to realize that this point of view can constructively be incorporated into her or his definition of engineering. A course like this will also provide the individual with resources with which to begin to evaluate problems or situations in which one finds oneself. Finally, such a course may help students to realize that they are not alone in facing issues like this and that by discussing problems like these with their co-workers or with other sympathetic persons in their lives, they may find resources available to them of which they were not aware. In this way they can be helped to realize that they can maintain integrity both as persons and as professionals.

In particular, the concept of justice must stand at the heart of such a course and also at the heart of a revised concept of engineering. Justice operates not only at the formal level of "giving each his or her due" or "treating equals equally," but must engage in the difficult task of assessing competing loyalties and interests on a personal and professional level. The question of justice is at the heart of product-liability and whistle-blowing concerns. Both suggest a high standard of justice on the part of the engineer, but the standard transcends a calculation of justice as an individual ethical reality and serves as a means of evaluating social implications, the relations among designer, company, and consumer, as well as profound issues of the social responsibility of both the engineer and the company. Such responsibilities will not be resolved by simply calculating one's interests only. So a revised understanding of justice as well as an understanding of its social dimensions will mean a significant reevaluation of one's personal and professional responsibilities as well as how these relate to the interaction of society and engineering.

This is why I chose to organize the course outline in the way I did. My sense is twofold: first, one must have some understanding of the various options for ethical decision-making; second, the most profound justice issues occur at the intersections of personal and professional loyalty and individual and social/corporate relations. To minimize abstractness, one must begin to examine, study, question, and test the hard justice questions: conflict of interest, product liability, trade secrets, whistle-blowing, and issues related to defense industries. There are no clear answers to justice issues raised here, or at least no answers that would be similar to ones raised about padding one's expense account or using the firm's credit card to cover a personal debt.

Our pressing need is to examine justice issues that arise within the context of the practice of engineering and the social structure of business. This requires an examination of the status quo of engineering, an evaluation of the role of the engineer, as well as consideration of the social responsibilities of both the engineer and one's company that are based on a social understanding of justice.

NOTES

1. Thomas Ogletree, "Values, Obligations, and Virtues: Approaches to Biomedical Ethics," *Journal of Religious Ethics*, no. 1 (Spring 1976): 105–30.
2. *WPI Operational Catalogue* (1978), p. 7.
3. Ibid.

SELECTED READINGS FOR FACULTY

Alger, Philip L.; N. A. Christensen; and Sterling P. Olmsted. *Ethical Problems in Engineering*. New York: John Wiley, 1965.

Baum, Robert. "Ethics Scene in Engineering Education: A State of the Field Report." *Professional Engineer* 47, no. 12 (December 1977): 21–23.

Beauchamp, Tom L., and Norman E. Bowie, eds. *Ethical Theory and Business*. Englewood Cliffs, N.J.: Prentice-Hall, 1979.

Bonnell, John A., ed. *A Guide for Developing Courses in Engineering*. NSPE Publication 2010. Washington, D.C.: National Society of Professional Engineers, 1976.

Chalk, Rosemary; Mark S. Frankel; and Sallie B. Chafer. *AAAS Professional Ethics Project*. Washington, D.C.: American Association for the Advancement of Science, 1980.

Chalk, Rosemary, and Frank Von Hippel. "Due Process for Dissenting Whistle-Blowers." *Technology Review* 81, no. 7 (June–July 1979).

———. "Engineer's Professional Rights." *Issues in Engineering* 106 (October 1980): 389–96.

————. "Ethical Responsibilities of Engineers in Large Organizations." *Business and Professional Ethics Journal* 1, no. 1 (Fall 1981): 1–14.

Flores, Albert, ed. *Designing for Safety: Engineering Ethics in Organizational Contexts.* National Science Foundation Grant. Troy, N.Y.: Rensselaer Polytechnic Institute, 1982.

Flores, Albert, and Deborah Johnson. "Collective Responsibility and Professional Roles." *Ethics* 93 (April 1983): 537–45.

Fruchtbaum, Harold, ed. *The Social Responsibility of Engineers.* The Annals of the New York Academy of Sciences, vol. 10, art. 10 (proceedings of a symposium held in 1972).

Knight, Kenneth T. "Engineering Ethics." *Mechanical Engineering* (November 1979): 38–41.

Ladenson, Robert F.; James Choromokos; Ernest d'Anjou; Martin Pimsler; and Howard Rosen. *A Selected Annotated Bibliography of Professional Ethics and Social Responsibility in Engineering.* Chicago, Ill.: Center for the Study of Ethics in the Professions, 1980.

Layton, Edwin T., Jr. *Revolt of the Engineers: Social Responsibility and the American Engineering Profession.* Cleveland, Ohio: Case Western Reserve Press, 1971.

Martin, Mike, and Roland Schinzinger. *Ethics and Engineering.* New York: McGraw-Hill, 1983.

Nader, Ralph; Peter Petkas; and Kate Blackwell, eds. *Whistle Blowing.* New York: Grossman, 1972.

Perrucci, Robert, and Joel E. Gerstl. *Professional without Community: Engineers in American Society.* New York: Random House, 1969.

————. "The Philosophical Bases of Engineering Codes of Ethics." In *Engineering and Humanities,* ed. James H. Schaub and Sheila K. Kickison. New York: John Wiley, 1983; pp. 269–76.

Pritchard, Michael S. "Moral Reasoning and Engineering." *Technology and Society* 8, no. 3 (September 1980): 3–13.

Schaub, James H., and Karl Pavlovic, with M. D. Morris, eds. *Engineering Professionalism and Ethics.* New York: John Wiley, 1983.

Weil, Vivian, ed. *Report of the Workshops on Ethical Issues in Engineering.* National Science Foundation Grant. Chicago, Ill.: Center for the Study of Ethics in the Professions, Illinois Institute of Technology, 1980.

Weinstein, Deena. *Bureaucratic Opposition: Challenging Abuses at the Workplace.* New York: Pergamon Press, 1979.

Westin, Alan F. *Whistle-Blowing: Loyalty and Dissent in the Corporation.* New York: McGraw-Hill, 1981.

13

Social Work

PATRICIA L. PILGER
SAINT MARY'S COLLEGE

Historically, the profession of social work has always addressed issues of social justice. Whether one wishes to trace the religious concerns of the poor, the philanthropic background of many of our predecessors, the advocacy roles of such outstanding figures as Jane Addams and Dorothea Dix, or the functions of voluntary interest groups, social workers have constantly exhibited concern for the poor, minorities, and persons unable to function at levels expected by the broader society.

The modern social worker tends to assume a multiplicity of roles. Because we practice in a variety of settings, using a number of methods to meet needs, it is often difficult to design curricula that address current socioeconomic problems, minority and cultural differences, and policy issues. In addition we must meet the needs of our students in preparing them for practice, while being conscious of clients' problems and the broader aspects of our national character and the third world. This essay presents a possible model for undergraduate social work educators, which may be adapted for the graduate school level.

The Council on Social Work Education (CSWE) has provided a broad-based liberal-arts requirement for the undergraduate degree in social work. In designing the curriculum, the council recommends that four general areas be included: human behavior in the social environment, research, social work theory and practice, and social welfare policy and services. The details of specific courses are left to the individual institution for development in accordance with its values and goals. Within these guidelines provided by CSWE, the faculty of the Department of Sociology, Anthropology and Social Work at Saint Mary's College (where the author teaches) has carefully structured the Social Work Program to include justice themes in all courses from the sophomore through the senior years. This author has chosen "Social Welfare Policy and Services" and "Social Work Theory and Practice" as the courses that best lend themselves to the teaching of values clarification and social justice.

Although this essay is specifically addressed to two courses within the Social Work Program, and provides a syllabus for one of the courses, it may assist the reader to understand the infusion concept if we briefly consider the total curriculum. In the first semester of the sophomore year, students are required to take the "Introduction to Social Work" and "Social Welfare Policy and Services" courses. In the introductory course, the National Association of Social Work's Code of Ethics is presented. After studying the history and practice areas of the profession in the first half of the semester, students visit selected agencies in the community in order to see the physical settings and to talk with staff.

In the second semester of the sophomore year, the required courses are "Human Behavior in the Social Environment" and "Social Welfare Theory and Practice." The latter will be discussed below. In the "Human Behavior" course, students are required to keep a diary of their responses to the lectures, the intent of which is to sensitize them to their own feelings. Since the surrounding area is rich in both traditional and nontraditional agencies, guest speakers from the community are invited to lecture to the class. Among the groups supplying lecturers have been Divorced Catholics, Compassionate Friends (a support group for parents who have suffered the death of a child), and DuComb Center, an alternative to the state penitentiary for convicted felons. This method allows students to converse with real people who have experienced problems in coping in society.

The junior year focuses mainly on the development of skills. The "Methods I" course emphasizes community organization and administration. The class forms itself into a board and subcommittees after identifying a social problem of the surrounding community. The semester's assignments address the problem and the possible means of correcting it. The final examination is a presentation of specific problem-solving scenarios to selected members of the community. In the past, students have successfully implemented programs for off-campus crime prevention and a Hunger Coalition.

In the spring semester, "Methods II" further expands personal skills. While traditional methods of casework and group work are taught, taped interviews of the students are used to move them from the tendency to give advice to working with the client's strengths in order to try to solve the client's problems. Justice issues in this course strive to integrate the knowledge base from previous courses into the student's awareness of self and attitudes.

The senior year is the capstone of the curriculum. All students work in social agencies of their choice for two full days per week during both semesters. This is the learning experience from which they bring cases to the accompanying senior seminar, a procedure that combines experiential and academic learning. The students are thus able to discuss the realities of inequality against a theoretical background of problem-solving.

TEACHING SOCIAL WELFARE POLICY

There is disagreement among social work educators as to the specific approach and methods to be used in teaching social welfare policy. This is sometimes taught as a beginning-level course; at other times it constitutes an upper-division area—and occasionally it is offered at both levels. The educator may teach it in historical perspective as suggested by Wilensky and Lebeaux,[1] or based on issues as evidenced by Piven and Cloward,[2] or a combination of the two methods. Unlike other curriculum areas, it is difficult to find a text suitable for both teacher and student needs and interests. A particular problem of current students is their lack of historical perspective, a lack that must be addressed if the program is to be successful.

In order to establish a workable orientation for students entering the profession of social work, the course in "Social Welfare Policy" begins with an overview of the definitions of "social welfare." This includes cultural definitions of poverty. Students are directed to various references as sources of discussion.

Class instruction is initiated with the categories of "deserving poor" as defined by the Elizabethan Poor Laws in England. We continue our study of how these concepts were brought to the United States and gradually codified into laws in various states. Historical events, precepts from philosophy, and an understanding of religious values are brought to bear on this research.

As taught at Saint Mary's College, "Social Welfare Policy and Services" has a different focus from similar courses taught at other colleges and universities. It differs from those taught at public institutions in that it emphasizes the traditions of the Roman Catholic Church, especially its attitudes and commitment to the care of people in society. This course may be similar to courses taught in other colleges and universities with a Catholic heritage, but because of Saint Mary's institutional commitment to justice issues, this theme is more clearly defined. Also, because we are encouraged to share ideas and teaching methods across disciplines, it is accepted practice to have faculty members from other departments lecture on their special areas in a variety of related courses.

Although the course as it will be described appears to be about justice, "Social Welfare Policy and Services" is not considered by social work educators to be a course about justice. Elizabeth Huttman has written: "The National Association of Social Workers (NASW) touches more on the mutual support-interpersonal relations aspect saying, 'Public social policy . . . consists of those laws, policies and practices of government that affect the social relationships of individuals and their relationship to the society of which they are a part.' "[3] Because policy issues are also addressed by voluntary organizations, policy is sometimes defined as follows: "In whatever loci it occurs, policy is above all strategies, actions, or plans for alleviating a social problem or meeting a social need after analyzing alternative choices."[4]

SOCIAL WELFARE POLICY AND SERVICES *(three credits)*

PURPOSE

"Social Welfare Policy and Services" is designed as one of two introductory courses to the Social Work Program, the other being "Introduction to Social Work." In this course the student is introduced to (1) the general concepts of social welfare, (2) the historical development of current social welfare programs, (3) an understanding of the social, economic, and political factors that influence policy-making, and (4) a selected group of current social welfare programs.

READING LIST

Text: Prigmore, Charles S., and Charles R. Atherton. *Social Welfare Policy: Analysis and Formulation.* Lexington, Mass.: D. C. Heath and Co., 1979.

Romanyshyn, John. *Social Welfare: Charity to Justice.* New York: Random House, 1971.

Sheehan, Susan. *A Welfare Mother.* Boston: Houghton, Mifflin Co., 1976.

Additional materials will be assigned during the course.

COURSE OUTLINE

Unit I. Social Welfare (two weeks)
   a. Definitions of social welfare
   b. Definitions of poverty
   c. Philosophical approaches to solutions
   d. Definitions of social policy
Unit II. Types of Needs and Programs (two weeks)
   a. Family policy
   b. Income maintenance
   c. Medical care
Unit III. Social Security Act (three weeks)
   a. Historical beginnings
   b. Changes through time
   c. Title XX of the act
   d. Current problems
Unit IV. Child Welfare Services (two weeks)
   a. Foster care
   b. Adoption
   c. Juvenile justice
   d. Day-care programs

e. School social work

Unit V. Health-Care Services (two weeks)

　a. Medicare and Medicaid

　b. Public health

　c. Mental health

Unit VI. Volunteer Action Programs (one week)

　a. Referral services

　b. Battered wives

　c. Runaway shelters

　d. Recreation programs

　e. Educational programs

Unit VII. Third World (two weeks)

　a. United Nations

　b. Comparative cultures

　c. Cultural context

　d. Problem definitions

ASSIGNMENTS

1. For 50 percent of the course grade: To reinforce concepts of justice education in social work, the students are given a semester-long project: Accessing Government Documents. The class is separated into teams of two persons. Each team is assigned a specific piece of legislation, for example, the Runaway Youth Act, Medicare, Medicaid, Food Stamps, Missing Children's Act. The college librarian presents a lecture on accessing government documents. The class, professor, and research librarians attend a demonstration lecture at the Government Repository at Notre Dame. Following these formal instructions, the students must trace the history of the legislation back through issues of the *Congressional Record.*

   At the end of the semester, the teams make a formal presentation to the class as their final examination. This assignment includes: (a) identifying the social problem addressed in the legislation; (b) determining what social, economic, and political climate caused the problem to be addressed by Congress at a particular point in history; (c) tracing the bill in and out of committee in its passage through Congress; (d) interviewing agency social workers as to how the services are delivered to the clients; (e) understanding the political use of lobbying and compromise to achieve social welfare aims.

   The purpose of this assignment is achieved when the students realize the necessity of political compromise. The most important lesson they learn is that much of United States congressional legislation is *not* motivated by charity, rarely by justice, and nearly always to satisfy political constituencies.

2. For 20 percent of the course grade: Each student will select a current

social welfare program and write a report to include: (a) a brief
historical statement; (b) an interview with a person in the program as
to how service is delivered; (c) reflection of the student's attitude.
3. For 15 percent of the course grade: Each student will write an evaluation of a current service for oral presentation and discussion following
the outline in the text.
4. For 15 percent of the course grade: Each student will research a third-
world country. A paper and oral presentation on a policy for that
country is required as the final examination.

Note: All students are required to attend class and participate in discussion. Any unexcused absences will lower the grade in the course. All
written work will be due on the assigned date.

The text for the "Social Welfare Policy and Services" course outlined
above—*Social Welfare Policy: Analysis and Formulation* by Charles S.
Prigmore and Charles R. Atherton—was chosen because these particular
authors use an analytical approach to a few selected social welfare policies.
This approach helps students to address a particular piece of stated policy from
the viewpoint of the practicality of its implementation. The definitions in the
text are first compared with those in the *Encyclopedia of Social Work,* a
reference that provides a current perspective on defining poverty and social
welfare. In order to appreciate the historical attitudes toward the poor, students are required to read Romanyshyn's *Social Welfare: Charity to Justice.*
During the second week of the course, lectures are given by the college
reference librarian on the topic of general research in the social sciences (social
work in particular), and accessing government documents.

Once the students have refreshed their sense of history and the interplay of
social, economic, philosophic, and religious values in influencing policy and
legislation, they are introduced to Catholic teaching on justice by reading
Rerum Novarum, Quadragesimo Anno, and *Laborem Exercens.*[5] Emphasis is
again placed on the historical perspective of these documents and why they
were written for the social problems addressed in them. Particular consideration in class discussion is placed on how these same principles may be applied
to current policy issues of poverty, unemployment, and family support systems.

Students are then referred to Ronald Federico's *The Social Welfare Institution: An Introduction,*[6] which presents an outline of the Capitalist-Puritan,
Humanistic-Positive, and Judeo-Christian perspectives on the existence of
humankind. This presentation is referred to later in the course when discussion
is centered around specific legislation. The intent of this referral is to evaluate
the influence of values on each piece of legislation.

It is helpful when discussing definitions of poverty to give the students an
experiential learning assignment that shows them, in a practical way, what

being poor means. I do this by asking my students to imagine that they are single parents with one child, who are given $300 to furnish a three-room apartment. They are then assigned one week to visit the shops run by the Salvation Army, the Saint Vincent DePaul Society, and Goodwill Industries. The teams report back to the class, not only on their "purchases" with that budget, but particularly on their feelings about being in such a situation. The reactions have ranged from anger with the instructor for the assignment and frustration with the limited income, to the loneliness of feeling like an "outsider." Once these feelings are addressed, emphasis continues throughout the course on personal reactions to clients and situations.

The next two weeks of the class focus on problem areas, client groups, and specific federal social welfare programs (namely, Income Maintenance, Health Insurance, and Housing programs). When possible, students read the original piece of legislation as it was enacted by the United States Congress. (Generally, these documents are available through one's congressional representatives.) Discussion is focused on why this legislation was necessary and the various arguments pro and con with regard to the issues addressed.

At this point in the course, one of the professors from the Government Department of Saint Mary's College is invited to lecture on how a bill is introduced and eventually becomes, or does not become, law. Included in this content area is a discussion of the United States budget. Emphasis is placed on the function of lobbyists for special-interest groups. When the course topic is Income Maintenance, we study unemployment compensation, Aid to Dependent Children, and the Food Stamp program as major support programs. A professor from Saint Mary's Department of Business Administration and Economics is invited to lecture on the negative income tax and its consequences. This presentation includes the economic definitions of poverty.

Following these presentations, the class reads *A Welfare Mother* by Susan Sheehan. This book is an account of a Puerto Rican family living in New York City. The author details the living conditions of the family and presents the multifaceted problems of being a cultural minority. The book describes some of the ways in which clients operate outside the formal social welfare system (which is trying to modify the clients' behavior) in an effort to solve their own problems.

The students find this reading particularly frustrating, as they tend to be judgmental toward the client and at the same time recognize that this attitude is not acceptable in social work. Discussion centers around the efficiency/ inefficiency of the welfare system in delivering service to this family, the methods by which the mother manipulates the system, and attitudes of morality and justice in society as they relate to institutional structures. However, students also identify with the client. The main character of the story is the mother of the family. Using their knowledge base, students identify her right to the basic necessities of life, but do not condone her methods of trying to improve the quality of her life by "playing the numbers" and not providing information to the social worker. Their application of the principles of distributive justice causes them to recognize injustices in the system and to suggest advocate roles for change. At the same time, the students develop a sensitivity to cultural contexts in which clients find support and identity.

The following few weeks are devoted to the Social Security Act of 1935 and amendments through Title XX (Social Services). In teaching the original intent of the act, there is little difficulty in understanding the need for this legislation in its historical context, nor are there problems in regard to the categories of clients to be served. Problems arise when students attempt to understand current implementation of the laws, with the attendant rules and regulations that appear to cause inefficiency in delivering services to needy clients. Negative sentiment arises particularly in discussions of taxable-base incomes for Old Age Survivors Disability and Health Insurance, since students recognize how the double taxation of gross annual income directly affects actual income and purchasing power. It is crucial that students appreciate the social, political, and economic factors that contributed to the original passage of the act and the subsequent amendments. Most important to their understanding is the impact of historical conditions. Students must write to their home states for a copy of that state's Title XX. Since the inception of the Reagan administration, a few states have opted for block grants to support these programs while the federal legislation still stands. Students are required, during their semester break, to determine why some states have gone to block grants for program support.

The major issue of health-care services in the United States occupies a large portion of the course. Students read the original legislation for Title XVIII (Medicare) and Title XIX (Medicaid). To develop an understanding of the current issues in these programs, students are referred to the *Congressional Record*. Again, there is little evidence of a lack of understanding of the need for the programs, or their intent. The difficulty arises with the implementation process.

While perusing Title XVIII, an in-depth presentation of the Older Americans Act is given. This enables the students to become acquainted with the problems of older adults, problems that may lead to, or increase the possibility of, people being at risk in terms of health problems and/or access to health care. In debating the pros and cons of institutional versus independent living for the elderly, a primary consideration is cost accountability.

The assignment to interview health-care professionals and client recipients provokes a social consciousness for this client group. Students tend to sense a developing community responsibility in reviewing functions of policy in the state's Nursing Home Review Board and the Ombudsman of the state Agency on Aging. The function of this board is to review all applications and referrals to nursing-home facilities to determine the appropriate action with individual clients. In this content area, principles of commutative justice are more easily observed, since decisions are related to the well-being of the client as well as of family members. Because this issue involves the nursing-home industry, the policy is seen as a community's just response to a client group's needs as well as the prevention of abuses in practice.

Title XIX presents a very different orientation because it serves the medically indigent. Questions of justice focus around the delivery of services. A severe values-orientation crisis arises from the obvious wealth of physicians, the need for modern technological equipment, the cost of care and equipment, and the blatant differences in care received by the poor both because of their economic status and because of the types of facilities and care available to them. Most students develop a sense of outrage at the lack of preventive health measures available to the poor of our society.

This attitude becomes especially intense when a comparative study is made of the health insurance system of the United Kingdom. Serious debate is held about social attitudes that are incorporated into legislation. A major issue is the obvious tendency in the United States to assuage one's sense of individual moral responsibility by placing it within an organizational structure.

At midsemester the class begins to focus on private-sector policy. I have found it instructive to use Saint Mary's College itself as an example. The first assignment is to read the Student Government *Manual* and to obtain a copy of the chart of the organizational structure of the college. Discussion centers on various college policies, why they exist, what the *Manual* says, and how, in fact, the policy is promulgated in the informal organizational structure.

When the students understand these concepts, they are then assigned to study private-agency policy. The major focus here is on adoption, foster care, and abuse. All students are required to visit an agency in order to define one social problem and policy regarding it. The emphasis of this assignment is on developing self-awareness at an emotional level while grasping an intellectual understanding of social welfare problems.

Once the students understand this two-pronged emphasis, the course focuses on defining justice and its application to policy issues, and then on identifying particular policy issues in which injustice occurs. To assist in determining a definition of justice, we turn to traditional church teachings and read Thomas Aquinas, *Summa Theologiae*, part II-II, questions 57 through 61. By understanding justice in this context, students later are able to distinguish the differences between justice and charity, and more importantly, the concepts of commutative and distributive justice. Commutative justice offers guidelines for the mutual dealings between two persons. Distributive justice addresses the problems of distributing common good proportionately.

To begin a study of a major social issue—unemployment—the students are referred to current literature to obtain statistics as well as media coverage of attitudes of the formerly employed toward their employers, their communities, and society in general. Discussion specifically relates to the moral responsibility of employers who decide to move a business or corporation, leaving hundreds or thousands of persons unemployed.

To understand this many faceted problem better, students interview a business owner, a representative from the employment service, and a benefit recipient. Following this experience, discussions are centered on individual rights and the application of principles of justice by the organization and community support services.

At this time in the semester, the students have generally mastered an understanding of broad societal issues and values. In studying the effects of unemployment and community response, they perceive the effects of situational stress on families. Learning is then highlighted by contact with private agencies who care for children who have suffered abuse or handicapping conditions. Generally, the study of this service area is less problematic because students perceive children as a helpless group for whom it is necessary to establish rights by legislation. It is clearer that this client group requires advocates in all areas of their lives because they are unable to speak or act for themselves.

In order to develop a broader sense of justice and peace, it is incumbent upon the instructor to introduce issues of ethnicity. For this purpose, a representative of the Midwest Hispanic Ministry is invited to lecture to the class and respond to questions about the emphasis on family life and child care within the Hispanic community. Also, since our students have virtually no experience with Native Americans, the Indian Child Welfare Act is required reading. Emphasis is placed upon the cultural context of the family and tribe, and the manner of working within the culture, even when it may cause problems in the executing agency or legal policy.

The course concludes with a study of social welfare in the third world. Since policy in this area was not developed by the individual countries until the 1950s, with the establishment of their independence from Western industrial nations, they had little expertise in this area. UNICEF (United Nations Children's Fund) worked mainly in the area of service delivery rather than development of policy within the cultures. Due to the urbanization of many countries, material needs such as providing housing and developing agriculture took priority. Social workers tended to use skills developed in Western societies, which proved inappropriate in new settings.

To appreciate better the problem of justice in the third world, students are required to research the culture of a third-world country and to address a common need, for example, housing. The intent of this research report is to develop a policy aimed at solving the problem within the cultural context of a specific country.

To support the class lectures with social experiences, students in the class are required to become members of the Social Action Club at Saint Mary's College. Most of the activities of this campus organization are focused on developing a social conscience among the student body, particularly through the World Hunger Coalition, which at this writing is addressing the issue of waste in the college dining hall. A second club activity is a fortnight-long program during which films and guest lectures are presented. These will include speakers who have worked, or at least lived, in third-world countries.

The students are also required to participate in a Mini-Urban Plunge. This event is planned through the Justice Education Office of Saint Mary's College. It includes a visit to, and participation in, a community soup kitchen, visits to various agencies serving the poor, and a lecture by a neighborhood self-help group.

Many of them also share in the full Urban Plunge (see Donald McNeill's "Afterword" in this volume) in cities throughout the United States during winter recess. This requires students to live for a few days in poverty neighborhoods, in various cities close to their homes, where they talk with welfare recipients about the latter's experiences with delivery systems. They also visit agencies that deliver services to the poor. Following this experience, faculty members and student participants share their feelings in group meetings.

Since social welfare policy is a required content area in both undergraduate and graduate school curricula, it is an ideal course for the infusion of social justice themes for several reasons. First, it directly addresses questions of poverty and the identification of who is poor and deserving of assistance. Second, it concerns itself with legislation at federal, state, and local levels. Third, it emphasizes the importance of voluntary agencies, which meet specific needs of particular client groups. Fourth, it develops a sensitivity to the stress undergone by social workers trying to meet client needs efficiently while trying also to satisfy a community demand for cost effectiveness.

SOCIAL WORK THEORY AND PRACTICE

The students' first formal experience in community service occurs as part of the course in "Social Work Theory and Practice." At Saint Mary's this course is required of social work majors in the second semester of the sophomore year, following "Social Welfare Policy and Services." The goal of this course is to teach how classroom theory applies in practice. The students are required to do three hours per week of volunteer work for a full semester.

Therefore, the most critical issues facing the students are the choice of agencies and supervisors with an orientation to justice and peace concepts. Since most communities have traditional agencies, such as a Department of Public Welfare, and Catholic Charities, as well as more recently-developed services, for example, shelters for battered women and for runaways, it is important to educate supervisors on how to include a content area on the subject of justice.

This is accomplished in three ways. Supervisors are involved in the ongoing educational process through seminars held at the college, both those sponsored by the host department and those sponsored by the university community as a whole. Seminars encourage supervisors to bring from practice to the classroom real problems that they have experienced with the delivery systems. Problem-solving methods centered around advocacy are presented for discussion by supervisors and students. An emphasis on justice issues, including clients' rights, helps develop a sense of professional ethics to which all volunteers must adhere. Most students develop a sense of professional responsibility through their study of values and behaviors as they relate to distributive justice.

Hence the emphasis should be on the selection of the supervisors and their commitment to justice education. It is incumbent upon the educators in the classroom to know their individual supervisors and to confer with them continually on practice problems. The resources of the college community should be made available to these supervisors. This includes open access to the library and the expertise of faculty from all departments for consultation and in-service training. It is also important that a "Guide for Supervisors" be written, specifically stating the focus of justice education, suggesting possible issues and experiences for the students to investigate, and providing outlines for possible assignments. (This guide is for use by outside supervisors in supervising students.)

At the conclusion of the practicum experience, educators should solicit feedback from students and supervisors as to their reactions. If specific recommendations are forthcoming, they should be acted upon with revisions of course content for the following semester.

I recommend that teachers of courses in social welfare policy also consider team-teaching, with faculty from government and economics departments. With this format, the students should more clearly understand the interplay of these forces in society that affect the creation and enactment of legislation and policy at all levels of government. Using different perspectives also enables students to appreciate different value orientations.

At Saint Mary's we have a method of teaching "in tandem." In this framework, the same group of students enrolls in two related courses, for example "Social Welfare Policy" and a government course. The two professors meet before the semester and select particular justice themes to be discussed in both courses. The professors then "audit" each other's courses so that specific references made to the justice topics and particular writing assignments and discussion periods will coincide. The students are thus able to approach the discussion from an interdisciplinary point of view.

CONCLUSION

Education is an ongoing process for all the persons concerned. Because social work historically has been in the vanguard of identifying social problems and developing methods of solution, it is the profession's moral responsibility to continue the personal development of its members and the social conscience of the profession.

Since the Bachelor's degree in social work has been recognized as the credential for entrance into the profession, it is critical for undergraduate social work educators to instill a sense of justice in students. Most of them are at a critical stage in their own personal development as human beings, as well as in their careers. A commitment to justice in society must be made by teachers and students. Social workers are caring people, sensitive to the needs of individuals and groups. Social workers must try to ensure justice for those unable to function according to society's demands, by serving as advocates for the disadvantaged, and by using their professional knowledge and skills at whatever level of government is needed and in whatever area of practice they function.

NOTES

1. Harold L. Wilensky and Charles N. Lebeaux, *Industrial Society and Social Welfare* (New York: Free Press, 1967).
2. Frances Fox Piven and Richard A. Cloward, *Regulating the Poor: The Functions of Public Welfare* (New York: Pantheon Books, 1971).
3. Elizabeth D. Huttman, *Introduction to Social Policy* (New York: McGraw-Hill, 1971), p. 6.
4. David Gil, "Incidents of Child Abuse and Demographic Characteristics of Persons Involved," in *The Battered Child,* ed. Ray E. Helfer and C. Henry Kempe (Chicago, Ill.: University of Chicago Press, 1981), p. 6.
5. Leo XIII, *Rerum Novarum* ("Of New Things," 1891) (Washington, DC: National Catholic Welfare Conference, 1942). Pius XI, *Quadragesimo Anno* ("Fortieth Year [after *Rerum Novarum*]," 1931) (Washington, DC: National Catholic Welfare Conference, 1942). John Paul II, *Laborem Exercens* ("On Human Work," 1981) (Washington, DC: USCC, 1981).
6. Lexington, Mass.: D.C. Heath and Co., 1980.

SELECTED READINGS FOR FACULTY

Akabas, Sheila H., and Paul A. Kurzman, eds. *Work, Workers and Organizations.* Englewood Cliffs, N. J.: Prentice-Hall, 1982.

Bird, Caroline. *The Invisible Scar.* New York: Longmans, 1966.

Burr, James. *Protective Services for Adults.* Washington, D.C.: U.S. Administration on Aging, Office of Human Development Services, 1982.

Caplan, Arthur L., and Daniel Callahan, eds. *Ethics in Hard Times.* New York: Plenum Press, 1981.

Constable, Robert. *School Social Work: Practice and Research Perspectives.* Homewood, Ill.: Dorsey Press, 1982.

Derthick, Martha. *Policy Making for Social Security.* Washington, D.C.: Brookings Institution, 1979.

Encylopedia of Social Work. Vols. 1 and 2. Washington, D.C.: National Association of Social Workers, 1977.

Federico, Ronald. The *Social Welfare Institution: An Introduction.* Lexington, Mass.: D. C. Heath and Co., 1980.

Feldman, Frances L. *Family Social Welfare.* New York: Aldine Publishing Co., 1979.

Frankfather, D. *Family Care of the Elderly.* Lexington, Mass.: D. C. Heath and Co., 1981.

Garraty, John. *Unemployment in History: Economic Thought and Public Policy.* New York: Harper & Row, 1978.

Graham, James. *The Enemies of the Poor.* New York: Random House, 1970.

Hancock, Betsy. *School Social Work.* Englewood Cliffs, N. J.: Prentice-Hall, 1982.

Heidenheimer, Arnold; Hugh Heclo; and Carolyn T. Adams. *Comparative Public Policy.* New York: St. Martin's Press, 1975.

Johnson, Otis S. *The Social Welfare Role of the Black Church.* Ann Arbor, Mich.: University Microfilms International, 1982.

Leo XIII. *Social Wellsprings.* Vols. 1 and 2. Milwaukee, Wis.: Bruce Publishing Co., 1940, 1942.

Midley, James. *Professional Imperialism: Social Work in the Third World.* London: Heinemann Educational Books, 1981.

Moynihan, Daniel P. *The Politics of a Guaranteed Income: The Nixon Administration and the Family Assistance Plan.* New York: Random House, 1973.

Munnell, Alicia. *The Future of Social Security.* Washington, D.C.: Brookings Institution, 1977.

Nelson, Margaret, and M. Frances Walton. *Ohoyo Ikhana: A Bibliography of American Indian-Alaska Native Curriculum Materials.* Austin, Tex.: Ohoyo Resource Center, 1982.

Organization for Economic Cooperation and Development. *Socio-Economic Policies for the Elderly.* Paris: OECD, 1979.

Romanyshyn, John. *Social Welfare: Charity to Justice.* New York: Random House, 1971.

Rousseau, A. M., *Shopping Bag Ladies.* New York: Pilgrim Press, 1981.

Sheehan, Susan. *A Welfare Mother.* Boston: Houghton Mifflin Co., 1976.

Social Services in Britain. London: Great Britain Central Office of Information, Reference Division, 1966.

Starr, Paul. *The Social Transformation of American Medicine.* New York: Basic Books, 1982.

Stevens, Robert. *Welfare Medicine in America.* New York: Free Press, 1974.

Titmuss, Richard. *Commitment to Welfare.* New York: Pantheon Books, 1968.

Trattner, Walter. *From Poor Law to Welfare State.* New York: Free Press, 1974.

United States Laws and Statutes. Public Law 95-608, Indian Child Welfare Act, Nov. 8, 1978; Title 42, Public Health and Welfare, Sept. 17, 1980.

Words of Today's American Indian Women: Ohoyo Makachi. Austin, Tex.: Ohoyo Resource Center, 1981.

PART IV

INTERDISCIPLINARY COURSES

14

World Hunger
from a Christian Perspective

SUZANNE C. TOTON
VILLANOVA UNIVERSITY

One of the most rewarding educational experiences I have had has been teaching a course entitled "World Hunger from a Christian Perspective." I was teaching part-time at a small, private Catholic college, Cabrini College, in Radnor, Pennsylvania. Being at Cabrini has its own advantages: cutting through the bureaucracy of introducing a new course into the curriculum, familiarity with faculty in other disciplines, getting the word out and attracting students to the new course, and the freedom to experiment. It was 1974, and the problem of hunger was very much in the news. The Soviet Union, experiencing serious problems with its wheat harvests, was turning to the United States for much of its grain. India's food supply had fallen perilously short due to inadequate monsoons. Drought plagued several areas of the globe. Fish harvests were dropping off. The price of fertilizer was soaring. The Organization of Petroleum Exporting Countries (OPEC) raised the price of oil, and the price of bread, poultry, beef, fish, and even beans was steadily increasing worldwide. The media carried stories weekly of large numbers of people dying of hunger, especially in Bangladesh and the Sahel region of Africa.

One of the professors at Cabrini, John DeTurck, a biologist who had a special interest in ecology, was keeping a close watch on the world food

---

An earlier version of this essay appeared in Suzanne C. Toton, *World Hunger: The Responsibility of Christian Education* (Maryknoll, N.Y.: Orbis Books, 1982).

situation. I was also keenly interested in the situation, but primarily from a religious and educational standpoint. Over lunch John DeTurck and I often shared thoughts and ideas about how to deal with the problem of hunger. He knew much more than I about the suffering that human beings undergo who are deprived of food, their loss of immunity to disease, and what nutrients it takes to keep the body functioning. He also had a wealth of knowledge about the ecosphere, its delicate balance, the desertification process, soil erosion, the ocean as a source of food, the implications of the green revolution, and genetic research being done on plant life. On the basis of his technical knowledge, DeTurck was convinced that hunger was unnecessary, and furthermore he believed hunger to be immoral. Because of my interest in global poverty, I in turn had more understanding of how the international systems of trade, aid, and investment contributed to shortages of food and capital in the third world. I was also familiar with the Roman Catholic Church's social teaching on these systems and was working on the implications of liberation theology and the pedagogy of Paulo Freire for North Americans. Looking back now, it seemed only natural that we should team-teach a course on world hunger, drawing on each other's strengths in the subject matter.

In planning the course we had a number of objectives in mind: to create a greater awareness of the magnitude of the problem of world hunger in our students and the college community, to examine critically the root causes and proposed solutions to the problem, and to reflect seriously on what our response as Christians might be. In designing the course, John DeTurck and I decided that it would be important to draw on as many resources in our geographical community as possible. We also wanted to provide students with experiences working with or for hungry people. The course was very well received—so well that we repeated it several times. Since I left Cabrini, John DeTurck and Mary Anne Duthie, a teacher in the Religion Department, have offered it and plan to repeat it.

Changes, naturally, were made in the course each time it was taught. What follows, however, is an overview of our pedagogical approach, the issues covered, and some of the results.

TEACHING A WORLD HUNGER COURSE

It is important to state at the outset that the educational methodology and goals we employed in our course were influenced by the Brazilian educator Paulo Freire. The primary purpose of education, Freire maintains, is to humanize, that is, to become sensitive to the suffering of others and to act to alleviate it. Our educational task must begin by developing an awareness of the magnitude of human need and suffering, analyzing the underlying causes, and taking the personal and structural steps needed for change. We understood our role as teachers to be primarily "problematizers." In Freire's terminology, "problematizers" make problems out of what is generally perceived to be the normal, the acceptable, and the taken-for-granted. The reality is presented as abnormal or unacceptable in a humane society. We also felt that, in the course, it was our responsibility to move beyond raising critical consciousness. The course itself, as we saw it, should contribute in some way to changing the values, systems, and structures that produce the problem.

WORLD HUNGER FROM A CHRISTIAN PERSPECTIVE
(three credits)

COURSE OBJECTIVES

One of the essential characteristics of being human, development ethicist Denis Goulet writes, is the ability to perceive the suffering of others and to respond to it. Over a half-billion people in the world today suffer from hunger. They lack the nutrients that they need to carry out everyday, normal human activity. A lot of reasons have been given for world hunger and a number of steps have been taken to alleviate it. The question is, Are the reasons that have been given and the steps already taken correct and appropriate? Is more needed? As Christians who have a special obligation to the poor and hungry, we must also ask what our personal responsibility and the responsibility of the churches are. This course should provide some clarity on these questions.

The purpose of the course is (1) to get a basic understanding of some of the theories for world hunger; (2) to look at the problem of world hunger within a broader context, that is, global poverty; (3) to determine what our responsibility as first-world Christians is toward the poor and the hungry of the world; and (4) to take some first steps to alleviate this form of human suffering.

REQUIRED READING

Agency for International Development (AID), Washington, D.C. *Facts about A.I.D.* (April 18, 1981, issue).
———. *World Development Letter* 4, no. 13 (June 24, 1981): 49–52.
Lappé, Frances Moore, and Joseph Collins. *Food First: Beyond the Myth of Scarcity.* Rev. ed. New York: Ballantine Books, 1979.
Marstin, Ronald. *Beyond Our Tribal Gods: The Maturing of Faith.* Maryknoll, N.Y.: Orbis Books, 1979.
Paul VI. *Populorum Progressio* ("On the Development of Peoples," 1967). In *The Gospel of Peace and Justice,* ed. Joseph Gremillion. Maryknoll, N.Y.: Orbis Books, 1976.
Presidential Commission on World Hunger. *Overcoming World Hunger: The Challenge Ahead.* Washington, D.C.: U.S. Government Printing Office, 1980.

Synod of Bishops, Second General Assembly. "Justice in the World,"
1971. In *The Gospel of Peace and Justice*, ed. Joseph Gremillion.
Maryknoll, N.Y.: Orbis Books, 1976.
United Nations General Assembly, Sixth Special Session (May 1, 1974).
"Declaration on the Establishment of a New International Economic
Order." Available from American Friends Service Committee, New
England Regional Office, 48 Inman Street, Cambridge, MA 02139.

COURSE OUTLINE

 I. Why Study World Hunger? (two weeks)
    Reading: Marstin, *Beyond Our Tribal Gods.*
 II. Overview of Theories about World Hunger (two weeks)
    Reading: Lappé and Collins, *Food First.*
 III. Putting World Hunger in Context (four weeks)
    Reading: AID materials; Lappé and Collins, *Food First;* Presidential
    Commission on World Hunger, *Overcoming World Hunger*;
    United Nations General Assembly, "Declaration on the Establish-
    ment of a New International Economic Order."
 IV. Relating Hunger in the United States to Hunger in the Third World
    (one week)
    Reading: Lappé and Collins, *Food First;* Presidential Commission
    on World Hunger, *Overcoming World Hunger.*
 V. The Responsibility of Christians (three weeks)
    Reading: Paul VI, "On the Development of Peoples"; Synod of
    Bishops, Second General Assembly, "Justice in the World."
 VI. Sharing Project Experiences (one or two weeks)

COURSE REQUIREMENTS

Since the success of this course depends to a large extent on student input,
it is imperative that students complete the assigned readings, actively
participate in class discussion, keep an up-to-date clipping file, attend
required lectures, and participate in extracurricular activities.

Students will receive a total of five grades for the course. They break
down as follows: (1) one grade per take-home exam. The take-home
exams will be given upon completion of each of the three major sections
of the course (first section, Units I and II; second section, Units III and
IV; third section, Unit V), which means a total of three take-home exams;
(2) one grade for the final project; (3) one grade for class participation.
This also includes keeping an active clipping file and participating in
required lectures and extracurricular activities.

The Clipping File

Each student is expected to keep a file of newspaper and magazine
clippings that relate to the issues discussed in class. The date and

source of the news item should be noted on the clipping itself. All important information in the clipping should be underlined.

Students who do not have personal copies of newspapers and magazines may either Xerox library copies or prepare a typed summary of the news piece.

Extra Credit

From time to time lectures or workshops on the topics under study are held on and off campus. Students can receive extra credit by attending these functions and by writing a brief (one or two pages) summary of the major issues discussed. Students may also earn extra credit if they take one or more of the optional class trips.

The Project

Each student is required to do a project. While it takes the place of a final examination, students will need to work on it throughout the semester. Students say that the project is interesting and fun, and that they learn more from it than they would from taking a final examination.

There are three types of projects from which to choose: (1) The student tries to determine through interviews and research how his or her chosen profession is presently contributing, or could contribute, to alleviating poverty and hunger in the United States and the third world. (2) The student interviews and researches religiously affiliated organizations working with and on behalf of the poor and hungry for structural and systemic change. (3) The student volunteers time on a regular basis and interviews the personnel working in a house of hospitality in the geographic area of the college.

Students will be expected to complete a six- to ten-page report, due the day scheduled for the class's final examination. Time will be given in the last few classes of the semester for students to share and reflect upon their project experiences. If a student needs assistance in organizing or making contacts for a project, the teacher will be on hand to help. Each student will receive a set of questions that may be helpful in conducting interviews and research, and guidelines for organizing the written report.

We began the course with the question of why hunger exists today (Unit I). The point was to make explicit some of the commonly held assumptions about hunger, such as that people in the third world don't take advantage of birth control, their governments squander all the aid the United States gives them, the people of India would rather spare their cows and allow their people to starve, the people of the third world lack the drive of the forefathers of the

United States to pull themselves out of their poverty, and the third world lacks the land and resources to feed its own people. In asking the question "Why?" we were also trying to raise a deeper issue, namely, in an age that has the technology to put people on the moon and to destroy the world several times over, why is it that over a half-billion people do not have enough to eat? We also wanted to raise the question, Can individuals be called "morally mature" or nations "developed" when they ignore or accept as inevitable the suffering that the majority of the world's people endure?

In discussing these deeper questions, we found a number of sources helpful. *The Cruel Choice* by the development ethicist Denis Goulet,[1] for example, raises the issue of the relationship of goods to the good life. He asks whether the so-called developed societies of the West have not confused the two. Has their obsession for economic prosperity and political and military superiority put them into a situation where they can no longer see beyond their immediate self-interest and make the profound value choice to eradicate world poverty and hunger? Goulet also asks if we can honestly call societies "developed" that place priority on military spending or providing luxury goods when the vast majority of humankind lacks the basic necessities of life. Can those societies even be called "human," since one of the most fundamental characteristics of being human is the ability to respond to the suffering of others? Another helpful source for this first section is *Beyond Our Tribal Gods* by Ronald Marstin.[2] Marstin raises the question of whether a faith that ignores such massive human suffering can truly be mature, or not. Drawing on the work of Jean Piaget, Lawrence Kohlberg, and James Fowler, Marstin argues that mature faith is characterized by a broadening of one's vision and concern, the ability to put oneself in another's shoes, and the ability to see that one's explanations for the way things are, are just that—one's *own* explanations. Finally, Marstin raises the question of whether or not maturity should be measured by the changes that come about in people's heads or by the changes people bring about in society.

This discussion of one's perception of reality lends itself quite nicely to moving into some of the explanations given for world hunger—Unit II of the course. We reviewed the Paddocks' theory of overpopulation, and contrasted it with Georg Borgstrom's theory that it is not the third world but the first world that is overpopulated. Countries are overpopulated, he says, when they are forced by limited natural resources to draw on other countries' resources to maintain their standard of living. We also looked at Lester Brown's approach, which places more emphasis on the natural causes of hunger. Brown maintains that hunger is due largely to the pressures that overpopulation and affluence exert on the ecosphere. These pressures have resulted in the devastation of land, water pollution, shortages of fuel and fertilizer, and depletion of the world's fish supply. By indicting the affluent along with the poor for the devastation of our ecosphere, Brown, in effect, set the stage for examining the costs in human terms of pursuing affluence in a world of limited resources. This led us into the third Unit of the course, in which we attempted to identify the hungry and pursue the economic, political, and social causes of hunger.[3]

We begin this unit by defining terms such as "the third world," "the underdeveloped nations," and "the periphery." We were careful to point out that the terms we use to speak about the poor determine to a large extent how we relate to them. We looked at some of the characteristics these nations have in common: low gross domestic product, high mortality rate, high rate of illiteracy, and so forth. After this, we found it helpful to study the demands that the poor nations expressed in the United Nations Declaration for the Establishment of a New International Economic Order. This provided the opportunity to discuss such issues as the colonial history of these countries, various theories relating underdevelopment to development, the objectives and failures of the first and second United Nations development decades, the meaning of the term "neo-colonialism," and a preference for the term "liberation" over "development" by a growing number of poor nations.

It was now time to examine the charges leveled at the first world in the United Nations Declaration for the Establishment of a New International Economic Order, with an eye to ascertaining the effect the systems of trade, aid, and investment have had on increasing poverty and hunger. We found the filmstrip *Sharing Global Resources*, from the American Friends Service Committee, good for providing a general overview from the third world's perspective on how these systems work to their detriment. In the area of trade, we focused on the question of why the third world is unable to meet its import demands despite the steady increase in its production rate and export volume. To treat this adequately we tried to explicate theories that account for unequal trade; the influence that organizations such as the General Agreement on Tariffs and Trade (GATT) and the United Nations Conference on Trade and Development (UNCTAD) have on world trade; the effect of tariffs, quotas, and nontariff barriers on third-world production and export; and proposals that have been made to rectify the inequitable situation. We tried to relate this discussion of trade to the situation of many of the poorest third-world countries during the food crisis of 1972–75. When forced to purchase grain at inflated prices from commercial markets, the poorest countries did not have the export revenue to compete with financially better-off countries.

If the third world could diversify its production, gain access to first-world markets, and receive a decent price for its products, it might not have to rely so heavily on aid. The next segment of Unit III takes up problems of third-world debt. We reviewed the various channels through which aid is transferred to the third world, noted the very small portion that such assistance represents of the first world's gross domestic product, pointed out the increase in the third world's indebtedness, and examined its implications for the world monetary system. Our focus, however, was on the conditions under which aid is transferred through multilateral agencies such as the World Bank Group and bilateral agencies such as the United States Agency for International Development (USAID). Our question was: Given the types of projects approved by the lending agencies and the conditions attached to the aid, is financial assistance a help or a hindrance to the poorest sectors of the third world? The United States Food for Peace Program, the major program through which food assistance is transferred to the third world, was our case study. We looked at the purposes for which it was developed, the modifications that have been made by the United States Congress, its performance during the food crisis, and the criticisms that are leveled at it by various religious-oriented hunger lobbies. We found it very useful to have students read material that USAID has published on aid in general and food aid in particular.

As the final part of Unit III, we looked at the criticisms that have been leveled at transnational corporations: their wage scales, working conditions, transfer pricing, investments, and interference in the internal affairs of developing countries. Our main concern, however, was the effect cash cropping has on hunger. Could land that is used for growing sugar, coffee, and bananas, and for grazing cattle, be used to grow food for local consumption? What are the obstacles to doing so? Were a significant portion of land diverted to growing food for domestic consumption, would there be any guarantee that the poor would eat? We found guest speakers from the regional interreligious coalition for responsible investment or a spokesperson from a transnational corporation to be invaluable for clarifying the issues raised in this part of the course.

After leading students through this examination of world trade, aid, and investment, it became clear that hunger is not an isolated problem but is integrally connected with the larger problem of global poverty. Hunger, we felt, could not be eradicated without fundamental changes in the systems and values that produce poverty. We asked whether the reforms called for in the New International Economic Order (NIEO) are radical enough. Do they merely tamper with the symptoms and leave the root causes of poverty undisturbed? Is it possible to change fundamentally the inequitable relationship between the first and third worlds without radically restructuring the economic system that produced that relationship and continues to make it necessary? On the other hand, if we adopt a more radical position, must we abandon the NIEO reforms? Or is it possible to view those reforms as steps in the longer process of radically transforming the market system? In other words, is it possible to approach the NIEO reforms in such a way that they become not palliative but creative incremental changes—changes that spur us on to work for deeper and long-lasting change? Since hunger by no means is confined to the third world, we spent some time (Unit IV) examining hunger in the United States and in our own geographic area. This included an attempt to identify the hungry and the systemic causes of hunger in the United States, and to understand and evaluate government programs set up to eradicate hunger. We also tried to make whatever parallels we could to the situation of hunger in the third world. Again, we found speakers helpful in this section. At times we called upon administrators from our diocesan feeding program, volunteers staffing food pantries set up by local parishes, religious who staff a house of hospitality, and community organizers.

Unit V of the course takes up the issue of our responsibility, as Christians, to respond to the problems of poverty and hunger. We found it extremely helpful to review the Catholic Church's teaching on the rights of workers, the role of the state, the right to private property, and systems of capitalism and socialism. To get the church's perspective on the international systems we had just covered, the students read Pope Paul VI's encyclical, *Populorum Progressio* ("On the Development of Peoples") and the statement by the Second General Assembly of the Synod of Bishops, "Justice in the World," both reprinted in *The Gospel of Peace and Justice*, edited by Joseph Gremillion. We also tried to give students some understanding of the church's struggle for justice in the third world. This included an overview of the statements of the Latin American Episcopal conferences at Medellín, Colombia (also reprinted in the Gremillion volume), and Puebla, Mexico (*Puebla and Beyond*, edited by Eagleson and Scharper and published by Orbis Books), and an introduction to the methodology of Latin American liberation theology and some of its key concepts. (See books by R. M. Brown and Gutiérrez cited at end of this essay). The Maryknoll Missioners have been invaluable in this segment of the course. Their Philadelphia, Pennsylvania, development house has provided films, at no cost, on the church in the third world. Priests, brothers, sisters, and lay missioners stationed in Philadelphia or visiting the area came to our class from time to time to share their personal experiences of poverty and the peoples' struggle for justice in the third world. Our class also spent an evening at the Maryknoll House in Philadelphia, having dinner, informally sharing experiences, and reflecting on our responsibility to the poor and hungry. Through the generosity of Brother Ray Tetrault, the director of the Philadelphia Maryknoll House, we stayed for a weekend at Maryknoll's headquarters in Ossining, New York. There we spent the better part of the morning with the Maryknoll Sisters and an afternoon with some of the lay volunteers. We had the opportunity to meet Father James Noonan, then superior-general of Maryknoll, and the directors of the Peace and Justice Office, the Peace and Justice Academic Program, and the Office of Communications. We also had sessions with some recently returned missioners from Asia, Africa, and Latin America. The most meaningful part of the weekend, however (the students told us), was the opportunity to talk with missioners on a one-on-one basis at meals. The purpose of these contacts with Maryknoll was not simply to provide information about the church and the struggle in the third world, but to begin to reflect together in very specific terms about the responsibility of the first-world church and individual Christians to change the structures and systems that keep the third world poor and hungry.

There have been other field trips, also, for participants in the course in different years. For example, some members of one class went to Washington, D.C., for the day, for a seminar on the lobbying process, a seminar designed for them by Network, the Catholic social justice lobby. One year we visited the United Nations and were briefed by an official from the United Nations Development Program. Another year we took a trip to Rodale Organic Farm at Emmaus, Pennsylvania. There we learned about various forms of experimental farming that restore nutrients to the soil and avoid the use of expensive pesticides and fertilizers that are often destructive or harmful in various ways. We also learned about various forms of experimental technology that are less energy- and capital-intensive, which could be adapted for use in the third world. We visited the Rodale Press, and the class also had a vegetarian meal prepared at Rodale's Fitness House, in addition to visiting the test kitchen and the dining room for Rodale employees. Some students noted the fact that the visit to the Rodale facilities gave them an insight into how social concerns could be combined with a career.

We invited United States Representative Bod Edgar, himself a minister, to our class. He spoke on the importance of Christians' learning to lobby effectively on behalf of the poor and hungry. Each student also keeps a clipping file of newspaper and magazine articles that relate to course issues. Through these files the students keep abreast of the latest developments and learn to read between the lines of the media coverage. They also begin to sense that what we are studying together is no mere abstract "academic" concern but a very real problem, which we have the potential to change. The clipping files kept by the students have the added benefit of involving the students' families and neighbors, so that these people, too, are on the lookout for articles of interest. This frequently results in worthwhile discussions on topics about which the students are learning through such reading.

An increased sensitivity to the food we eat, its nutritional value, and the amount of food wasted by Americans was a by-product of the course. The students began to take note of the nutritional quality of food, what foods they ate in the college cafeteria, and the amount of food that they and their peers wasted. Several times during the course selected students prepared snacks high in nutrients to share with the class. One semester, we prepared a complete vegetarian dinner together. We used the opportunity to discuss the protein-complementarity theory, the American diet, and the arguments for eating foods lower on the food chain.

One aspect of the course that has been perhaps most meaningful for many students is the student projects (reported on in Unit VI). The value of the projects is based on the old adage: "I hear and I forget; I see and I remember; I do and I understand." Student projects fulfill the following purposes:

1. They help students to see that this study is not just academic. The lives of millions of people in the third world are affected by the actions of individuals and of society in the first world.

2. They help students to identify the hungry in their society and to develop a feeling of identity with those people.

3. They can help students to relate their major field of study and their future occupation to the problem of hunger.

4. They put students in touch with people and organizations in society that are striving to combat world poverty and hunger. In this way students can see firsthand the channels available to us to work for global change.

The projects are worked on throughout the semester by students individually or as members of a group. After students become involved in their projects and begin to relate their own experiences in the projects to the problems we are confronting in class work, a change can be seen in the teacher/student relationship. In my opinion the students come very close to what Freire would call "student/teachers." They actually begin to take possession of the teaching/ learning act. Although we remain the teachers, we are no longer perceived as the sole source of information. The students themselves become experts and problem-posers. It was exciting for us as teachers to witness the change as students began to take over their own educational process. Brief descriptions of some student projects, and benefits derived, follow.

Typical Projects

Understanding Undernutrition and Powerlessness: A group of biology students chose a project in which they could study the effects of malnutrition and undernutrition. Under the supervision of John DeTurck, the students fed one group of mice an adequate diet and another group an inadequate diet. As the semester went by, the students kept close tabs on the mice, charting the physical development of both groups. It was noticed that the undernourished mice began to deteriorate physically and in time became so listless that they did not even have enough energy to respond when food was offered to them. Besides learning about the physical effects of undernutrition and malnutrition, the students made an unexpected discovery. They told the class how they had discovered the meaning of power through manipulation. They spoke of the ease with which the powerful can make decisions affecting the lives of the powerless and how, given the absence of personal or societal moral restraints, the power of the powerful is limitless. They also gained a new appreciation of the word "dependency" and learned something about the advantage of controlling resources and keeping others dependent.

Understanding Systemic Injustice: Another group of students volunteered for the Meals-on-Wheels program for the semester. They delivered frozen meals prepared by area volunteers to elderly and housebound people living in the vicinity. The students received valuable personal contacts with individuals in need of food. They discovered that the elderly in the United States are often hungry and dependent. They were disturbed that a so-called developed society could cast off those who were no longer economically productive, and that the reward for a lifetime of labor might be poverty and dependency. They wondered what might happen to their parents and themselves in old age. This experience led them to discuss with parents and grandparents the justice of the United States Social Security system, forced retirement, the tax system, and care for the elderly. The meaning of systemic injustice became a reality and not just an idea to students who saw firsthand that the hungry whom they encountered were hungry not through personal failure but through a failure of systems.

Understanding Bias in the News: A journalism major studied the coverage of hunger in several newspapers. Becoming adept at judging the quality of the reporting on hunger, she found that the political, more controversial aspect of the issue was rarely treated. Moreover, she began to see that so-called unbiased reporting was never really unbiased. All stories were written from a particular perspective. In the case of news reports on hunger, she found that they rarely challenged the United States government's perspective. As part of her project she wrote a column on hunger for the school newspaper and did a fine job of keeping the campus informed of issues related to global poverty and hunger.

Food and Clothing Drives: Food and clothing drives for the poor are common on campus. As their project, some students tried to make our campus food drive different. They set out to educate the donors about the complexity of the issues and the need for other, more long-term actions. The students who ran the Thanksgiving food drive found that contributors would much rather deal with hunger on the level of charity. They did not want to hear about the causes of hunger, and they preferred merely to give cans of food and not to make an effort, such as writing to their congressional representative, to address roots of the problem. The students also learned—much to their surprise—that their fellow students were as apathetic and insensitive (if not more so) as the older generation appeared to be.

Conferring with Organizations in Favor of Structural Change: Some students have opted to visit organizations like the Interfaith Center on Corporate Responsibility, the Interfaith Action for Economic Justice, the Campaign for Human Development, Catholic Relief Services, Church World Service, the Quixote Center, Network, and others. People at those organizations have been extremely helpful and generous of their time. Without the enthusiastic support of such representatives, the student projects could not have been as successful as they have been.

One student usually makes arrangements for a group of four or five students to spend a day visiting the organization. Information is obtained about the organization and its projects so that the group can become familiar with the organization before its visit. The students aim to obtain firsthand information about the purposes of the organization; projects in which it is involved; its function, funding, successes, and failures; obstacles to the achievement of its purposes; and specific contributions that individuals and churches are making to the work of the organization. The students generally meet as a group with a representative of the organization, who explains its operation and answers questions. Then, depending on the students' individual research interests, each student confers with an expert within the organization who is working in the area of the student's interest. Students on a visit to the Interfaith Center on Corporate Responsibility (ICCR), for example, met first as a group with Timothy Smith, director of ICCR. Afterward one student conferred with the resource person for the infant-formula project; another, with the expert on bank loans to South Africa; a third, with the expert on church holdings of securities issued by corporations producing military products; and a fourth, with the expert on agribusinesses in the third world.

After their visit the students carried on a fair amount of independent research in their areas of special interest. Using materials obtained about the organization and their own areas of special interest as well as the results of their own critical reflections, they drew up a report of their findings and shared it with the class.

Benefits from the Projects

The student projects have proved to be pedagogically invaluable for a number of reasons. First, they counter the common tendency to approach global poverty and hunger as theoretical, abstract, and academic problems. Through their projects, some students encounter for the first time people who are hungry, and hear about their situation. Other students get to know the people and to identify the faces behind organizations working to alleviate hunger. Still other students encounter people who are opposed to action on behalf of the hungry. Thus hunger becomes for students what it essentially is— a human problem.

Not only does the project highlight the concreteness and immediacy of the problem, but it also frees students from narrowly identifying education with schooling. The poor themselves, people in various organizations, the students' families, their friends, the churches, and the media all become sources of education as students draw them into dialogue.

Students who worked in the Meals-on-Wheels project, for example, received an outstanding course on aging in American society from the elderly men and women to whom they took meals. Timothy Smith, director of ICCR, made six aspiring corporate executives aware of the fact that religious institutions are a force to be reckoned with.

Beyond the immediate benefits just mentioned, the projects provided for many students an invaluable link between their chosen occupation and possible solutions to the problems of poverty and hunger. It became quite clear to many that unless they acted differently from their predecessors in business, law, politics, and other occupations, hunger and poverty would continue to plague global society.

Although the students may not remember the content of readings or class discussion, what they learned from their projects will probably stay with them as a reminder of the fact that it is possible to work for change in one's society and in the world. After leaving school, they will know where to look for support of their own efforts on behalf of justice.

CONCLUSION

As with all educational endeavors, it is difficult to predict the long-term effect of our efforts, in the course just described, on the lives of students. This is especially true if we measure success not on the basis of test scores or financial and professional achievements but on change in consciousness and actions for justice.

The evaluations by our students at the end of the course gave us hope, however. Let me share just a few of their comments here:

> The most valuable aspect of this course for me was how it made me open up and question my own beliefs and thoughts as a Christian. Our class discussions forced me to take a stand. . . .

> The most valuable aspect of the course was the opportunity it gave the students to reevaluate their lives, the world, and the part they play in the world. . . .

> At times the course seemed very trying and unsettling. It raised questions about my beliefs, values, and responsibilities. . . .

Let me close with a note to teachers who are considering a course like the one I have described. John DeTurck, Mary Anne Duthie, and I have at times expressed the frustrations we felt during the course. It came not from the course or our students, but from teaching itself. Teaching seemed so removed from where the action was. How much more satisfying it would be to work in a refugee camp, a clinic, or even as a lobbyist on Capitol Hill! Yet, teaching is what we do best. And we knew that, in some way, we were enabling religious educational institutions to assume their responsibility to build a more just and humane world. Whenever I would rather be out in the field instead of preparing class, counseling students, or reading exams, I often think of a statement by one of the commissioners on the Independent Commission on International Development Issues, known as the Brandt Commission. He said, "New generations of the world need not only economic solutions, they need ideas to inspire them, hopes to encourage them, and first steps to implement them. They need a belief in man, in human dignity, in basic human rights; a belief in the values of justice, freedom, peace, mutual respect, in love and generosity, in reason rather than force." If we, as teachers, and our courses contribute toward that end, perhaps some day there will be no need for refugee camps, clinics, or even lobbies.

NOTES

1. Denis Goulet, *The Cruel Choice* (New York: Atheneum Publishers, 1971).
2. Ronald Marstin, *Beyond Our Tribal Gods* (Maryknoll, N.Y.: Orbis Books, 1979). Marstin provides an overview of the work of Piaget, Kohlberg, and Fowler.
3. For an overview of the theories of Borgstrom, Brown, and Paddock, see Toton, *World Hunger* (Maryknoll, N.Y.: Orbis Books, 1982), pp. 5–12.

SELECTED READINGS FOR FACULTY

Barnet, Richard J., and Ronald E. Müller. *Global Reach: The Power of the Multinational Corporations.* New York: Simon and Schuster, 1974.

Brandt, Willy, et al. *North-South: A Programme for Survival*. Cambridge, Mass.: MIT Press, 1980.

Brown, Robert McAfee. *Theology in a New Key: Responding to Liberation Themes*. Philadelphia, Pa.: Westminster Press, 1978.

Freire, Paulo. *Pedagogy of the Oppressed*. New York: Seabury Press, 1970.

George, Susan. *How the Other Half Dies: The Real Reasons for World Hunger*. Montclair, N.J.: Allanheld, Osmun, 1977.

Goulet, Denis. *The Cruel Choice: A New Concept in the Theory of Development*. New York: Atheneum Publishers, 1971.

Gremillion, Joseph, ed. *The Gospel of Peace and Justice: Catholic Social Teaching since Pope John*. Maryknoll, N.Y.: Orbis Books, 1976.

Gutiérrez, Gustavo. *A Theology of Liberation: History, Politics and Salvation*. Maryknoll, N.Y.: Orbis Books, 1973.

Harrington, Michael. *The Vast Majority: A Journey to the World's Poor*. New York: Simon and Schuster, 1977.

Lappé, Frances Moore, and Joseph Collins. *Food First: Beyond the Myth of Scarcity*. Rev. ed. New York: Ballantine Books, 1979.

Marstin, Ronald. *Beyond Our Tribal Gods: The Maturing of Faith*. Maryknoll, N.Y.: Orbis Books, 1979.

McGinnis, James B. *Bread and Justice: Toward a New International Economic Order*. New York: Paulist Press, 1979. Also the accompanying manual, *Bread and Justice: Toward a New International Economic Order Teacher's Book*.

Nelson, Jack A. *Hunger for Justice: The Politics of Food and Faith*. Maryknoll, N.Y.: Orbis Books, 1980.

Payer, Cheryl. *The Debt Trap*. New York: Monthly Review Press, 1974.

Presidential Commission on World Hunger. *Overcoming World Hunger: The Challenge Ahead*. Washington, D.C.: U.S. Government Printing Office, 1980.

Sivard, Ruth Leger. *World Military and Social Expenditures*, published 1974ff. Write to World Priorities, Box 25140, Washington, DC 20007, for copies and for information on editions available.

Toton, Suzanne C. *World Hunger: The Responsibility of Christian Education*. Maryknoll, N.Y.: Orbis Books, 1982.

United States Senate. Prepared for the Subcommittee on Foreign Agricultural Policy of the Committee on Agriculture, Nutrition and Forestry by the Congressional Research Service. *Food for Peace 1954–78: Major Changes in Legislation*. Washington, D.C.: U.S. Government Printing Office, 1979.

Wren, Brian. *Education for Justice: Pedagogical Principles*. Maryknoll, N.Y.: Orbis Books, 1977.

15

Science, Technology, and Society

MONA CUTOLO AND DENIS M. MIRANDA
MARYMOUNT MANHATTAN COLLEGE

We live in an age characterized as the "socio-technical" civilization; an age that has witnessed an unparalleled scientific explosion and technological growth. "Socio-technics," a term introduced by Herbert Richardson, refers to "the new knowledge whereby man exercises technical control not only over nature but also over all the specific institutions that make up society, i.e., economics, education, science and politics."[1]

This new technological order has transformed our physical environment, shattered our traditional values, destroyed or modified our social and political institutions, and radically altered our cultural perceptions. The unprecedented growth and innovations in science and technology during the second half of the twentieth century have spawned a new subculture that has produced some unique problems for modern society: on the one hand, the social dynamics of this technocracy dominates our economics, politics, and culture; and on the other hand, the complexities, the methods, and the language by which science and technology operate have created new levels of unrest and alienation among those outside this subculture.

While we are witness to the splendid achievements of science and technology around us and dream of possibilities for dramatic enlargement in human fulfillment, we are also oppressed by the possibility of an extinction of all life through nuclear war or of devastating the earth through overexploitation and environmental imbalance.

There is a world crisis in values and unassessed technological backlashes. These are traceable to the uncontrolled technological growth, its rapid spread among the nations of the world, and the consequent cultural lags resulting from the failure of social institutions and belief systems to adjust accordingly.

The modern world is confronted with, among other things, the fourfold specter of environmental crisis, nuclear threat, population explosion, and growing disparity in distribution of health care, wealth, and justice between the rich and the not-so-rich.

The "Science, Technology, and Society" (STS) course at Marymount Manhattan College grew out of the authors' own need to come to grips with the issues outlined above and from personal encounters, in the 1960s and 1970s, with the movement for relevance in liberal education, particularly with regard to science, scientific research, and technology. The course was designed to give liberal arts students a better understanding of the scientific process and the nature of current technological developments. At the same time, the course was intended to give science as well as humanities students a deeper understanding of the need to assess the social, cultural, economic, political, and environmental impact of scientific and technological advances on societies at different levels of technological development.

We have deliberately avoided making this a course *in* science and technology, where the emphasis in the course is usually upon the subject matter of science, the history of ideas and innovations—in other words, the substance that makes up science. Our course is *about* science and technology. This approach allows one to look at the basic nature of science and its relevance to human beings and society. The pedagogical emphasis is on the analysis of the pervasive historical and ongoing interaction of scientific endeavors and technological innovations, and the social and cultural environments that nurture or constrain such activity and that are changed by them. Relevance in science is taken to mean the study and identification of social problems arising from science and technology, the process that sets priorities for the direction of research and development, technology assessment, instruments for social assent and control, and future planning. There is a certain amount of risk involved when one sacrifices substance in favor of relevance in that a meaningful discussion of relevance may be impossible without a comprehension of what it is that is relevant. Thus, in order to minimize this deficiency, where appropriate the subject matter of science is discussed and supplementary readings are suggested.

STRUCTURE OF THE COURSE

"Science, Technology, and Society" is an interdisciplinary course team-taught by a physicist and a sociologist. Both faculty members are present for all class meetings to discuss and comment, from the perspective of their disciplines, on the issues raised. They plan each class session together. There is considerable flexibility in how this team concept is used. One may lecture for several classes, with the other commenting to round out the presentation. They occasionally alternate class lectures, and both develop and discuss the issues at hand in preparation for the class session. Usually both members of the team are active participants to some degree in each class session. As the course progresses, the role of the faculty team changes from that of lecturer to discussion leader.

The use of a team faculty for the STS course has two purposes. First, the interdisciplinary nature of the material requires the expertise of both a natural scientist and a social scientist. The second purpose in using a team of teachers is to encourage the enrollment of students from a cross section of academic disciplines. This was viewed as important, because the course was designed to fill in perceived gaps in the education of students from the sciences and the humanities and because the diversity represented by this mix was considered valuable for the success of projects and class discussions. The presence of teachers from different segments of the academic spectrum encouraged diversity in enrollment. The STS course is currently required of all "International Studies" majors and is expected to be listed among the six or seven courses singled out by the college as special-core "Liberal Studies" seminars, at least one of which must be taken by all students as a graduation requirement.

SCIENCE, TECHNOLOGY, AND SOCIETY (three credits)

This is an interdisciplinary, team-taught course focusing on the interaction of science and technology with society. Among the areas considered are the impact of scientific and technological developments on thought throughout history and on the structure of societies; the place of human values in a technological society; the relationships among technological innovations; the functioning of economic and political institutions; and the values that influence social behavior. Some of the specific issues discussed are problems of genetics and genetic engineering; cybernetics and automation; energy and the population explosion; science, industry, and warfare; future shock; artificial intelligence; and space travel.

TEXTS

Required:
Pytlik, Edward C.; Donald P. Lauda; and David L. Johnson. *Technology, Change and Society.* Worcester, Mass.: Davis Publications, 1978.
Teich, Albert H., ed. *Technology and Man's Future.* 3rd ed. New York: St. Martin's Press, 1981.
Supplementary:
Truitt, W. H. and T. W. G. Solomons, eds. *Science, Technology and Freedom.* Boston, Mass.: Houghton Mifflin Co., 1974.

COURSE OUTLINE

Chapter numbers refer to Pytlik, et al. Readings from Teich, relating to particular issues being discussed, are assigned in class.

I. The Nature of Science and Society (chap. 1; two weeks).
1. What is science?
2. The relationship between science and technology
3. What is society?
4. The impact of science on society (and vice versa)
II. Revolutionary Change: Case Studies (chaps. 2–7; four weeks).
1. The Industrial Revolution
    a. the technological revolution
    b. the social revolution
2. Science and technology in twentieth-century societies
    a. science in the modern world
    b. the status of technology
    c. social changes and adjustments
        . . . in underdeveloped and primitive societies
        . . . in developing nations
        . . . in technologically advanced countries
III. Science, Society, and Human Values (chaps. 8–12; six weeks).
    Issue-oriented debates and discussions on selected topics, such as
    population growth, medicine, the environment, war and aggres-
    sion in the nuclear age
IV. Planning for the Future (two weeks).
1. Models for the future
    a. anticipating new technology
    b. alternative forms of social organization
2. Space: new frontier, new opportunities
    a. space industrialization
    b. space colonization

COURSE REQUIREMENTS

1. Participation in class discussions (assumes regular attendance)
2. Assigned readings in text and other sources
3. Short assignments (e.g., additional reading or writing; field trips;
   etc.)
4. Major research project: An impact analysis
5. Final examination

Grade for course will be based on fulfillment of all of the above requirements.

TECHNIQUES IN PRESENTATION OF THE COURSE

We begin the course by presenting the basic concepts that define the nature
of science and its methodology, and discuss the distinction between science and

technology. Similarly, concepts explaining the nature of society, of social and cultural organization, of the basic institutions found in some form in all societies, and of the processes by which social and cultural change occurs (or fails to occur) are explored. The vast range of cultural diversity in values, social structures, religious, political, and economic systems and their varying impacts on how scientific and technological advances are received in a society provide the foundation for developing the students' analytical skills. It is in this context that the differing roles and goals of the scientist and the technician (scientist-engineer) are presented, with special emphasis on the interaction of the scientist and the engineer with the society. (To what degree and in what manner does society support scientific exploration? Is it publicly, privately, or independently supported? Do cultural values encourage, support, shape, or even depend on scientific achievement? Is public support predicated on practical applications and marketable accomplishments? How are scientists and engineers perceived by the society—as gods, miracle workers, lunatics, devils? Is science perceived as the hope of humankind or the destroyer of worlds?)

One cannot be expected to assess fully and accurately the impact of science and technology on society without first understanding and respecting the different needs, perspectives, and worldviews of our neighbors with whom we share this fragile planet. The issues discussed in the course—issues such as the environment, population control, energy, industrial development, nuclear weapons, biomedical technology, space exploration—encourage a global-village perspective. While political divisions are real and meaningful boundaries for citizens, they are not for scientific and technical research and development. Social and cultural diffusion of improved technologies as well as spreading pollution and disease are evidence of the limited usefulness of political boundaries. We are all residents of the same planet. Our interdependence is heightened by the fact that the same planetary life-support system sustains one and all, rich and poor. The supra-nationality of the nature of science and technology forces on us a social and ethical worldview of an essential oneness of humanity, a world community. The global consciousness required of this one worldview parallels the corporate and universal aspects of Christian faith: the wholeness of creation and the implied unity of all peoples.

By broadening the students' cultural perspectives and giving them the conceptual tools for analysis of social benefits and risks of new technologies, students are encouraged to make impact assessments. The course suggests an ethical framework of very general principles for students' own analyses of issues. In their impact-analysis assignment, students are to incorporate an ethic recognizing a standard for justice for all, giving priority to respect for human life and the quality of that life and respect for cultural values. Students must identify the cause of a problem and must avoid quick technological fixes, which often create inhuman conditions and rarely deal with the source of the problem.

And finally, the point is made that failure to keep oneself informed on social, political, and scientific issues, failure to analyze data and evaluate it and, in some cases, failure to act (to speak out, to write a congressman, to organize a protest, to vote for or against an issue) may, in itself, be a major issue in human ethical responsibility. To do nothing, to remain in ignorance, is not being neutral. "Doing nothing" is not doing nothing. It is abdicating responsibility— a responsibility that we have to ourselves, our children, and our world.

After lectures and discussions early in the course on the nature of science and of society, the relationship between science and technology, and their collective impact on society, the students should have the conceptual tools they need to begin to analyze the process of social and cultural change that is set in motion by the developments in science and technology.

To assist the students, we distribute a guideline suggestive of the content expected in any analysis of the impact of science and technology on society. The guideline consists of a series of questions, which are not to be answered separately but are to provide the framework for a comprehensive impact assessment. We use this framework consistently in our lectures and discussions, and the students follow it in their varied assignments.

GUIDELINE FOR ANALYZING THE IMPACT OF SCIENCE AND TECHNOLOGY ON SOCIETY

NOTE: This is offered merely as a guideline. It does not have to be followed exactly or in any specific order, nor must each question be answered separately. It is suggestive of the content expected in the analysis of the process of social change.

THE PROCESS OF SOCIAL CHANGE

In analyzing the impact of any change, note the following:
1. Scientific and technological environment:
   a. What is the status of the technology in the area of study (e.g., experimental stage, tested but not yet marketed, advanced technology with broad areas of application)?
   b. Was the particular development under study a response to a "felt need" of society or an application of a by-product of other research? (Serendipity?)
   c. From what sources did research in this area have financial support (government, industry, private foundations)?
2. The innovators:
   a. Who are they (scientists, industrial researchers, inventors)?
   b. What is their role and position in the society?
   c. How will acceptance or rejection of innovation be influenced by 2b, above?

3. Communication:
   a. How was the innovation introduced into the society?
   b. How and by whom was this innovation communicated to the society?
4. Sociocultural environment:
   a. Is the innovation compatible with existing patterns (norms, values, expectations), a logical development from existing patterns, or the direct antithesis of existing patterns?
   b. What existent forces in society are conducive to acceptance of this change?
   c. What existent forces in society are directed against acceptance?
5. Social relationships:
   a. Which groups will be most directly affected by this change? How?
   b. What other groups, institutions, and so forth might be affected by this change?
   c. What adjustments would have to be made in other sectors of life if this innovation were accepted by society?
6. Stress, strain, or equilibrium:
   a. What are the manifest functions of the innovation?
   b. What are the latent functions of the innovation?
   c. Will the innovation produce a stress or strain in the society, or is it intended to return society to a state of equilibrium?
   d. Is the innovation a fairly self-contained one, or will it set in motion a chain reaction throughout the society?
7. Physical environment:
   a. Will this change have any impact on the physical environment?
   b. If so, specify the positive and/or negative effects on the physical environment.
   c. What segments of society will be most affected by these changes?
   d. How might these segments of society respond to the original innovation that brought about these environmental changes?
8. Acceptance or rejection:
   a. Given sufficient trial time, do you see greater acceptance or rejection of the innovation? Explain.

The second part of the course develops the analytical skills of the students. The Industrial Revolution is discussed as both a technological and a social revolution. The role of the culture of eighteenth-century England in fostering scientific and technological advances, and the social and cultural changes that the new technologies engendered, are analyzed. The factors that contributed to the Industrial Revolution in England, and not elsewhere until later, are discussed, emphasizing the role of culture.

Students then move on to analyze the role of science and technology in twentieth-century societies. Cultural values supporting scientific research and technological development are discussed. The status of the scientist in society is viewed critically with the specific objective of demythologizing the deification of science and scientists. (The role of the scientist on the teaching team is crucial for this discussion.) The tentativeness of scientific theory, based on observations and experiments, and requiring a language for its explication that may be wholly or partially technical, must be recognized and both the scientist and the citizen need to overcome their mutual fears that each is incapable of communicating effectively with the other. Explanations following the Three Mile Island nuclear-power-plant disaster in Pennsylvania and the recent proliferation of popular scientific magazines in bookstores give ample evidence of public interest in, and ability to deal with, scientific information and a genuine willingness on the part of scientists to communicate with citizens in a less technical language that can be understood by the latter.

An understanding of twentieth-century science must include a study of the culture of the scientific community—its concepts and language, motivations, values, views, and perspectives. Students must learn to distinguish between scientific and political decision-making power. They must distinguish between the neutrality of a scientific breakthrough (e.g., harnessing the atom) and its use or misuse for political or economic purposes.

Modern technologically advanced societies expect and anticipate change, and often express a blind faith in science to bring about change for the better. The complexity of structures of these societies often renders an analysis of the impact of the changes very difficult. The multitude of changes make identification of causality of a particular change nearly impossible. Unanticipated changes are not often linked to their source.

However, in underdeveloped and developing nations an analysis of the process of change instigated by the introduction of scientific and technological innovations presents a very different set of problems. The introduction of an advanced technology, even if only into a very specific sphere of activity (health, agriculture, industry), may set in motion a chain reaction of impacts resulting in the serious disruption of a culture, an economy, a social or a political system. An anticipatory analysis of what the impact of this innovation might be on such a society requires a thorough understanding of the culture of that society. Such a broad cultural understanding is often lacking among those making such assessments. Students are impressed with the responsibility of the analyst to respect cultural values and not impose the values of his or her own society in assessing "benefit." The fact that one of the authors of this essay was born and raised in India has been of some advantage to the discussion on the experiences of the third-world countries.

By this point in the course (about halfway through the semester), students should be aware of social, cultural, scientific, political, and religious perspectives that they bring to bear on any analysis of the impact of a scientific/ technical change on a society.

Two case studies from Spicer's *Human Problems in Technological Change* are used to exemplify these issues. The successful introduction of a wagon into the culture of an Indian tribe in southern Arizona is contrasted with the unsuccessful attempt to introduce a hybrid-corn seed into a Spanish American farming community in New Mexico.[2] In the case of the wagon, little planning and a lot of serendipity combined with the culturally adaptive mechanisms of society to effect a relatively quick, nondisruptive acceptance of the innovation with widespread changes in the way of life of the people and their culture. The second case emphasized the role of the planner, here the agricultural extension agent, who conscientiously prepared the community for the change. He followed a prescribed set of procedures for introducing the hybrid corn in a way more conducive to community acceptance. The initial results were very favorable, but ultimately the hybrid corn was rejected and the community returned to its weaker variety of corn. The social, cultural, and institutional elements affecting the outcomes in each of the cases are fully analyzed.

Students are then asked to anticipate the consequences of technological change. After reading Alvin Weinberg's article "Can Technology Replace Social Engineering?"[3] students are assigned the task of suggesting both a social and a technical solution to a social problem. They also analyze the differing impact each would have on society.

In the third part of the course, the instructors shift roles. Having lectured on the nature of science and of societies at different levels of development, the faculty now give students a larger responsibility for the class by having them assess the impact of technical innovations on society and human values in addressing specific social problems. Students engage in issue-oriented debates and discussions on selected topics such as energy and resource depletion, population growth, nuclear weapons, environment, medical technology, and space industrialization. An extensive bibliography and a major written project analyzing the impact of specific changes on a society support their classroom activities.

During these discussions the students are encouraged to participate actively in the dialogue, express opinions freely, be willing to criticize incomplete arguments, point out gaps in each other's analysis, and suggest alternative conclusions. There is often a tendency on the part of some to get too involved emotionally and blame "them." Very often "they" are the government, the military, an industry, or simply the folks across town or on the other side of the river. This occasions a discussion on fairness and justice: that social malfunctions, unlike malfunctions in science and technology, are rarely resolved by looking for simple solutions or quick fixes.

The discussions regarding the collective malfunctions in the adaptive mechanisms of the social fabric, and the attempts to identify their causality and to understand the resulting conflicts, form the important experiences of the course. It is pointed out that the need to be emotionally involved is essential to the business of taking a social or political action but that reason and charity should temper and guide our emotions so that the rights of others are not violated and justice is allowed to prevail.

The last two meetings of the class deal with the future. The natural scientist describes anticipated new technologies currently being developed or perfected and leads discussion on the nature of the changes that these innovations might bring about. The social scientist discusses possible alternative forms of social, political, or economic organizations among the member states of our global village.

Finally, we step out beyond the global village into the new frontier—space. The new opportunities made possible by the truly unique environment of the weightless vacuum of space for industry, medicine, and science are discussed. Possibilities for space agriculture, space industrialization, and space colonization are demonstrated with slides.

The following are examples of some of the recurrent themes that have generated the most interest and discussion. This is the way we approach the issues.

Scientific Endeavor

While science is generally understood as a human activity in search of knowledge, the public perception of science is that it is comprised of truths that tell us right from wrong, and that it has answers to all questions. This thinking can lead to unreasonable expectations from science and technology, particularly when the products of science and technology misbehave or are misused. What is less understood is the way the scientific outlook itself has changed in modern times. The goal of scientific research, at least in the field of applied science, is not knowledge for its own sake, but power. Power gives one control over nature; if one can "synthesize" it then one has understood it. What is implicit in this conquest of nature "for the relief of man's estate," as Francis Bacon admonished, is the power wielded by some persons over other persons, using knowledge of nature as their instrument. Lynn White has pointed out another side to this attitude of dominance over nature. According to him, Christianity bears "a huge burden of guilt" for the ecological nightmare we face today. "By destroying pagan animism," White argues, "Christianity made it possible to exploit nature in a mood of indifference to the feelings of natural objects."[4]

Somewhere along here, the plight of a modern scientist is compared with that of the legendary Daedalus. In many respects an archetypal scientist, Daedalus was dedicated to his discipline but not to his time, offering his services to whomever in exchange for opportunities to explore his fantasies and the wonders of the world. However, Daedalus was able to undo some of the mischief caused by his creations, first by confining the Minotaur in the labyrinth, and second, by helping Theseus to kill it and then escape from the labyrinth. Modern Minotaurs, such as nuclear bombs, chemical defoliants, and poisons in the environment, refuse to go away.

Distributive Justice

Social malfunctions and social tensions result from conflicts of interest whether it be individuals competing for scarce resources or nations seeking raw materials for their industries. Garrett Hardin, in his paper "The Tragedy of the Commons," discusses this point by illustrating the situation in a New England village where every man is allowed to graze his cows free on the village commons.[5] The commons is destroyed if each individual attempts to maximize his advantage. The interests of the individual are clearly at odds with those of the community. One can clearly draw similar lessons on the national level, where the growing benefits of technical development tend to go largely to a small elite. On the international level, the disproportionate consumption of the world's resources by the advanced nations is another example.

A similar point, with regard to human ecology, was made by Julius K. Nyerere, the Tanzanian president, in his address to Maryknoll Sisters in 1970:

So the world is not one. Its peoples are more divided now, and also more conscious of their divisions, than they have ever been. They are divided between those who are satiated and those who are hungry. They are divided between those with power and those without power. They are divided between those who dominate and those who are dominated; between those who exploit and those who are exploited. And it is the minority which is well fed, and the minority which has secured control over the world's wealth and over their fellow men. Further, in general that minority is distinguished by the color of their skins and by their race. And the nations in which most of that minority of the world's people live have a further distinguishing characteristic—their adoption of the Christian religion.[6]

Biomedical Technology and Human Engineering

A discussion involving any issue in this area usually turns very emotional. Nevertheless, it is necessary to explore some basic questions because they are current and controversial. How have developments in medical technology changed our definitions of "life" and "death" and our understanding of the meaning of life and the quality of life? Should there be any limits on organ transplantation and the use of bio-electronics? What are the potential benefits and dangers of continued research in genetic engineering? Can a program of eugenics be justified? If so, who shall determine what constitutes a superior individual worthy of special attention; who shall determine which individual may or may not reproduce and by what method? Further questions revolve around the use of dehumanizing technologies in health care, experiments on or manipulation of the unborn, protection and confidentiality in health matters, and balancing efforts aimed at prevention against those aimed at cure. The questions come easily. The answers do not.

Social Engineering

In our discussion on space colonies, we encourage the students to apply the techniques of analysis considered during the course and their own sense of justice, equality, fair play, and tempered idealism to design a community that would comprise a space colony in orbit around the earth. Students decide whether the colony would be best served by a homogeneous or a socially and culturally diverse population and then devise procedures for a process of screening and selecting the colonists. Dominant values that will permeate the culture are identified. Students are charged to consider that a community to be healthy and prosperous needs all the social support systems, and therefore they need to plan the nature of the institutions—such as family, education, government, economy, religion, and the arts—that will provide the structural framework for a viable social system responsive to the needs of its people. Students, given the opportunity to create their own small world, unfettered by existing cultural patterns and able to draw upon the most advanced technologies, envision a future that could be. Perhaps they will be motivated to work toward creating such a better world.

NOTES

1. Herbert Richardson, *Toward an American Theology* (New York: Harper and Row, 1967), p. 16.

2. Edward H. Spicer, ed., *Human Problems in Technological Change* (New York: John Wiley & Sons, 1952), pp. 23–29.

3. Alvin Weinberg, "Can Technology Replace Social Engineering?" in *Technology and Man's Future* (3rd ed.), ed. Albert H. Teich (New York: St. Martin's Press, 1981), pp. 29–39.

4. Lynn White, Jr., "The Historical Roots of Our Ecologic Crisis," *Science* 155 (Mar. 10, 1967): 1203–7.

5. Garrett Hardin, "The Tragedy of the Commons," *Science* 162 (Dec. 13, 1968): 1243–48.

6. Julius K. Nyerere, "Division Is the Problem of the Third World," in *Education for Justice: A Resource Manual,* ed. Thomas P. Fenton (Maryknoll, N.Y.: Orbis Books, 1975), pp. 87–98.

SELECTED READINGS FOR FACULTY

Applebaum, Richard. "The Future Is Made, Not Predicted: Technocratic Planners vs. Public Interest." *Society,* May/June 1977.

Ash, Brian. *Faces of the Future.* New York: Taplinger Publishers, 1975.

Barzun, Jacques. *Science: The Glorious Entertainment.* New York: Harper & Row, 1964.

Bell, Daniel. *The Coming of Post-Industrial Society.* New York: Basic Books, 1973.

Berry, Adrian. *The Next Ten Thousand Years.* New York: Mentor Books, 1974.

Bluth, P. J., and S. R. McNeal, eds. *Update on Space.* Vol. 1. Grenada Hills, Calif.: National Behavior Systems, 1981.

Boreano, Philip. *Technology as a Social and Political Phenomenon.* New York: John Wiley & Sons, 1974.

Burke, James. *Connections.* Boston, Mass.: Little, Brown, 1978.

Calder, Nigel. *Technopolis: Social Control of the Uses of Science.* New York: Simon and Schuster, 1970.

Carson, Rachel. *The Silent Spring.* New York: Crest Publishers, 1966.

Clarke, Arthur C. *Profiles of the Future.* New York: Harper & Row, 1962.

Commoner, Barry. *The Closing Circle: Nature, Man and Technology.* New York: Bantam Books, 1972.

Congdon, R. J., ed. *Introduction to Appropriate Technology.* Emmaus, Pa.: Rodale Press, 1977.

Ellul, Jacques. *The Technological Society.* New York: Vintage Books, 1964.

Etzioni, Amitai. *Genetic Fix.* New York: Harper Colophon Books, 1975.

————, ed. *Social Change: Sources, Patterns, Consequences.* New York: Basic Books, 1964.

Fenton, Thomas P. ed. *Education for Justice: A Resource Manual.* Maryknoll, N.Y.: Orbis Books, 1975.

Ferkis, Victor. *Technological Man: The Myth and Reality.* New York: New American Library, 1969.

Friedlander, Michael W. *The Conduct of Science.* Englewood Cliffs, N.J.: Prentice-Hall, 1972.

Gremillion, Joseph, ed. *Food/Energy and the Major Faiths.* Maryknoll, N.Y.: Orbis Books, 1978.

Hall, Edward T. *The Silent Language.* New York: Fawcett Premier, 1959.

Hardin, Garrett. *Stalking the Wild Taboo.* Los Angeles, Calif.: William Kaufman, 1973.

Hardy, John. *Science, Technology and Society.* Philadelphia, Pa.: W. B. Saunders, 1975.

Heppenheimer, T. A. *Colonies in Space.* New York: Warner Books, 1977.

Holdren, John P. "The Nuclear Controversy and the Limitations of Decision-Making by Experts." *Bulletin of the Atomic Scientists* 32 (March 1976): 20–22.

Kahn, Herman, and Anthony J. Weiner. *The Year 2000.* New York: Macmillan, 1967.

Kardestuncer, H., ed. *Social Consequences of Engineering.* San Francisco, Calif.: Boyd and Fraser, 1979.

Kranzberg, Melvin, and William Davenport, eds. *Technology and Culture.* New York: Schocken Books, 1972.

Mead, Margaret, ed. *Cultural Patterns and Technological Change.* New York: New American Library, 1955.

National Academy of Sciences. *Science and Technology: A 5 Year Outlook.* San Francisco, Calif: W. H. Freeman, 1979.

Price, Derek J. de Solla. *Little Science, Big Science.* New York: Columbia University Press, 1965.

Schumacher, E. F. *Small is Beautiful.* New York: Harper & Row, 1973.

Spicer, Edward, ed. *Human Problems in Technological Change.* New York: John Wiley & Sons, 1952.

Spiegel-Rossing, Ina, and Derek J. de Solla Price, eds. *Science, Technology, and Society: A Cross-Disciplinary Perspective.* London: Sage Publications, 1977.

Stine, G. Harry. *The Space Enterprise.* New York: Ace Books, 1980.

————. *The Third Industrial Revolution.* New York: Ace Books, 1975.

Toffler, Alvin. *Future Shock.* New York: Random House, 1970.

Afterword

Experiential Justice and Peace Education: Reflections on Forms and Foundations

DONALD P. McNEILL, C.S.C.

UNIVERSITY OF NOTRE DAME

It is encouraging for me to share these reflections after reading the other articles in this book. Experiential justice and peace education is often viewed in the academic world as "extra-curricular." I seek to indicate here a few hopeful signs of forms and foundations of justice and peace education that are—like the courses described in this book—integrated with, not extraneous to, the educational mission of Catholic institutions.

My major emphasis will be on the process and forms of linking field-based justice education with academic courses. In the first and most comprehensive section I shall reflect on programs at the University of Notre Dame and at Boston College.[1] The final two sections will center on possibilities for developing foundations for continuity of justice and peace education with various constituencies of Catholic colleges and universities.

These reflections are written with the hope that they lead to new forms of justice education. I also hope that the reflections are considered within the broader perspective articulated by Peter Henriot, S. J., in his address "The 'Second Founding': Commitment to Education for Justice and Peace":

> Difficult days. Hence days for profoundly reconsidering . . . fundamental questions about the very nature of the institution's existence. The very best days for looking at the issue of education for justice and peace! For if your college or university can clearly grasp the implications of the *context* within which we live, can critically analyze the *problematic*

facing Catholic schools in the United States today, and can creatively design a *response* worthy of the challenge, then you will have shaped a *vision,* a life-giving vision, for your institution. Dealing with education for justice and peace is indeed integral to the challenge of a "Second Founding." It is an exciting challenge to be caught up in.[2]

LINKING EXPERIENTIAL LEARNING WITH ACADEMIC COURSES

In this section we shall concentrate on programs and courses that enable students to reflect on justice and peace questions and issues that emerge from experiential learning opportunities. I shall focus on forms of experiential learning where the method of discovery is more inductive than deductive. These forms enable students in their own lives to experience the absence of justice and peace as data for reflection. William Byron, S.J., reflects on experiential learning of the meaning of justice in this way:

> I would want to argue that our images of justice, our symbols, can be immensely helpful in preparing the way for personal appropriation of the principles of justice. I would also be prepared to argue that the experience of injustice is an excellent, at times the best, pedagogical route toward a grasp, quite literally a comprehension, of the idea of justice. One person's experience will differ perhaps from another's. Hence, there is likely to be conceptual diversity but not necessarily contradiction relating to the idea of justice.[3]

The University of Notre Dame's Center for Social Concerns

At Notre Dame the Center for Social Concerns helps to coordinate a variety of programs that are linked with academic courses. There are two educational areas within the center: (1) Social Analysis, and (2) Service/Learning. In the first reflection, I shall focus on the "Urban Plunge" as a model of education for justice in the area of social analysis. In the second part I shall describe the course "Theology and Community Service" as an example of service/learning.

The brochure of the center describes the Social Analysis area in the following way:

> Through educational events, courses and experiential programs, the Center enables students, faculty and alumni to study and explore contemporary ethical and moral issues from a variety of perspectives. A special focus is provided by the social teachings of the Catholic Church concerning justice and peace.
>
> All the disciplines are employed in the analytical process of seeking to understand the issues facing society now and in the future. An additional component to social analysis is exploring possibilities of how to respond to injustice in today's world.

Since the Urban Plunge program began in 1975, more than 1,600 undergraduate students have made "the Plunge," in fifty-two cities in the United States and Mexico, to learn more about poverty, criminal justice issues, the church's social programs, and other aspects of inner-city life. The Plunge is a forty-eight-hour immersion into the kind of urban life that most of us have never seen and a live-in experience with persons working for social justice. It enables students to experience and learn for themselves the problems of injustice, poverty, and apathy in the urban areas of the United States. To prepare for the Plunge, students undertake both reading and a workshop. The best article to prepare students for the experience is "Social Sin: The Recovery of a Christian Tradition," by Peter Henriot, S.J.[4]

The actual Plunge, which takes place over Christmas vacation, allows students to experience firsthand some of the critical issues that can be encountered in cities. Returning to the university, they bring back new questions, which are articulated in a four-to-seven-page reflection paper and then discussed with faculty at meetings in their homes. Following these meetings, students are linked with courses that enable them to reflect on the Urban Plunge in a more comprehensive way.

As part of the Learning Agreement for the Plunge, students are required to participate in an additional workshop, reflection session, or course. For example, in January and February 1985, the students were provided the following options: participation in a lecture/discussion with Archbishop Weakland on the "Pastoral Letter on Catholic Social Teaching and the U.S. Economy"; a workshop on the church and the economy by Sr. Amata Miller; small-group discussions in the colleges where students are majoring with faculty of that college; or small-group meetings to watch and discuss Peter Henriot's video cassette on *The Option for the Poor* and to reflect in these sessions on how the issues relate to their experience of the Urban Plunge.[5]

In November, during advance registration for the Plunge experience described here, and also in January, students are provided with a list of academic courses in various disciplines which explore issues that commonly emerge from the Urban Plunge experience. All students who sign the Learning Agreement and participate in the Urban Plunge are participants in the "Church and Social Action" course, and they receive one credit in the Department of Theology and a grade of "Satisfactory" if they complete all the structured learning experiences following the brief experience of the Plunge. A few three-credit or follow-up courses specifically relate to issues of the Plunge and are coordinated by the center with various academic departments; for example, "Theology and Social Ministry" in the Theology Department and "Power in American Society" in the Department of American Studies.

We continue to face questions about the length of time of the Urban Plunge (forty-eight hours) and whether or not it achieves an in-depth learning experience. However, over the years we have found it to be an excellent initiation into the exploration of issues as well as a useful means of discovering various students and faculty who are concerned about this form of learning and studying social issues. For many students this sparks their interest in other film series, seminars, and social action experiences during the summers and after graduation. Many articulate in their own words that this is a form of "displacement" that opens their eyes to new questions about the mission of the church in acting for social justice.[6]

Service/Learning is the second educational area of the Center for Social Concerns. In this area, the center's goal is to provide students with multiple opportunities to serve the needs of others on campus, in South Bend, in the nation, and abroad and to enable as many as possible to reflect on these experiences within the perspective of Christian compassion. To this end, academic courses complement the service activities of the students. There are courses which involve readings and discussions on service, aging, suffering, compassion, and poverty. Currently, there are approximately twenty different volunteer service groups, made up of almost 1,500 undergraduates, directly serving persons in South Bend, Indiana.

The majority of students who participate in the service experience come to it without any formal reflection on the comprehensive learning possibilities of the experience. Consequently, since 1971 there has been an academic course, related to student experiences of service, called "Theology and Community Service." More than 500 undergraduates have participated in this course. The course size varies each semester, naturally. The model (which is fashioned after Clinical Pastoral Education, the formal educational process found in both Protestant and Catholic ministerial training) necessitates a facilitator for small groups of eight as part of the course. It is based in the Department of Theology and meets once a week for two and one-half hours. The students' other two-and-one-half hour commitment is spent at a nursing home visiting two residents with whom the student meets regularly each week throughout the semester. There is also a workshop, which helps introduce students to the reality of nursing-home life. Staff from the nursing homes help with the workshop, and also during the semester the Department of Pastoral Care at a local hospital helps with the course section on death and dying.

The "Theology and Community Service" course is based on the issues that emerge from the students' visits to the nursing homes. The course is completed by a comprehensive case study, which emerges from reflections on the individual student's journal, group discussions and directed readings throughout the semester, and specific readings related to the questions that were raised in the students' visitations. Although there are continual changes each year, the basic structure of the course follows the model as I have described it in another article.[7] There are several books that we have found helpful in structuring this course.[8]

A person in the Department of Theology who has had background in pastoral theology is especially qualified to teach this course. It is possible to use resource persons in the residence halls or staff as facilitators of the small groups. They ought to have at least a Master's degree in theology, or equivalent graduate education, in order to help students process the materials and raise questions from their experiences.

A major complication for this course is the students' diverse backgrounds in theology. Many want the answers to their experiential questions without exploring through their own faith some of the dimensions of those questions. This is a struggle throughout the semester when students have other courses competing for their time. However, for those students over the years who have entered into these questions with academic discipline, the learning has had a lasting impact in the various careers and lifestyles they have chosen. The case studies are normally fifteen typewritten pages and are placed on reserve in the library for students in the seminar to read before the presentation by each member in the class. The process of reading each other's case studies before the presentations and discussions enables students to enter into a form of learning that is seldom possible through the dynamic of seminar discussions and individual presentations without preparation by others in the class.

In addition to the "Theology and Community Service" course, there are one-credit-hour offerings (which are also related to service activities in the local area) and sixty Summer Service projects (which are funded by more than thirty-eight Alumni clubs and the Andrews Scholarship Fund for eight weeks during the summer). These are shorter than the course just described, are based on the journals kept by the students, and provide appropriate readings in relationship to the depth of the questions in a more limited academic commitment. The one-credit-hour courses are graded either "Satisfactory" or "Unsatisfactory."

In sum, the Center for Social Concerns attempts to link the awareness and service involvements of students with their own academic majors and career interests. This program of formative education is based on a model by Bernard Lonergan and others, which relates directly to questions from experience and moves toward more critical thinking and broader theoretical understanding in a variety of disciplines. The center has as its mission "the integration of justice and peace concerns into everyday life through formative educational experiences." It is hoped that these formal courses will provide a stimulus for other people, who do not have time to take courses for credit, to participate in events and programs that often build on the experience of students who have become more intensely involved with the overall dynamics of the center and its educational mission.

Boston College's Pulse Program

The PULSE Program at Boston College is another form of experiential learning that provides students with a variety of educational opportunities that are linked to service and social action projects in the local area and abroad. The rationale for the PULSE Program is presented as follows:

The PULSE Program involves students in works of social service and advocacy with communities and institutions throughout Greater Boston and in disciplined philosophical and theological reflection in the classroom. Through such involvement, the program hopes to promote a deeper self-understanding, engage the student in a sophisticated analysis of the causes and complexities of social order, and foster a commitment to assume personal responsibility for addressing these injustices and disorders.

The various placements offer a context for discovery. In the process of working with indigent and oppressed people or of lobbying on behalf of a piece of legislation, a student begins to discover his/her strengths, limitations, biases and insights. The field placement can also serve to illuminate the ways in which personal history and circumstances have formed the student. This newly awakening appreciation of what might be called one's personal "story" develops as the student confronts a plurality of life-stories and circumstances in the field work. Besides offering an opportunity for self-discovery, the placement will confront the student with one or more aspects of social injustices or suffering.[9]

Dr. Patrick Byrne, who originated the PULSE Program, and Richard Keeley, its director at this writing, provided consistent continuity for the program during its first fifteen years. I am indebted to them for the following reflections, which they prepared for this "Afterword":

Since 1972 the PULSE Program at Boston College has enrolled an average of 180 students each year. Roughly 20 percent of the students involved have sustained a commitment for more than two years. A first incentive to involvement is that the initial two-semester PULSE course, "Personal and Social Responsibility," fulfills core requirements in philosophy and theology. Four sections of this course are offered yearly. Beyond the foundational course, students may elect further PULSE courses in philosophy, theology, psychology, social work, or management. In the 1983–84 academic year, course offerings included "Faith, Work, and Vocation," "Suffering and the Challenge to Belief," "Psychological Perspectives on Justice," "International Social Work," "Environment, Welfare, and Social Action," "Values in Health Care and Human Services," "Economic Justice," "Housing: A Guide for the Perplexed," "The Structure of Community Life," and a special seminar for students involved in a summer program in Belize, Central America.

The linkage of field and classroom work constitutes the PULSE Program's greatest achievement, its continuing struggle, and the source of a fair amount of misunderstanding. These misunderstandings arise from preconceived notions as to how field work and class work interrelate. A word about the three most common preconceptions might clarify what distinguishes PULSE's pedagogical aims.

Preconception no. 1: "The academic component serves to *motivate* students toward social responsibility by focusing on, say, activist-oriented Catholic social teachings." In fact, the social encyclicals and episcopal documents play only a marginal role in but a few of the courses. The relationship of theology to work with the poor and afflicted is integral, not inspirational.

Preconception no. 2: "The academic component stresses technique (e.g., how to be a good counselor, welfare advocate, or community organizer) under the guise of theory." We made this mistake in the early years of the program—and rectified it. We have found that issues of technique can be better addressed in supervision, special workshops, and discussions; class time focuses on theory in a special sense and its relationship to concrete field experiences.

Preconception no. 3: "The academic component should engage in 'social analysis of structures of injustice.' " Although we are sympathetic to the critique of a privatized understanding of social evil and injustice, we are chary of the blend of socialist economics, neo-Marxist sociology, and democratic populism that pervades most "social analysis." Such methods have already identified a set of villains and assumed an answer to the question, What needs to be done? In our experiences as teachers, we have found these questions much more difficult to solve in ways that respect the integrity of those raising the questions—the students themselves. In many cases the enemy, in the words of Pogo, is us.

It is easier to say what the PULSE academic component is *not* than to say what it *is*. On the surface the academic component may seem indistinguishable from ordinary college curricula. In PULSE courses students read traditonal works, including Plato, Aristotle, the Bible, Machiavelli, Locke, Marx, and so on. Yet the PULSE approach to these texts is quite different from the usual one. In PULSE the texts are treated as *formational* rather than *informational*. That is, the reading material is presented as raising questions that every human being faces, and as setting forth fundamental paradigms for just, happy, and holy living.

This approach seems to work because PULSE faculty members endeavor to show students in what ways these texts are the products of people who have struggled with issues very similar to those that the students are encountering in their field placements—questions of proper action, fidelity in friendship, institutional justice, ignorance, evil, and redemption. The extent to which PULSE faculty succeed is in large part due to the new perspectives that the best in modern scholarship has brought to the understanding of these classical texts. And among these, the works of Bernard Lonergan, S.J., and his students have been most helpful.

Two examples from PULSE teaching experiences will serve to illustrate these points. The first focuses on interpersonal dimensions, the second on structural issues.

1. Each year, several PULSE students volunteer at "Rosie's Place" (one of the field placements). Rosie's Place provides dinner, shelter, and a limited number of beds for Boston's homeless women. The lives of the

women who frequent Rosie's Place are in stark contrast with those of the PULSE students. Yet these students often say they have learned lasting lessons about generosity, courage, beauty, and friendship from these women.

One of the students' most common reactions to what they witness in these women is a kind of despair at the possibility of ever helping any of them to lead a "normal life." This despair is gradually overcome as they learn to look more carefully, with the guidance of our readings (especially Aristotle's *Ethics* and the Gospels). In particular, Aristotle's discussions of virtue and friendship help them to discover that, as one student put it, "In their struggle for survival, some still take time to give what little they have to someone they think has less." Another volunteer spoke of the friendship she developed with an alcoholic woman because of the latter's courage in trying to stop drinking. She recognized that, despite their differences in age, socioeconomic status, and experience, there was a sameness, an *identity*, in courage, which was the basis of their "Aristotelian" mutual affection. Critical discussions of the Gospel accounts of the Beatitudes can occasion similar insights.

Through these kinds of reflections our students overcome the sense of despair. They find worth and hope in what they do at Rosie's Place. They cannot make over the women's lives, but their understanding of what a "normal life" entails is radically transformed. They discover that they can befriend, identify with, and support those parts of the women's lives that are authentic, healing, and growing.

2. The second example is drawn from a former PULSE student who is currently the director of a network of schools for adolescents in the juvenile-justice system. When this student was a senior, he developed a "Senior Thesis Project" that combined responsibilities to a local Catholic Worker house with a theoretical study of community. He expected to learn about the internal workings of a community of service to the destitute. But the unexpected learning that occurred—inspired in equal parts by the field experience and the persistent, judicious questioning of a team of faculty members—eclipsed his original intention. He came to understand firsthand the mechanisms of "gentrification" and its social consequences for the poor. He discovered a set of surprising facts about rooming houses. Most notable among these was that, far from being symbols of urban problems, rooming houses contribute in a positive and complex way to the social and economic climate of a neighborhood. He had the opportunity to confirm and expand upon a set of analytic tools assembled from the theoretical study by Jane Jacobs, *The Death and Life of Great American Cities.* Finally, his study became the basis for an effort on the part of several members of the Catholic Worker house to preserve rooming houses.

The PULSE staff—director, administrative intern, faculty—also devote considerable time to a more subtle style of education: the formation of a community of leaders. Experience suggests that the liberation of thought and affect, which occurs through the intersection of field placement and classroom activity, remains subject to countervailing pressures from campus life and from the culture at large. Accordingly, the PULSE staff nurtures peer leadership in formal and informal ways.

The paradigmatic case is that of the PULSE Council, a group of approximately twelve undergraduates who assist in the coordination of the program. The council, whose members are selected on the basis of outstanding field and classroom performance as well as evidence of leadership potential, receives special attention from the PULSE staff. In a training weekend council members explore work and vision. Most council members also participate in a year-long seminar that offers an opportunity for extended, higher-level reflection upon the PULSE Program. Retreats and workshops add a further dimension to their formation. In short, the staff tries to foster a community among these students in response to the difficulties and injustices encountered in the field. In turn, the PULSE Council is an indispensable source of encouragement and support in the face of those pressures issuing from campus and society at large. Together, the staff and Council of PULSE tries to embody a *living response* to the problems of human living.

The elements of experiential learning provided by these comprehensive programs at the University of Notre Dame and at Boston College offer students an opportunity to enter into other courses with an experiential base of questions and an inquisitiveness to search for further understanding in the midst of uncertainty. These are only two of various programs offered by many Catholic colleges and universities involved in a similar process.

IDENTIFYING, INVITING, AND COUNSELING STUDENTS WITH JUSTICE AND PEACE CONCERNS

One of the greatest challenges for faculty and staff is to identify, invite, and counsel students with justice and peace concerns. Every campus has a small minority of students who are explicitly looking for programs and courses related to previous family and high school experiences with justice education. However, the majority of students seem to arrive at universities with many other concerns as top priorities. Every campus has some organizations and groups that need to collaborate in fostering an environment in which justice and peace education and action are an important part of a holistic view of value education. Many of these areas have been outlined in the Winter 1981 issue of *Current Issues in Catholic Higher Education,* to which I refer the reader.[10] In this section I briefly reflect on the identification process through Notre Dame's Office of Admissions and Freshman Year; the invitation process through programs and events; and the counseling process through Placement and Career Development offices.

Many colleges and universities are now admitting some high school students who have had an initial exposure to justice education. In some instances, they come to a particular institution because of its emphasis on value and justice education. It is critical to find ways of identifying these students and putting them into early contact with faculty and others concerned to build on their previous foundation. A few of these students have been overseas, or were involved in experiences in Appalachia, or have worked in inner-city areas and helped with peace and hunger concerns. Some have even had thorough courses, in their junior and senior years, which linked their experiences with courses in religion, social science, and English. These students can become isolated from their early experiences and take these experiences no further in their college career.

Catholic educators in particular must be cautious not to assume that the emphasis in Confirmation classes on "required service" and in Catholic schools on "required service projects" are foundations for justice education. Often such service activities are performed in a "do-gooder" and "volunteerism" context with no broader reflection on such activities and society at large. We cannot assume that any distinctions are made between service and social action at that level. However, there is great potential.

At Notre Dame and other universities, value questionnaires have been developed that are part of the package given to incoming freshmen before they begin classes. These questionnaires help to identify the overall response of the incoming classes to justice and peace questions. The students also participate in the UCLA/American Council on Education annual national survey of incoming freshmen.[11] The specific questions related to justice and peace are then asked again before the students receive their diploma, usually in April of their senior year. This research is being explored and studied at the present time, and the questionnaires are available to interested faculty members from other institutions.[12] This research can relate directly to the various colleges chosen by students, and it may eventually indicate what impact the "incorporation" or "infusion" method of education described in other chapters in this book has.

One of the questionnaires in the freshman packet mentioned above concerns student interest in various programs and events related to justice and peace matters. Various student groups on campus plan to meet with interested freshmen during their first few weeks in order to explore their possible involvement in programs sometime during the year. An area of further investigation for all of us is the possibility of working more closely with freshmen counselors (or, at the University of Notre Dame, with the Freshman Year of Studies staff). They are often able to identify students who are frustrated both by the gap between the stated goals of the university or college and the reality of their dorm life, and by the competitive atmosphere of studies. The PULSE program at Boston College, described above, identifies motivated students early, and they can begin the six-credit-hour comprehensive introduction on the social responsibility of the person during their first year.

There is an increasing need to find creative ways of inviting students to participate in justice- and peace-related courses, events, and meetings with professors who share these concerns. The usual posters and bulletin boards announcing campus events and programs are important and draw a small group that is often supportive of each other. However, few programs have come to my attention that provide a comprehensive coordination of justice and peace concerns with campus ministry, residence-hall staff, retreats for faculty and students, events with follow-up, and preparation in the overall curriculum in each college. Student groups are often isolated from the faculty and the latter's concern for solid education, which explores a variety of options on major issues of justice and peace. These linkages need to be explored and shared among colleagues and campuses. In my experience, programs attempting to link faculty members with students in residence halls, as a group, in either formal or informal ways, have consistently failed. Faculty members with the greatest interest in justice and peace issues are more often linked with students with explicit interests in Amnesty International, Bread for the World, or Central American issues. An outreach and coming together of diverse groups of faculty and students is almost nonexistent in the departmentalized structure of larger universities.

One of the greatest challenges for justice and peace educators in the future will be the counseling of students concerning the relationship of social concerns to their vocation/career explorations in whatever field. When justice and peace issues are introduced in a creative way and are included in courses related to professions, this often leads to confusion among students who want to be person-oriented and yet are being educated in technical skills and professional knowledge. It is very easy to advise motivated students to work with one or another service-related group for a year or two in order to have an experience of social action in whatever job or profession they choose. These experiences, however, often attract no more than 3 to 5 percent of the graduating seniors in any particular college or university. What about the remaining 95 or more percent? Is it possible for faculty members to provide all students with perspectives on integrating justice and peace into their vocation to serve through whatever careers they may follow?

It is my hope that more discussion will take place in light of this book and the reflections within the colleges and universities reported herein. We do not often have role models of alumni who are struggling with the tension of responding to the social teachings of the church while maintaining sustenance for their families. Nevertheless, many graduates of our programs are attempting to find the best way to integrate social concerns into their law practice, their medical practice, decisions required of them as engineers, and the like. The students at Notre Dame invited Peter Henriot, S.J., to address himself to this issue in January 1984. His talk was entitled "A Call to Care: Career Planning for a Social Conscience."[13] Many of the students attending the workshop at which Henriot spoke felt that this perspective enabled them to have a vision and a direction on which to base their decisions. Often students are lacking a framework and become lost at the Placement and Career Development Office. A

great deal of attention needs to be paid, by the faculty and staff of programs
related to justice and peace, to dialoguing with persons in the career-
exploration area.

ENCOURAGING INSTITUTIONAL WITNESS AND COMMITMENT TO JUSTICE AND PEACE EDUCATION

The budget of a well-managed college or university should reflect that
institution's priorities. Unfortunately, many people who have committed themselves to years of teaching and working on justice and peace programs have not
also had the time and energy to assert the importance of these programs and
the need for adequate funding of all aspects of the work. True, in many
Catholic educational institutions these programs are singled out in fund-raising
campaigns as part of the school's "Catholic character." Nevertheless, it is clear
that many institutions do not have a budget consistent with their stated vision
and goals. As we have learned through the various essays included in this book,
faculty members have discovered ways within "the system" to include justice
and peace concerns in their courses. However, for others reading this book who
might be interested in attempting this, the questions arise: Would the university
(or college) support a summer leave for me to read and study in this area?
Would I be funded for travel to a conference where colleagues from similar
disciplines are meeting to share possibilities for these forms of inclusion?

In this brief section, I shall concentrate on three areas of concern related to
the institutional witness and commitment to justice and peace education of a
Catholic college or university. These or similar concerns can, of course, be
related to any educational institution, Catholic or non-Catholic, but I write
here out of my own experience. First, the relationship between mission or goal
statements and research and evaluation will be explored. Second, questions
will be posed concerning the relationship of offices of public relations, alumni
affairs, and development to justice and peace teaching, research, and programs. Finally, there will be a few concluding reflections on the importance of
spirituality.

Catholic colleges and universities have developed mission and priority statements about their "Catholic character" in recent years. It is extremely difficult
to make these statements operational in ways in which a thorough evaluation
and research project related to the statements can be made. However, it would
seem that justice and peace educators ought to be more assertive in the future
concerning the importance of asking questions like: What institutional witness
in the area of justice and peace do we expect from our faculty and graduates in
the year 2000? What percentage of students graduate with a minimum amount
of time spent in courses and service/social action projects related to justice and
peace concerns? Are some colleges more consistent than others in raising
ethical and moral concerns in the context of their core curriculum? If so, why?
Are most justice and peace issues expected to emerge in theology and philosophy courses rather than in other curricular programs within the colleges?

What budgetary allotments are consistently made for faculty development related to justice and peace issues? What percentage of the budget (in priorities in departments, colleges, and programs) is specifically focused on justice- and peace-related concerns?

Educators for justice and peace must avoid approaching these secular and "bottom-line" questions as if they are the *most* important. However, there is a tendency for those in disciplines considered "soft" not to work hard enough for the necessary budget and endowment to make sure that their programs and teaching will continue for at least another decade or two. These questions and many others need to be raised by appropriate groups in order to assess the consistency of mission or goal statements when there are budget constraints in the future.

The relationship between justice and peace education and offices for public relations, alumni affairs, and development needs to be explored at all Catholic colleges and universities. This exploration will lead to a serious assessment of the values and concerns of those who receive honorary degrees, of members of boards of trustees and advisory councils, and of persons who receive major student and alumni awards and are publicized in college magazines and newsletters.

Often those who speak a great deal about the commitment of students to service and about exploring values, and being involved in peace studies, and other important value questions are in development offices and public relations roles related to the university. Many alumni and other donors respect the institutional commitment to these important areas, which can often distinguish a religiously-based institution from others. Talks to alumni and other persons helping to encourage students to attend a Catholic institution often stress the importance of value education. Are these groups meeting with the faculty and staff and students concerned about justice and peace education? Are various program directors, faculty members, and college representatives allowed to speak about their own involvement in value questions and education and to have some funds earmarked for specific programs of the university that focus, for example, on justice and peace? Will the Alumni Office identify persons with social concerns in various cities who can be supportive and help with the educational process at the institution?

The institutional exploration into these questions will be extremely important as donors seriously question what might be special about the Catholic institution. Many alumni and donors are impressed when they meet students who are involved in justice- and peace-related programs and who have a challenging perspective. Are these students encouraged to become part of the Development Office strategy? Many who would take a prophetic stance relating to finances might question the importance of endowment to undergird justice- and peace-related programs in both student affairs and academic curriculum. However, an approach including both endowment and other forms of undergirding the continuity of justice and peace education in the years ahead is vitally important. There are tremendous competing and important needs at our universities, all requiring financial aid. A book like this ought to stimulate faculty and staff to see the importance of undergirding a commitment to justice and peace education through specific commitments in various institutional settings in the university.

The importance of spirituality as an institutional commitment in the future cannot be underestimated. Students, faculty, and administrators are bombarded by a tremendous number of concerns. There will be increasing stress in many institutions as budget constraints and questions about future continuity of justice and peace concerns continue. A spirituality needs to be developed for persons committed to the academic excellence of Catholic colleges and universities and who share in the mission in a variety of ways. Time priorities are continually being assessed by all persons in such institutions. The commitment to family, career, students, recreation, and social and other aspects of life is complex. A proper religious spirituality will enable persons and small groups to help each other in the process of integration. This integration process is a lifelong quest. Structures and persons within the university are needed to enable creative space to be developed for persons searching for inner peace in the midst of complex decisions.

My reflections on forms and foundations of experiential justice and peace education have raised more questions than answers. It is my hope that such educational programs as those offered by PULSE and the Center for Social Concerns will, in their linking of field-based learning with academic courses, show readers how experiential learning can complement the other forms of teaching described in this book. All of us need to continue to explore ways of identifying, inviting, and counseling undergraduate students with a justice and peace orientation. Without an explicit effort in this area, however, it will be impossible for us to be serious about our institutional witness and commitment to justice and peace education in the future. It is my hope, and that of many who have been part of the Advisory Council on Justice and Peace Education of the Association of Catholic Colleges and Universities over the years, that this book will be a step in the right direction, helping readers to ask the right questions and to assist each other in discovering the best *forms* of education, and helping them to find ways to undergird the forms with *foundations* in both the academic and the student-affairs worlds.

NOTES

1. For descriptions of programs at institutions other than these, see *Occasional Papers on Catholic Higher Education* 4, no. 2 (Winter 1978), and *Current Issues in Catholic Higher Education* 1, no. 2 (Winter 1981). Both of these editions of the journal (*Current Issues* is the present title of the former *Occasional Papers*) of the Association of Catholic Colleges and Universities are devoted exclusively to justice and peace education, and are available from ACCU, Suite 650, One Dupont Circle, Washington, DC 20036.

2. Peter Henriot, S.J., "The 'Second Founding': Commitment to Education for Justice and Peace," a presentation at ACCU Conference on Justice and Peace Education, University of Notre Dame, June 1981.

3. William J. Byron, S.J., "Ideas and Images of Justice," *Loyola Law Review* 26, no. 3 (1980): 445.

4. Peter Henriot, S.J., "Social Sin: The Recovery of a Christian Tradition," in *Method in Ministry,* ed. James and Evelyn Whitehead (New York: Seabury Press, 1980), pp. 127-44.

5. Peter Henriot, S.J., *The Option for the Poor,* video cassette available from the Center of Concern, 3700 13th Street, N.E., Washington, DC 20017.

6. Donald P. McNeill, Douglas A. Morrison, and Henri J. M. Nouwen, *Compassion: A Reflection on the Christian Life* (Garden City, N.Y.: Doubleday Image Books, 1983), pp. 62-66.

7. Donald P. McNeill, "Learning and Teaching Experiential Theology: An Intergenerational Journey," *Notre Dame Journal of Education* 5, no. 2 (Summer 1976), and Donald McNeill and Karen Ann Paul, "Theology and Field-Based Learning," *Occasional Papers on Catholic Higher Education* 1, no. 2 (December 1975).

8. Gregory Baum, *Men Becoming: God in Secular Experience* (New York: Seabury Press, 1979); James T. Burtchaell, *Philemon's Problem: The Daily Dilemma of a Christian* (published in 1973 and available from Life in Christ, ACTA, Foundation for Adult Catechetical Aids, 201 East Ohio St., Chicago, IL 60611); Arthur C. McGill, *Suffering: A Test of Theological Method* (Philadelphia, Pa.: Westminster Press, 1982); Donald P. McNeill, et al., *Compassion: A Reflection on the Christian Life* (see n. 6 above); Henri Nouwen, *Aging, the Fulfillment of Life,* written with Walter J. Gaffney (Garden City, N.Y.: Doubleday Image Books, 1974); Nouwen, *Creative Ministry* (Garden City, N.Y.: Doubleday Image Books, 1978); Nouwen, *Intimacy: Pastoral Psychological Essays* (Notre Dame, Ind.: Fides/Claretian Press, 1969); Nouwen, *Reaching Out: The Three Movements of the Spiritual Life* (Garden City, N.Y.: Doubleday, 1975); Nouwen, *The Wounded Healer* (Garden City, N.Y.: Doubleday, 1979); Evelyn and James Whitehead, *Christian Life Patterns* (Garden City, N.Y.: Doubleday, 1979).

9. From a PULSE brochure (1983-84). For information on the PULSE Program, write to Richard Keeley, Director, PULSE, Boston College, Chestnut Hill, MA 02167.

10. *Current Issues in Catholic Higher Education* 1, no. 2 (Winter 1981).

11. These data from the University of California, Los Angeles/American Council on Education provide the University of Notre Dame with an opportunity to contrast its students with those at other independent and public institutions. See Alexander Astin et al., *The American Freshman: National Norms for Fall, 1984).* (Los Angeles, Calif.: Cooperative Institutional Research Program, 1984). This is an annual publication which summarizes the UCLA data.

12. Drs. Kathleen Maas Weigert and C. Lincoln Johnson are exploring the best way to analyze the data and share them with other constituencies at peer institutions. Interested faculty may write to Weigert and Johnson in care of the Social Science Training Laboratory, University of Notre Dame, Notre Dame, IN 46556.

13. Peter Henriot, S.J., *A Call to Care: Career Planning for a Social Conscience,* cassette available from the Center of Concern, 3700 13th Street, N.E., Washington, DC 20017.

Contributors

DAVID B. BURRELL, C.S.C., holds a B.A. degree from the University of Notre Dame, an S.T.L. from Gregorian University in Rome, and a Ph.D. degree in philosophy from Yale University. He is currently professor of philosophy and theology at the University of Notre Dame in Indiana.

WILLIAM J. BYRON, S.J., earned his B.A. and M.A. degrees at St. Louis University. He holds a Ph.D. in economics from the University of Maryland. Father Byron is now serving as president of the Catholic University of America in Washington, D.C.

MONA CUTOLO was awarded a B.S. in sociology at Fordham University in 1964. She holds the M.A. in sociology, awarded by Fordham in 1966, and is currently an assistant professor at Marymount Manhattan College in New York City.

JOSEPH J. FAHEY earned his B.A. in philosophy at the Maryknoll Seminary in 1962, and his M.A. in theology at the Maryknoll School of Theology in 1966. He holds a Ph.D. in Christian social ethics, awarded by New York University in 1974. Dr. Fahey is the director of the Peace Studies Institute and professor of religious studies at Manhattan College in New York City.

DON FORAN earned B.A. and M.A. degrees at Gonzaga University before achieving the Ph.D. degree in English from the University of Southern California. He also holds the M.A. degree in theology from the Jesuit School of Theology in Berkeley, California. Dr. Foran teaches at Centralia College, Centralia, Washington.

MARGARET GORMAN, R.S.C.J., graduated from Trinity College in Washington, D.C., with a B.A. in English. She completed her M.A. in philosophy at Fordham University, and the Ph.D. in educational psychology at the Catholic University of America in Washington, D.C. She is currently an adjunct professor of psychology and theology at Boston College.

MILDRED HAIPT, O.S.U., attended Fordham University, which awarded her both B.A. and M.A. degrees. Her Ph.D. was awarded in education by the University of Maryland. Dr. Haipt is currently associate professor and chairperson of the Department of Education of the College of New Rochelle in New York.

MONIKA K. HELLWIG was awarded the LL.B. in British law by Liverpool University. Her M.A. and Ph.D. degrees in theology were earned at the Catholic University of America. Dr. Hellwig is now professor of theology at Georgetown University in Washington, D.C.

DAVID M. JOHNSON holds a B.A. from the University of Notre Dame, an M.A. in sociology from the University of Connecticut, and a Juris Doctor degree from Fordham University. Formerly associate professor of sociology at Mount Saint Mary College in New York, he is now associate executive director of the Association of Catholic Colleges and Universities in Washington, D.C.

DONALD P. McNEILL, C.S.C., earned his B.A. at the University of Notre Dame before completing the S.T.L. program at the Gregorian University in Rome. He also holds a Ph.D. in pastoral theology from Princeton Theological School. Dr. McNeill holds concurrent appointments as an associate professor of theology and director of the Center for Social Concerns at the University of Notre Dame.

DENIS M. MIRANDA did his undergraduate work in Bombay, India, before completing both the M.S. and Ph.D. in physics at Fordham University. He is currently assistant professor of physics at Marymount Manhattan College in New York City.

JANE F. MORRISSEY, S.S.J., graduated from the College of Our Lady of the Elms before earning both the M.A. and Ph.D. degrees in English at the University of Massachusetts. She is now assistant professor of English at the College of Our Lady of the Elms in Chicopee, Massachusetts.

MARIE AUGUSTA NEAL, SND de Namur, attended Emmanuel College in Boston as an undergraduate. Her M.A. in sociology was taken at Boston College, and her Ph.D. at Harvard University. She is currently professor of sociology at Emmanuel College.

DAVID J. O'BRIEN earned his B.A. in history at the University of Notre Dame, and his Ph.D. in United States history at the University of Rochester in New York. Dr. O'Brien is associate professor of history at the College of the Holy Cross in Worcester, Massachusetts.

PATRICIA L. PILGER took her B.A. degree in social science at Saint Mary's College in Notre Dame, Indiana. She later earned her M.A. degree in social work at St. Louis University. She is currently assistant professor of social work at Saint Mary's College.

DANIEL T. REGAN earned a B.A. degree in philosophy at the University of Toronto, and his M.A. degree in the same discipline at Villanova University. He is currently director of the Peace and Justice Program at Villanova.

THOMAS A. SHANNON attended Quincy College as an undergraduate before earning both S.T.M. and Ph.D. degrees in social ethics at Boston University. Dr. Shannon is now professor of social ethics at Worcester Polytechnic Institute in Massachusetts.

SUZANNE C. TOTON earned both the B.A. and M.A. degrees in religion at Temple University before completing an Ed.D. in religion and education at Columbia University's Teachers College. Dr. Toton is assistant professor of Christian living and religious education at Villanova University in Pennsylvania.

OLIVER F. WILLIAMS, C.S.C., earned the B.S. and M.Th. degrees at the University of Notre Dame before moving on to Vanderbilt University for the Ph.D. in theology. He also conducted research at Stanford University's Graduate School of Business Administration. Dr. Williams is currently co-director of Notre Dame's Center for Ethics and Religious Values in Business and serves on the faculty of the Department of Management.